GET ON THE PURPLE LINE

GET ON THE PURPLE LINE

A Memoir

By
Bill Rigali

© 2025 by Bill Rigali

All rights reserved. This book or any portion thereof may not be reproduced or used in any manner whatsoever without the express written permission of the publisher except for the use of brief quotations in a book review.

ISBN: 979-8-9920122-0-0 (Hardcover)
ISBN: 979-8-9920122-1-7 (Paperback)
ISBN: 979-8-9920122-2-4 (Digital)

INTRODUCTION

On June 28, 2019, on the magic island of Martha's Vineyard, my thirty-six-year varsity basketball coaching career at Holyoke High School (HHS) came to a disappointing end. Sandy and I were on the Vineyard to celebrate Kiely, our oldest daughter, and Saiid's wedding anniversary. The wash-ashores were working hard at building their new lives and careers in teaching and the trades. They were also facing the challenges of acclimating their two children to island life. Syius William, eleven at the time, was kind, smart, and empathetic to others. Marianela Juliet, just turning two, had the makings of a fighter pilot.

    They left Holyoke and came to the island to take new employment in the face of the uncertainty of a school system that had been placed in receivership by Massachusetts's Department of Elementary and Secondary Education (DESE). Kiely, along with many other teachers and citizens of Holyoke, had opposed the takeover with call-to-action rallies and informational sessions. The main issue was the loss of local control and democratic principles of self-governing. Their efforts were ignored, and the takeover was put in place. I had retired from teaching at that point, and my initial concern was for my daughter's career and grandchildren's education. Little did I know that I too would soon be impacted by the state's takeover.

    Midmorning my cell phone rang in the kitchen at Kiely and Saiid's home in Edgartown. "Hi, Bill. We have made a decision regarding your application for the basketball job. The committee has decided to go in another direction."

I was thanked for and congratulated on my career and offered a ceremony by Holyoke Public Schools (HPS) before one of next year's home games, but I respectfully declined. I did not want to stop coaching. I was, and still am, in good health and loved coaching basketball and tennis, as well as contributing to my community. Our program was incredibly successful, and I had been chosen as MBCA (Massachusetts Basketball Coaches Association) coach of the year two out of the last three seasons for the West Division 1 (D1) boys. My teams had continually qualified for state playoffs, competing in twenty-eight D1 state tournaments. I missed zero days of practice and games in thirty-six seasons. I had no MIAA violations for breaking rules or cutting corners. A clear, clean record of working hard day after day to be the best teacher and coach for my students, players, and community.

I had hoped to close out my coaching days in Holyoke on my own terms. Sixteen victories shy of five hundred career wins, I had hoped to deliver that milestone to my community and family. But just like that, I was gone. Now it was up to me to heed one of my own teachings to my family and the kids I taught in the classroom and coached on the hoop and tennis courts: "When you get knocked down, get up and keep moving forward."

CHAPTER 1

HOMETOWN

Having grown up in Holyoke, a baby boomer from the "Greatest Generation," Dad, Chelso "Chic" Rigali, served in the South Pacific during World War II. After the war, he worked in the dry cleaning business and as the club steward for the local Elks Club #902, where he was much beloved. Mom, Margaret "Pego" Rigali, née Kiely, worked part time in retail but mostly stayed at home to raise their three children. They provided us with a simple childhood that was not filled with monetary wealth but tons of love and social equity for my two sisters and me. I grew up in a community that provided me with a safe environment. I had plenty of neighborhood friends, recreation, and great schools. You pretty much had to have a plan to fail in those days. Growing up I wanted to make my family and community proud of the person I was and to give back. My parents and community taught me to be honest and respectful to people. You helped people climb the ladder of success by reaching down and pulling people up with you, and never at someone else's expense.

My teaching and coaching career, closing in on forty years, were the vehicles I drove to connect with my family, school, and community—and they continue to be. These places gave me my focus Qs to navigate each day. The following writings are remembrances of the people, places, and events that shaped my teaching and coaching career. Most of this work was written during the COVID pandemic lockdown and the 2020 presidential election, so there are a few thoughts on those events. To the best of my recollection, here I offer the lessons I learned along the way.

In September 1975, I started my teaching career at John J. Lynch Jr. High School in Holyoke, MA, on the first Tuesday after Labor Day. Armed with my English and political science degree from Assumption College, I was ready to go. The teachers at Lynch primarily dealt with students from upwardly mobile families. Children from the most affluent section in our community sent their offspring there to get an education. The students were children from middle class working families along with families made up of successful doctors, lawyers, and businessmen who all mixed in well together. The school was a melting pot from Irish, Polish, Jewish, Italian, French, and African-American backgrounds all united by an overwhelming drive to be successful.

 I had grown up and was educated in this diverse community, and I was about to embark on my teaching career there. It is no secret that teaching is and has always been a hard job. But I have always believed that the real skill in doing a great job is something akin to the old basketball creed that one must "know the time and score." Ascertaining this information allows any great teacher or coach a much better chance at success in the classroom.

 I arrived bright and early that first day and went straight to my mailbox in the main office. I could not wait to get my schedule and soon discovered it was as follows: four grade-seven social studies classes and one eighth grade English class. *Not bad*, I mused. *I can handle this.* As I set out to explore the landscape of the two story L-shaped building, I quickly noticed that only one of my classes had a room number. The rest of my classes were given the following designations: Stage, Boys Entrance, Home Economics. That's right. I started my teaching career in the sewing room and boys locker room, as well as the left side of the school auditorium. There were no concerns or worries about a quiet, safe, and equitable learning environment, let alone lighting, desks, and teaching materials for the students or me. Later in the day, I mentioned to the principal my classroom situation, or lack thereof. He simply smiled and related to me that the school had such a good reputation it was much packed to the limit with students.

The gym and social studies kids poured into the boys locker room in which I was immediately confronted with my first teaching challenge. A number of students on my class roster were girls. While my students were reporting to a period of social studies, there still remained other male students who were changing for gym class and the beginning of the period and showering at the end of class (kids actually took them back then). How to manage this seemed a bit more challenging than getting them to know the capitals of the US states.

The students were abuzz with nervous chatter and laughs, confused and at a loss how to navigate this situation. Inevitably, some rude remarks from a male student named Roger were directed toward the girl students: "Hey! Didn't I see you down on High Street last night?" Before I could respond, the cavalry showed up in the form of our gym teacher.

"All right! Cut the crap! All gym kids up the stairs. Change in the boys bathroom outside the gym." With that authoritative voice, out they went. The teacher then told Roger to "Hold on" because he wanted to speak with him. "Step over here."

Apparently this veteran teacher had overheard Roger's rude remarks to the girls. I fumbled to get my class list for attendance. All of a sudden from the other side of the locker room came a very loud dressing down of Roger. There was a heavy emphasis on respect, opportunity, and a final but effective threat about calling home. I think Roger was getting the message. The talk ended with a couple of hard slams of a locker door for effect.

The conversation had its intended result, and for the rest of the school year, Roger was the first to show up in our social studies / gym boys locker room class space. He carried in the box of textbooks we used for class and passed them out politely to each student as they entered. Roger would then excuse himself and go upstairs to change for gym class. Thinking back, Roger and I both learned an important lesson that day about knowing the time and score.

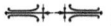

During my first year of teaching, I also started my forty-three year basketball coaching career by taking on the freshman team at Lynch. I held that position for five seasons until budget cuts eliminated the program, and while I was sad to see the program cut, I can assure you five years of coaching ninth-graders was plenty! There should be a term limit or guidelines in place to protect the social-emotional well-being of adults coaching freshman teams. In truth, there really is not a lot to say about those five years spent as a freshman coach except for mentioning a few foundational experiences to the rest of my coaching career.

The first memorable experience was my first game as a coach on the road at the JFK School in Northampton, MA. I cannot recall if we won, but I do remember by the time we got back to the Lynch parking lot I was angry. It was not the outcome of the game that incited my anger but my team's rude and obnoxious behavior on the bus ride home. The players trash-talked each other, the opposing team, the bus driver, and the team manager. Even inanimate objects like the ball bag took abuse. Despite my status as a first year teacher and coach, I knew I could not let these freshman ballers dictate who was running the show.

Get on the Purple Line

A number of warnings failed to quell any of the riotous activity on the trip home. As the bus pulled into the Lynch parking lot, I could see the lot was full of cars. Parents were waiting to get their sons home, while an adult recreational league basketball game was going on inside the school's gym. As my players got up and were pushing to the front of the bus to race out, I rose from my seat and blocked the exit. "Sit down, please. We need to talk," I stated firmly.

"F this!" sprang from the back of the bus, but I did not relent my position and they slowly sat back down. I went over a number of expectations I had for future away games and future travels. As I continued to list clear guidelines for appropriate player behavior, the kids grew impatient and nasty again. It was then that I realized they had lost any ability to listen and fully comprehend my lecture.

"All right, into the gym and change back into your uniforms!" I said in a low, controlled voice."

Once again a chorus of opposition and obscenities rang out.

"F this!"

"I'm not going!"

"My mom's waiting in the car!"

"Well, gentlemen," I replied, "you have a choice: you can go inside and run for a while and think about how you behaved, or you can turn in your uniform."

"I am going to the principal!" one player shouted.

"Go ahead," I stated, calling his bluff.

Once inside we marched into the gym, one grumpy freshman after the other. My next step was to commandeer the court away from the adults for a few minutes, which I surmised might be trickier than getting the players off the bus and into the gym. As the adult league game raced back and forth, I walked to center court and announced that our school team needed to run. I explained what had happened. Several of the adult basketball players looked a bit bemused and reluctantly sat on the sidelines watching as my team ran up and down the court.

At the end of the sprints, something interesting happened. Our better angels surprisingly showed up. A few of the adult players got up and started to run with the team, even talking with them. They offered advice such as "You guys should behave on trips" and "You need to respect your coach."

Another gentleman warned, "You better not let this happen again 'cause we ain't giving up our gym to you punks again." While another still commented, "My taxes are paying for your damn bus and driver, so you best respect it."

The adults who did not run started to clap and cheer as the sprints were completed. Still, I remember to this day how just a few minutes of running became a lifelong lesson on social equity and compassion.

I remember little about my actual first game as a coach. But what sticks with me is that bus ride home and running sprints afterward. What sticks with me is the tremendous privilege and pressure that comes with working with young people and helping them learn and grow into productive, compassionate adults.

This experience always reminds me of a speech I listened to many years later from the great Marquette coach Al McGuire during a basketball clinic in Boston. He definitely walked, marched, and rode his Harley to the beat of his own drum. In this talk he stated, "Never leave a game or practice as the only person pissed off. Your team and players will do that to you, so if they piss you off, make sure when they leave they are twice as pissed as you." As a coach, you need to know the time and score not only of the game but your players as well.

CHAPTER 2
TITLE IX

The Federal Civil Rights Law passed as part of the Education Amendments of 1972 has had a tremendous impact on our society. Title IX crossed my path for the first time during my tenure as basketball coach at Lynch. The law protects people from discrimination based on sex in education programs or activities that receive federal monies, ensuring equal access and opportunity to both male and female athletes.

At the time I was coaching the Lynch boys freshman basketball team, there was not a freshman program for the girls. Lisa Blake, a tall, thin young lady, tried out for the boys team as she was allowed to do so under Title IX. I soon discovered that Lisa had as much talent as all but a few of the boys. Her one disadvantage was that she lacked physical strength comparable to the stronger players on the team. The strength issue notwithstanding, I believed she should be selected to the team. The only questions were "How could I use her effectively in the games?" and "Could the boys handle a female teammate, focusing on playing basketball?" Creating team unity would be the biggest challenge for the season, and it was my job to put it together.

Lisa practiced well, she was a smart player, and she was an excellent student, as her degree from Bates College many years later would attest. There was the predictable problem of Lisa's teammates not wanting to play with a girl and an unwillingness to pass her the ball when she was open. The male junior-high ego was in full throttle on a number of occasions, but despite being frozen out on certain possessions, Lisa performed well in the games.

I remember her playing time to be about eight to ten minutes per contest. Lisa took her shots when she had them and passed the ball at the right time. One fundamental skill she had instinctively was to go to the ball when one of our players was trapped, and she had plenty of practice doing this throughout the season. Oftentimes inexperienced players overdribble. They go to parts of the court that have "No Exit" signs all over the place, getting trapped with nowhere to move the ball.

Lisa would always come to the ball to help. Most of her teammates would stand around, waving their hands, screaming, "I'm open! Over here! Here!" as if my trapped ninth-graders had LeBron James's superpower strength and skill to extradite themselves and the ball to safety. Lisa went on to a successful basketball career. She played for Hall of Fame coach Barbara Martino at HHS, who herself broke gender barriers as one of the first female athletic directors in the state of Massachusetts. Lisa's basketball career continued as she played for Bates College, which was no small accomplishment when you consider only about 7 percent of high school athletes go on to play in college (a ratio of about 1 in 13).

Being a member of the boys freshman basketball team and practicing every day against the boys made her a better player. A similar practice can be seen on the Women's Tennis Association tour: many female players employ a male hitting partner for practice. This can also be seen in many college women's basketball programs across the country that play against a male practice squad. It is a matter of strength and speed; it is a matter of knowing the time and score of one's opponent and what is necessary to improve. This overloading of strength and speed prepares the athlete for any situation they might encounter in their real-time competitions.

What did I think were the benefits of selecting a girl to a boys program? Three things come to mind. First, Lisa was one of the fifteen best players, so she deserved it pure and simple. Second, I hoped it gave Lisa and other girls who took notice confidence in themselves and their place in this world. It is important for young female students and athletes to understand they do not need to accept second-class citizenship to their male counterparts. Third, the world needs both young men and young women in leadership roles. One of the great powers of sports is that it can help develop the future leaders of tomorrow for a much more inclusive world and better society for all.

CHAPTER 3

WHO WE FIND AND WHO FINDS US

Most of us know or have heard about coaches who have a positive and lasting effect in the lives of their players and teams, students and schools, and families and communities. These essential relationships depend on many different characteristics and circumstances. When considering the type of coach I wanted to be and how to best get my team ready for the season, so many questions came to mind.

First, it was important to consider what was expected from the team and the season ahead.

What type of personality does the team and community have?

What experiences do I have that apply to my role as coach?

What are the areas and skills in which my players excel?

Will these strengths bring the team together or tear it apart?

Can any one player dominate a game?

Will the team demonstrate sportsmanship and maturity despite the game's outcome?

Will the team refuse to give up and persevere through hardships?

Have some of the players overcome great obstacles in their personal life to get on the court?

What do the players have to teach their teammates and me to help us learn and grow as a team?

How can we avoid circumstances in which we might let each other down?

Will there be a feeling that the players are a part of something special, something that is bigger than them?

Will there be a feeling or belief that we will be there for each other through both good and bad times? Are we really an extended family?

There are so many questions going into a season, but the answers are not discovered until the season is completed. And with each new team come more questions and surprises that can only be discovered by the relationships that are fostered between the players, coaches, families, and communities involved.

One such relationship was fostered during my early years as the boys varsity basketball coach at HHS, with a player named Mike and his family, the Laplantes. Later on Mike became the head coach for Jacksonville State University, a D1 men's basketball program in Alabama. Earlier in his career, Mike had landed the position of assistant coach to Cliff Ellis at Auburn University in the NCAA's Southern Eastern Conference (SEC). Presently there are around 350 D1 basketball programs in the NCAA. It is a special accomplishment to coach at that level. Mike Laplante is an excellent coach and a special person.

Mike was also the first captain on the varsity boys basketball team at HHS my initial year coaching. He was a six-foot-five, red-haired center who loved basketball and his teammates. His parents, Ed and Phyllis Laplante, were both essential members of the community, serving as a fireman and elementary school teacher, respectively, who raised their family on Hillside Avenue in the Elmwood section of our city. Mike's parents always had kids from the team over at their house: Rollie McCarter, Daren Hillman,

My first varsity team at HHS. Mike Laplante number 23 team captain.

Dan Gordan, Scott Jackson, Gil Sanchez, Jimmy Hart, Packy Fitzgibbons, and Paul Hobert. They even took in kids not on the team whose parents had pretty much given up on them.

It did not matter to the Laplante family if a kid was white, black, or Hispanic. If they needed a roof over their head or a meal, it was all taken care of by Ed and Phyllis. They were my version of a group text before such technology existed. If you needed to find a player, chances were you could call the Laplante household and find him there. I always knew where to find my players.

Their son Mike was a good high school player who improved each year as he grew into his body. After a year of postgraduate work at Suffield Academy in Connecticut, he landed a D1 scholarship to the University of Maine.

Our Holyoke teams with Mike were solid. We qualified for playoffs and even upset state champions Tech High School at the Springfield Civic Center during the regular season. I remember that defeat sent Tech head coach Howie Burns into a spiral. He announced to me in the handshake line that they would see us in the playoffs. Well, they certainly did, with the Tech Tigers pummeling us with pressure defense, high-flying dunks, and sharpshooting from the perimeter. At that point in our season, we were struggling with multiple injuries and had gone as far as we could go.

What made Mike special was that he had this great enthusiasm for the game of basketball. Over the years, I have found that you come across many high school kids who want to be on their school team because of status, bragging rights, or even for the approval of their parents. Their experience is seen as a check on the bucket list. These players more often than not are driven by self-interest, playing for "me" instead of "we." Mike played for the love of the game and supporting his teammates.

Defeats in the playoffs and the last game can be quite gut-wrenching experiences. Not only is it the final game of the season; for some graduating seniors it is the final game of their basketball career. It can be a difficult time to talk with players after the game in the locker room. However, as a coach it is your responsibility to finish your season as a team and help your players find some closure in the face of defeat. The season does not end at the final buzzer; it ends when you talk to your team.

The first player into the locker room after that playoff loss was Mike, with his hand out to every player. "Great job. Good season. You guys will get them next year." Captain Mike made it easy to talk with our team and coaches.

The end is always like running into a wall. Every team feels it after a playoff loss. I was incredibly lucky to have come across Mike and his family so early in my coaching journey. He made the game fun and he had an infectious effect on our team's chemistry.

Additionally, Mike's parents provided consistent positive reinforcement of both basketball and life skill experiences to the members of our team. Again, regardless of race, nationality, economic status, all kids were treated the same and welcomed.

What did I learn from Mike and his family in those early years? What lessons did they pass on to our team and me?

One of the best gifts you can give your team is to tell them you love them. Show respect for the game and others you come across on your journey. Win or lose, you will be better off through the nourishment of the relationships you forge along the way. Unconditional love and respect will transcend wins and losses.

Today Mike lives in Alabama with his family, where he is a practicing attorney undoubtedly passing on the same compassion and enthusiasm he learned from his parents and showed as a promising high school student athlete.

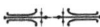

Note: You never know when or how you will reconnect with one of your former players. I remember Mike's dad coming back from a few weeks of helping out with the grandkids in Alabama.

"Boy, that Courtney is sure going to be something!" Ed told me as he watched our team practice one afternoon.

Turns out he was right. I turned on my television one evening and caught a few minutes on the 2024 Grammy Awards, where I saw that Courtney LaPlante, Spirit Box, was nominated for Best Heavy Metal Band and Vocalist. Alas, she lost the award to Metallica. But just like her father, it was clear she had a passion for and love of the game, win or lose.

CHAPTER 4

MENTORS—JINX, JOE, AND ALEC

No individual gets to where they are going on their own. Along the way, we find guides and mentors who help us develop into the people we are meant to become. John "Jinx" O'Connor, Joe O'Brien, and Alec Vyce are three legendary coaches who helped me develop as a person and coach.

The collective accomplishments of each man, as both athlete and coach in basketball and baseball, are mind boggling. Their concern and dedication to family, community, and athletics are top tier. My mentors' honors include inductions into school, state, and national sports hall of fame establishments. One man played on an NCAA D1 basketball final four team at New York University, another served as president of the Dr. James Naismith Memorial Basketball Hall of Fame, while the other played on arguably the best high school baseball team in the history of Massachusetts, at Chicopee High School. Each of these men carved out coaching and teaching careers at the high school and collegiate levels. On their journey, they took care of their families and contributed to their communities by helping many people from all walks of life. These three gentlemen teacher-coaches made a tremendous impact on my life that reached far beyond the basketball court and baseball diamond.

My high school basketball team with coach John "Jinx" O'Connor.
L-R Al Westbrook, me, T. Rohan, Ron Westbrook.
First row coach O'Connor and John "Elgin" Downey.

My mentor-coaches were giants in their specific sport. They provided plenty of analytics for the games of basketball and baseball long before it became popular to do so. They did not have high-speed supercomputers to track the data; instead, they used their experience, composure, and great communication skills to get their game plans across. An avalanche of victories was the eye test for their teams.

Today, with the internet, coaches and players have access to the same information. So without the benefit of the internet, what made these three men forge to the head of the class? What made them different from so many other coaches? The answer seems simple but has eluded many who have attempted to rule from the sidelines. O'Connor, O'Brien, and Vyce were honest, provided useful information to their players, and prepared their teams for all imaginable situations. As the young Prince Hamlet observes as he plans to avenge his father's murder, "the readiness is all."

These three mentors nurtured the soul of the team and modeled hope for the young people they worked with to ensure success. They emphasized the fundamentals of their sports with persistence, patience, and consistency. They earned the trust of their players, who in turn believed in what they were teaching them. Every member of the team needed a simple eye test to see the practice and preparation of fundamentals worked. And most importantly, they believed in how they were coaching players because it was all based on their core values as human beings. On the rare occasion when things didn't work out quite the way they wanted, they took responsibility for it. No surprise. Playing sports is all about wins and losses. That is a part of playing the game. It was through their triumphs and struggles that I learned how to be an effective coach not only on the field but also in my own life.

Jinx was my first mentor. He taught his teams the value of teamwork, and through him, I learned how to play together with my teammates. When he was my high school basketball coach, we won a lot of games. Not only that, but we won difficult games against teams that had stars but were defeated by our balanced focus on offense and defense. In fact, he introduced me to my first system of offense, the Auburn shuffle (3, 4, 5, 2, 1), which was a sequence of player movement that I used extensively throughout my coaching career. In the 1995 Western Massachusetts Championship game in which HHS played Longmeadow High School, we scored repeatedly on the shuffle, cut, and screen, leaving Wilfredo Cabrera, our screener, open for multiple three-point shots.

Jinx was smart. He understood intrinsically that basketball was a team game that could not be played individually but that we all needed to take individual responsibility for our actions and contributions to the team. That is why it is no surprise to me that Coach helped me acquire my first real job, as a counselor at Camp Holy Cross in Goshen, MA. I worked there with one of Jinx's sons, Brian O'Connor, who was and still is a friend, as well as an entrepreneur, singer-songwriter, and tennis teaching guru. We learned to work with kids and give back. The work also provided much-needed money for my family and me to cover some school expenses.

At the Goshen camp, I could play pickup basketball games with Joe McDowell, Cathedral and Villanova star, when the campers were back in their cabins. I met many people connected to the sports world through Coach O'Connor and his family, such as American League umpire Eddie Hurley, Al Grenert, Press and Pete Maravich, Dolph Shayes, Larry Costello, Lou Carnesecca, NBA referee Sid Borgia, NYU coach Howard Cann (who happened to be Jinx's coach for the final four team) and Celtic great Sam Jones.

As well as teaching the value of teamwork, Coach and his dedicated wife Annette always stressed the importance of education and modeled for us firsthand the value of learning in our lives. Jinx had a degree from NYU, while Mrs. O'Connor graduated from the prestigious all-girl school Mount Holyoke College. Together they scraped by to send all of their children off for a postgraduate year at some of the best prep schools in the nation. The O'Connors graced the halls of Deerfield and Northfield Mount Herman Academy before matriculating to four-year schools.

It is difficult to comprehend the extent of the role just one person can have in your life. Jinx was a coach to me but so many other things to so many others as well. When he passed away, his son Brian, one of six O'Connor children, posted the following remembrance to his dad:

> From Dillon's Block to Normandy, Sicily and North Africa
> From St Jerome's Gym to Madison Square Garden
> From Mckenzie Field to the Polo Grounds to the Basketball Hall of Fame
> Walked with Kings and never lost his common touch

What can't you say about my second mentor, Joe O'Brien? Part of the New England basketball mafia, along with Dee Rowe (University of Connecticut), George Blaney (Holy Cross), Ed Markey (Saint Michael's College), Joe Vancisin (Yale), Joe Mullaney, and Dave Gavitt (Providence College). This group of talented coaches put their schools' programs at the top of the college game. Coach O'Brien's accomplishments in basketball led him to the top as a coach, innovator, and global leader. He impacted basketball from local neighborhoods to international play as he served as president of the James Naismith Memorial Basketball Hall of Fame. During his tenure the game exploded and expanded to all parts of the globe.

Before he led the transformation of the Basketball Hall of Fame from its Springfield College site to its present state-of-the-art facility located on Columbus Avenue in Springfield, MA, however, he was both the baseball and basketball coach at Assumption College (presently Assumption University). Most importantly for me, he was my college baseball coach.

As basketball coach for the school, Joe was involved in classic New England battles each year. The Greyhounds advanced to the Elite Eight D2 Nationals in Evansville each year that I was a student at Assumption. Memorable games against Bentley and

Saint Michael's stand out, as well as a regular season win over Holy Cross and Jack Donahue. Donahue was supposed to deliver Lew Alcindor (Kareem Abdul-Jabbar) to the Cross as his high school mentor at Power Memorial. However, a visit to the West Coast sunshine changed the landscape of college basketball, and Lew became a Bruin.

D2 basketball has a history of great players, from Bo Lamar to Marvin Webster, George Gervin, and Earl "the Pearl" Monroe, to name a few. Coach O'Brien's teams competed with the best D2 teams in the nation. Assumption was fed by a New Jersey pipeline of hoop talent that included the likes of Jake Jones and Mike and Jim Boylan. Jim transferred to Marquette his junior year and was the starting point guard on Al McGuire's National Championship team. Western Mass also contributed to the Greyhounds' success, with Joe Klofas from Coach Vyce's Chicopee Comp team and John Grocholowski, who played at Holyoke Catholic. John benefited greatly from Coach O'Brien's innovative genius. Groch, a big man at six-foot-seven, could shoot, and from fifteen to seventeen feet away, he was money. Coach O'Brien used John to drag other teams' bigs out from the paint. This opened up space for the other smaller but faster Greyhounds to penetrate without the threat of a shot blocker confronting their forays to the rim.

If this sounds familiar, it's only because most of today's modern game of pace and space are replicated in Coach O'Brien's original game plan. Coach was way ahead of his time. He developed a team style that was unique in the early '70s, when D2 teams around the nation had many D1 players on their rosters. The explosion of ESPN and the Big East and other power conferences was on the horizon.

Coach O'Brien was also one heck of a baseball coach. He was an excellent pitcher in his day, as well as a great basketball player. I played baseball at Assumption for Coach O'Brien, and that is where I got to know him best. One of my work-study jobs at Assumption was to help out at Laska Gymnasium. This was a great gig for me because I watched firsthand as Coach O'Brien ran his basketball practices. Coach put a lot of energy into his team. He was a hands-on coach and demanded a lot from himself and his staff of assistant coaches during a practice session. Each year I played baseball for the Greyhounds, our men's basketball team advanced to the Elite Eight in Evansville, Indiana. There is nothing like March Madness on a college campus during the playoffs!

So what was coach O'Brien's gift to me, and what did I take away from our time together? I am sure Coach O'Brien was exhausted at the conclusion of a long basketball season. There was plenty of travel and stress to go around, trying to win a National Championship. I often wondered if the baseball season was going to be that important to him.

It didn't take long to find out. Joe O'Brien would show up at our first baseball practice and coach us for two hours like we were the most important thing going on in the world. I know he was physically and emotionally exhausted from basketball. However, he never let us feel that we were second to the basketball season. Coach O'Brien taught me to be present. He taught me to focus on the team in front of me. He taught me to try to make others feel important.

My third mentor was Alec Vyce, who achieved a wave of success at Chicopee Comprehensive High School when I first started coaching basketball at HHS. His championship teams were a blend of power, skill, and smarts, with players like Holmes, Drabinski, the Franklin brothers, and Klofas. His teams never beat themselves. I am sure Alec was busy teaching, coaching, and raising his family, yet he always had time to talk with me.

Through phone calls and preseason scrimmages, Coach Vyce gave me plenty of things to think about and implement against superior opponents. As we were playing out of the strong Valley League for my entire coaching career, there would be many games we would go into as the underdog.

"You have to give your team hope against superior talent. You can't go at them straight up all the time. If you have a better team, keep it simple. But if the other guy has the horses, mix it up."

Thus I learned to mix defenses, focus on one or two of our opponent's strengths, and work to minimize them. Our coaching staff would create a game plan that we presented and practiced with the team. For Coach Vyce's guidance and friendship I am forever grateful.

Alec Vyce hall of fame Chicopee Comp coach.

Jinx, O'Brien, and Vyce were important figures that modeled for me what being a coach can be for young people. I know mine certainly was not the only life they affected positively.

Mentors are by nature leaders, and there is no way to count how many other lives they touch. For example, Jim Moon Mullens was recently inducted into the Assumption University Sports Hall of Fame. Other than Coach O'Brien's family, he probably knows Coach O'Brien better than anyone. Mullen served as assistant director of athletics and was a manager for the Greyhounds basketball and baseball programs, where he got to spend a lot of time with Coach O'Brien.

When I called Jim to share some of his thoughts on Joe O'Brien, he stated, "Joe and his wife were special friends to me. They took me under their wings when I started out on Salisbury Street. As a manager I was treated like one of the players, not a second-class citizen. I was expected to follow all the rules as the players. Coach would always preach to the team family first, books second, and basketball a distant third."

Jim talked about Coach bringing him to work at the Basketball Hall of Fame in '85. "Time to get out into the world, Moon!" O'Brien had advised him. Jim said, "I think Coach knew I would pay attention to the smallest details to get things right."

So, with the hall of fame transitioning into a modern venue, Coach O'Brien believed Jim's opportunity to grow as a person and his value in the workplace would benefit both of them.

Their time and work together at the hall of fame came with many memorable stories and experiences, but one story stood out fondly for Jimmy. "As I was closing up the hall one evening, working my way down from the second floor to the lobby, I noticed a very tall man approaching the first floor entrance. 'Sorry, sir! We are just closing up.'"

The very tall man then asked Moon if he could just step inside for a few minutes, explaining he would not be long. Jim let the man in, explaining, "You might want to take the elevator to the third floor." The third floor is where the Ring of Honor is on display.

Assumption College baseball head coach, Joe O'Brien pictured in top row far right #20, I am #11 first row second from left.

The next morning Jim walked into Joe O'Brien's office. "We had a visitor last night."

"Oh, who was it?" O'Brien inquired.

"Bill Russell!" Jim exclaimed. "I told him to take the elevator to the third floor."

Without looking up from his coffee and paper, Joe O'Brien asked "What did he say?"

"He said, 'Don't tell anyone I was here.'"

Joe O'Brien turned the page of his newspaper and replied, "I knew he would show up sooner or later."

Bill Russell did not attend his enshrinement ceremony. Some feel it was his way of letting people know how unjustly other African Americans had been mistreated in our society. Some say it was because the hall had not acknowledged Chuck Cooper, the first to break the color barrier in the NBA. In a private ceremony on November 15, 2019, Russell tweeted, "I accepted my HOF ring. In 1975 I refused being the first black player to go into the Hall of Fame. I felt others before me should have that honor. Good to see progress. Chuck Cooper HOF 2019" (internet sportscasting.com). Like all great leaders, Joe O'Brien helped move the game in the direction it needed to go.

Note: Two coaches who also had special meaning for me as mentors were Abe Collamore and Dan Dulchinos. Abe Collamore was my junior varsity basketball coach my freshman year at HHS. Abe was an HHS and Saint Anselm's College hall of fame player on the hardwood and was one of only five Purple Knights to have claimed the Lahovich Award, the highest award for high school basketball players in western Mass. Abe was an incredible assistant coach for Jinx, and he stressed the importance of defense each night we took to the court.

The other coach was Dan Dulchinos from Chicopee Comprehensive High School. Coach Dulchinos skippered the Chicopee Comp baseball program for fifty seasons. He was also a Western Mass Championship basketball coach at Comp and logged many seasons as their freshman coach as well. Although I never played for him, I felt I had. When I watched Coach Dulchinos conduct himself during games and interact with his players, I knew these were things I wanted to emulate in my coaching one day.

Both men were regulars at high school games to support their communities. On many occasions we would make a point of talking with each other a bit before or after a Purple Knight game. Our talks never centered around winning or losing. Instead there was always a special reminder from them that "You're coaching kids, and this is supposed to be fun" or "Remember, they are only teenagers." Both men were always delivering the same important message: "Don't get full of yourself. We are here for the kids."

The cities of Holyoke and Chicopee were very fortunate these men dedicated their talents and time to work for so many years with the young adults. I was very fortunate that they took some time to watch the high school kids play and were supportive of my coaching career at HHS.

Sadly, in January 2023 Abe Collamore passed over to be with his beloved wife Marge. I am sure there is also a bit of basketball chatter going on with the "Wizard of Western Mass" Coach O'Connor. Heaven bless their lovely wives.

CHAPTER 5

THE MAN WHO JUMPS FROM SCHOOL TO SCHOOL

Eddie Acosta always found me. Wherever I taught in the Holyoke Public Schools, we came across one other. Eddie moved around a lot for many different reasons. As his family changed apartments, school lines were redrawn, and Eddie changed schools, he struggled to find a comfort level and a place where he felt he belonged. Additionally, the Holyoke Public Schools had flipped back and forth between a grade school, middle school, and junior high school model in their K–8 schools.

Eddie was a smart kid, but as his teacher, I always worried that the streets would get the best of him. One time he corrected me when I said "Ed, you are smart. You should be doing a lot better in school."

Offering a bit of genius that I have never forgotten, he said, "Mr. Rigali, being smart is only half of being successful. You need to feel you belong someplace." I must admit Eddie's insight really struck a cord deep within me.

Similarly to Eddie, I also moved around a lot in the early days of my teaching career. I connected with his need to belong to someplace too. I was near the bottom of our teacher seniority list and as a result was always one of the first to be riffed or reassigned to a different teaching position.

At this time the cracks had started to show in Holyoke, a city built for a blue-collar workforce that was starting to experience the influences of manufacturers moving out or closing up. The paper factories and other mills were on the endangered species list. As the school system started to take hits to their budget, I made the rounds from school to school: John J. Lynch Jr., unemployment, Peck Middle School, unemployment, Dean Vocational High School, adult education classes with ESL students, Magnet Middle School, the Holyoke Street School, and my last stop, HHS.

The Holyoke Street School, an alternative school on Race Street, was the last place Eddie and I found each other. I had Eddie as a student in six out of those seven venues. At times it seemed like I saw Eddie more than my own kids. Like I mentioned before, Eddie was smart, but he was also strong and athletic. He talked a lot about boxing and the Golden Gloves, but I am not sure if he actually trained or just had a passing interest.

The Street School was an alternative school to help struggling students obtain a high school diploma. Eddie was a student in my English block. Students like Eddie were fortunate for this opportunity. The school on Race Street was a well-designed safety net for thirty to forty kids per school year who had dropped out in the past or were on the verge of leaving traditional settings. The school was a bit too liberal for me, but I have to admit it worked for many kids due to many compassionate and skilled teachers (who could have doubled as Bill Walton's favorite band the Grateful Dead). Music aside, these teachers connected to their students, providing them the opportunity to get a good start to their adult life.

Eddie had gone through a lot in his short time on this planet. His defense mechanism to deal with life's hard knocks was to write. He especially liked to write poems, which was good for me as his English teacher as it allowed me to award him points toward graduation (a last chance, magical number computed with hours, assignments, and attendance to earn a high school diploma).

Before winter break the school was going to have a student-faculty basketball game. The game was to be played at Kelly School in a Holyoke neighborhood known as the Flats. However, we had to wait until three in the afternoon for the game to start. The Street School was usually done by 1:00 p.m. so the kids could get after school work in the afternoon or at early evening shifts.

As the game started, it was evident that no one in this student-faculty game was in danger of making any SportsCenter clips. I did not play but instead volunteered to referee the game. Some of the staff knew I coached high school basketball, so they were glad to pass that honor on to me.

Eddie, Biggie, and Miguel showed some basketball promise among the otherwise chaotic contestants. Despite their efforts, it became clear after a few minutes of refereeing I would have to make a few amendments to Dr. Naismith's rules.

The first rule change was that traveling with the basketball would be allowed. Second, a player needed to be assaulted at least three times before a foul could be given to the defender. Third, absolutely no technical fouls could be called for any reason. The game looked more like a rugby scrum than basketball, but the students were having fun and nobody was getting hurt. It was a great community building opportunity for staff and students, leaving everyone in good spirits.

Or rather, it seemed like a nice way to start the weekend until I went out to my car and found I was missing the two rear tires from my late-model VW. I am sure the neighborhood tire crew would have gotten all four had our student-faculty game gone into overtime. Perhaps the tire thieves were scared away by the final buzzer?

Regardless, I was angry but not as upset as my Street School students. At that time, we did not have cell phones, so I went back into the school to call for a tow truck. I half expected to come out and find my other two tires missing in action. Instead, what I found was my beat-up old VW jacked up with a bunch of Street School kids feverishly replacing my two stolen tires. They did not match and they were not new, but that really was not the point.

Mooky, one of the kids from the game, had raced home and pulled out a couple of tires from his garage. His dad was an auto mechanic and always had parts around. He then reached into his pocket and pulled out a sticker with a big blue dot on it.

"Here, Mr. R. Put this on your bumper. No one will ever bother your ride again."

They never did.

"My Teacher"
To my teacher
who stares like a preacher, William Rigali.
I had him in Lynch
There it was such a cinch.
I had him in street school:
There he taught me to be smart
Instead of a fool.
If only William Rigali could stay
A little longer in street school,
I could learn more reading and writing
Which would be very exciting
Especially from you William Rigali
The man that jumps from
School to school.
Yours truly,
Edward

Note: Many years later Eddie found me again. It was in my new English classroom, 108 Holyoke High School. HHS was my seventh and final teaching venue within the Holyoke Public Schools, where I taught thirty-eight September-to-June seasons.

This time, however, it wasn't exactly Eddie, but his daughter. She was quiet, calm, confident, and very smart. She wanted to go on to nursing school.

"My dad is Eddie Acosta," she announced to me as I called her name while taking attendance. She then got out of her seat and approached my desk. "He wanted me to say hi for him. He said you guys go way back and he loved writing poems in your class."

"Thanks!" I started to chirp before she cut me off.

"He also said you were the very worst basketball referee that he had ever seen!"

She smiled and walked back to her seat and opened her notebook. I hope she was writing a poem. It was clear she knew the time and score, just like her dad.

CHAPTER 6

SOCIAL DISTANCING

My first introduction to social distancing was not the global COVID-19 lockdown of 2020 but rather back in the late '60s at Technical High School in Springfield, MA. A number of new laws, particularly the Civil Rights Act of 1964, were enacted during this time period. Many of these laws were put in place under President Johnson's watch and driven forward by the great sacrifices of many civil rights leaders. Change was coming, and one of the first places affected by these changes were the neighborhood schools.

When it comes to social justice matters, I often say we can do our best to pass laws to provide fairness and equality to all but we can't legislate people's hearts. It takes a lot more than a pen and paper to move people toward more open, compassionate hearts. That is the real hurdle and work of social justice progress.

Nowhere was this more evident than our country's struggle with school integration and busing. For most Americans, including the people in the Pioneer Valley, these were relatively new social concepts. Like many places in America at that time, Springfield had its share of discontent and community angst concerning racial integration.

The Springfield Public Schools and one parochial boys high

school basketball team played out of the City League. The league was made up of the following schools: Technical, Commerce, Putnam, Classical, and parochial Cathedral high schools. Needless to say, five schools drawing from a large urban area produced amazing talent and teams.

Despite the talent, the City League members had trouble filling out a full schedule. You could argue that other Pioneer Valley teams did not want to play them because of their basketball prowess. However, my inclination is that the difficulty in scheduling games for the Springfield teams was due more to racial intolerance as well as a fear of fights and trouble that could possibly break out at games. At one point, some city teams were down to a dozen games for the season. Scheduling would become such an issue for the Springfield teams that eventually the league, including Holyoke, was merged into the Valley League.

Over the years, many Pioneer Valley schools tiptoed in and out of this league. Some schools flat out refused to be realigned into the top tier competition of the reimagined Valley League. In fact, the HHS boys basketball program remains the only non-Springfield team with continuous membership in the merged Valley League–City League since its inception. This realignment occurred nearly forty years ago.

My high school coach Jinx O'Connor scheduled our HHS team to play a city school each year. In my senior year, we played Springfield Technical in their tiny gymnasium. The Tigers' gym was very different from our spanking-new sixteen-hundred-seat facility back in Holyoke. Our games were always packed. At this time, high school teams were the main focus for their communities. That passion had not yet been eroded by sports on television and the internet, or the proliferation of for-profit school teams.

When the Knights walked out for the jump ball that December in the late '60s in the Technical High School gym, we played in front of zero fans. The only people allowed in the facility were the referees, coaches, players, school administrators, and police.

The game started at 3:30 p.m. Both the Holyoke Knights and the Tech Tigers had black and white players on their rosters. To this day, I still feel lucky I had the opportunity to play alongside my teammates against our opponents in that game. I was fortunate to have a coach like Jinx O'Connor who did not succumb to the hysteria of hate, fear, and prejudice that some people carried around with them, tainting their world view and the potential of a united society.

Tech always had excellent teams. The Tech Tigers provided the opposition for the Purple Knights in one of the initial contests played in the new Holyoke gym. Today, that facility bears the name John "Jinx" O'Connor Gymnasium, a fitting tribute to my late coach.

As a youth, I remember watching the Tigers play in the new HHS facility before a sold-out audience. As a young fan, I was mesmerized watching Tech's magical basketball talent Dwight Durante, a talented, left-handed, black player standing at only five-eight. He was lightning quick, had a great handle, and filled out his résumé with a picture-perfect jump shot. Double D, as Dwight became known, could do it all, and that night he had the crowd reacting to his every move. He could control the ball like it was on a string. Some would say that he would showboat when he had the ball, but that was not the case. Double D could get to wherever he wanted to be on the court. He just did it faster and better than the other players in western Mass. Behind the back, between the legs, crossovers, hesitation, right, left, and right again. It made the Purple Knights dizzy trying to defend him.

Bobby Cremins, the Georgia Tech coach who recruited Springfield Central great Travis Best, said the same thing about Travis: "He can get to any spot on the court he wants."

Double D was the first of many high school players I looked up to in my pre-high-school years. Durante went on to a great career at Catawba College in North Carolina. He was drafted by the New York Knicks but made his mark barnstorming for many years with the Harlem Globetrotters. Durante was also one of the first black students to register at Catawba College. What a gift to fans to see him and competitors to play against him.

On the other hand, what a loss it was for those who did not get the opportunity due to their inability to change and grow. We all lose as a society when we allow our hate, fear, and prejudice to close doors which keep us apart. So in that early season game in the late '60s, in my senior year, the doors were closed to the Tech High School gym. We were apart from everything that makes us human. No family, no friends, and no community. Hysteria, hate, and fear had won for that day, but Coach O'Connor would not let it prevail. All of us who played for him that day learned an invaluable life lesson of humanity. The doors were closed to the gym that day, but my teammates and I would start our adult lives keeping the doors open for whoever was on the other side brave enough and willing to walk through.

Note: How good was Dwight Durante? I believe in today's modern game, considering the NBA's progress toward a diverse and inclusive community, specifically in positions of influence around the league, that he would have been on any number of NBA teams.

In fact, in January 2017 Durante was inducted into the North Carolina Sports Hall of Fame. This is quite an honor since the hall includes such great NBA players as Michael Jordan, Walt Bellemy, John Lucas, Cedric Maxwell, and Jeff Mullins. Durante and Lawrence Bullock were Catawba's first black basketball players in the '65–'66 season. Many basketball insiders felt Durante's discouraging experience at the 1968 Olympic trials pushed him to go with the Globetrotters and not take a shot at the NBA. Pete Maravich, Calvin Murphy, Rick Mount, and Charlie Scott all had their hands full trying to guard the lefty wizard. Head to head it was reported Durante put forty-four points on Calvin Murphy, who had a long and distinguished career that led to the NBA Hall of Fame. Alas, Dwight was left off the team that went to Mexico City to compete.

CHAPTER 7

CAMP LIFE—NELSON-SANDERS AND THE SAINT

For many high school coaches who got into the game before the internet, the best way to keep adding to your coaching satchel was to work the basketball camp scene in the summer months. The pay was pathetic, but you put the time in to be around coaches from the professional, college, and high school ranks. It was not only a way to improve your craft; it also helped that some of your own players could attend to improve their game in the off season. Especially since attending a summer camp was not always an option for many of the kids I coached. Their families just did not have any extra money to spend on a week away at basketball camp. Additionally, MIAA rules prohibit schools from fundraising to pay for a camp experience, so players and families are on their own to fundraise and finance that experience.

I spent many summers at the Nelson-Sanders Camp. The basketball school operated out of a number of locations in Southern New Hampshire. The 1980s and '90s were a hot time for basketball camps. People from other disciplines had not caught on to the fact that they could make lots of money by teaching a skill or discipline during the school vacation months. During my coaching career, I witnessed parenting evolve from "Be back when the street lights turn on" to helicopter status, snow plowing, and finally to the college bribe scandal of the privileged few to scam their children into name schools. At this time, parents were starting to invest in all kinds of extracurricular activities to help give their child a slight advantage, or simply get them out of their hair for a week.

Camp photo from Nelson/Sanders basketball school. Don Nelson back row far left, I am in the middle with my shades and Tom Satch Sanders far right top row.

My attraction to the Nelson-Sanders Basketball School came from two influences. First, from my love for the Boston Celtics. I grew up listening to their games on the radio with gravel-voiced Johnny Most calling the games "high above courtside." No broadcaster has ever come close to being as much of a homer as Johnny Most. No insult to an opposing player, coach, fan, or referee was ever off the table. But it was fine with me as I lay listening to the C's games on my scratchy transistor radio. The Celtics were my team, and they were great. Russell, Cousy, Satch, Sharman, Nellie, Heinshon, Havlicek, KC, and Sam led by the guy with the cigar. Not to mention Bird, McHale, and Parish! Cities and fans hated Red Auerbach and the Celts because of their success year after year, but the Celtics were more than just champions. Auerbach and the Celtics helped advance the integration process for the black athlete in professional sports immensely. I certainly was not aware of it as a young fan, but the Celtics and Red had many firsts for the inclusion of the black athlete, from head coach Russell to an all-black starting five.

I was able to attend many Celtics games as a young fan. The NBA was struggling then, and you could go down the day of the game and pick up a ticket to an important playoff game with ease, never mind a regular season contest. I watched doubleheaders on Sunday, cheered for and against the Big O and Jerry West, procured tons of players' autographs and a few photos. One game I scooped up most of the Philadelphia 76ers' signatures with the likes of Hal Greer, who always stopped to talk with kids. Watching Wilt stroll in next to Hal Greer was an interesting sight. It did reinforce the fact that Dr. Naismith's game to this day has a place for you regardless of your size.

I was at Bob Cousy Day and can still hear the fan from the upper deck shout out, "We love ya, Cooz!" when the Celtic legend got choked up at the microphone. I was at game seven of the famous Celtics versus Sixers series in 1962. "Havlicek stole the ball! It's all over! It's all over! It's all over!" That night Al Grenert (Holyoke native) was in on the famous call from Johnny Most.

I have three important memories from that game. The first was the start of the game, when the Celtics came roaring out of the gate and Sam Jones knocked down one of his fast break bank shots. It was the loudest sound I had ever heard. The second was the haze. By the middle of the third quarter, the banners hanging from the rafters and upper seats were pretty much impossible to see. Back then you could smoke at public venues, and the nerves were definitely getting the best of the chain-smoking Celtic fans. Third was the silence after the Sixers scored with only a few seconds left to cut our lead to a single digit. The Celtics just needed to inbound the ball safely, and the game and series would be ours. Then the unthinkable happened. Russell grabbed the ball and stepped out of bounds to inbound the ball off the guide wire. Next thing, the Sixers had the ball under their own hoop and a time-out was called. The dread and dead silence overtook everyone in the Garden in a single moment. I am sure even the infamous Garden rats paused, waiting with baited breath. It was such a fearful feeling.

Most felt with the Sixers inbounding right under their own hoop they would send a lob pass to Wilt for a dunk, series over. But, as any true Celtics fan knows, that didn't happen. The basketball gods had other ideas, "Havelicek stole the ball!" and the Celtics move on to play another day.

Note: Grenert was a Holyoke native, professional player and college coach, a member of the Saint Anselm Hall of Fame, and a US Marine Corp veteran who served in World War II.

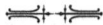

Tom Sanders, eight-time NBA champion, and Don Nelson, four-time NBA champion, were Celtic teammates and members of the hall of fame. Both players helped the NBA survive and grow into the global billion-dollar industry that it is today. Both went on to successful ventures after their playing careers were over. Their lives after playing in the "Association" focused on coaching, mentorship, consulting, and community driven partnerships. Their names were synonymous with success. Nelson and Sanders had helped build the league but played when it was on a financial shoestring.

One day over lunch in the cafeteria, Satch recanted his tough negotiations with the Celtics. His biggest contract was $31K. He noted playoff money was extremely important to the players. Number 16 related to me that many of his teammates went home to other jobs at the conclusion of the NBA season. Summer camps were a way to recoup some money on careers that in today's market would be worth millions.

Don Nelson was a hot item during the summers when I worked at the Nelson-Sanders Basketball School. Along with report cards issued to each camper, kids and their parents had the opportunity to purchase merchandise (which went flying off the shelves and were an indisputable cash cow).The camp investors wanted to make the most out of this business opportunity.

Don Nelson coached the Milwaukee Bucks and later the Golden State Warriors. He was on a run. He coached excellent teams with great players like Bob Lanier, Sydney Moncrief, Tim Hardaway, Mitch Richmond, and Chris Mullins. His Golden State Warriors created the foundation of the fast Nellie Ball offense, proving Don Nelson was an innovator in the league.

In fact, Nelson's Warrior teams were a precursor to how the NBA game is played today. Nelson was also ahead of the curve when it came to finding international players. He was constantly dispatching his son Donnie to Europe to find NBA talent. The Warriors led the NBA in offense during the '89–'90 season. They sold out every home game in '90–'91 and beat Denver 162–158, the highest-scoring regulation game in NBA history. His players loved to play that way.

I learned many things about coaching during my time working at Nelson-Sanders Camp. It cannot be emphasized enough the tremendous value that came with watching these two men in action on and off the basketball court. I learned so much about coaching and running my team during my work over the summer that I could directly apply it to my role as head basketball coach at HHS.

In particular, I learned how important it was to adjust each season not only to the ability of our team but also to the relative lack of size and height of our players. The era of a coach calling a set every time down the court was waning. On the other hand, Holyoke's Hispanic population was growing rapidly. As a result, I seldom had teams that featured big guys, leading to our coaching staff making adjustments every season. We taught a fast-break style with a mix of switching defenses, which helped the Purple Knights snap Central High School's streak of eighty-five consecutive wins. We were able to accomplish this great feat with every Purple Knight point coming at the foul line or in the paint. We were small, but we were fast. No midrange or three-point field goals. Just layup after layup. Our style was to sprint down on offense and sprint back to defend.

On the few occasions, when we had a lazy game on transition defense, we practiced the next day without a basketball. Together the coaching staff and the players perfected our transition game, and it led to a Western Mass Championship in 1993. This was one of the most important takeaways from my time at the Nelson-Sanders Camp: the necessity of adjusting your style to your talent. We might not have had size, but we were getting competitive, skilled players who could hold their own against bigger teams.

Another important lesson I learned from my yearslong work at Nelson-Sanders Camp was the importance of in-game adjustments. Most coaches know that there will be many games in their coaching career where they have to adjust on the fly. One such memorable games for me was during a sectional semifinal match at the University of Massachusetts gym, known infamously as the Cage, against Springfield's Central High School. We started out playing a more traditional three-out, two-in setup. We had some size with two players coming in at 6-foot-5 and 6-foot-3, so we could go inside a lot against most opponents. However, that was not the case against this Central team, with players from 6-foot-7 to 6-foot-10 who strutted around the court.

Hasan Ward, who went on to play for Virginia Commonwealth University, was blocking shots like he was the second coming of Bill Russell. At the end of the first quarter, we trailed thirteen to one. Our bigs could not score inside. At the half, we were still being smothered inside by their size. It was then that I decided to roll the dice and play some Nellie ball. Small ball, here we go!

We spread the Central players out and drove to the hoop. Nate Melero, inserted into the game as our fourth small, dragged their bigs away from the hoop. He went on to hit several three-pointers when they didn't step out to cover him and blew by any big they put on him if he was crowded. It opened up the lanes for us to get back into the game. Nate had played an important role at the time when we needed it most.

I was very proud of that team for being able to make such a significant halftime adjustment in such an important game. I was so happy for Nate that he had his moment to shine. He had missed 90 percent of his junior season due to a broken arm, and it took him almost his entire senior year to get back into top form. Still, Nate came through for us big that day when we needed him most. He was the quintessential sixth man, playing hard every possession that game. Ultimately we lost the game, but we were able to hold our heads high and know we left our best effort on the court. Central went on to win the championship but had to vacate the title due to a paper work technicality.

Another valuable lesson I learned during my time at Nelson-Sanders Camp and as a basketball player myself was how to work with parents. Obviously, the camp provided an excellent opportunity for families and campers to help their children develop new skills on and off the courts. The service and experience provided by the camp was top notch and saw the likes of many Boston professional athletes sending their own children to learn from the two Celtic greats.

However, working with parents and families can present many challenges as a coach. If you stay in coaching long enough, you will eventually get some fallout from parents who are not happy with the game plan or playing time of their son or daughter. They might even find offense in the fact that their offspring are not featured prominently in the team's offensive approach. I accepted my responsibility as a head coach of a varsity program, knowing I would have to make hard decisions. My job was to always put together the best team possible by placing the best players on the court to give my school and community a chance to win. I did this regardless of race, religion, or economic status. Family, friend, and foe were all given equal opportunity to earn their place.

At times the race card was played out from both sides. Black and white groups felt their kids were getting a raw deal. Hispanic and Latino groups felt the same. I only saw kids as students and basketball players at our school. I refused to be influenced by the noise of the community crowd. Each player who tried out was given a level playing field to compete for a spot on the team and playing time.

I quickly learned from my experience as a coach that you are not going to make everyone happy. You need to focus on your job and keep working with the kids on the team to get it right. I continually emphasized the roles and importance from the first player to the last. The rest is really up to the players. As a coach you can only hope the messages players hear from their parents, friends, and community are supportive of your program.

During my senior year in high school as one of the captains of our undefeated Valley League team, I learned a valuable lesson from Coach O'Connor concerning this topic. At the conclusion of a hard-fought win, a teammate's father confronted Jinx on the way back to the locker room. He started to scream at Coach about the lack of playing time for his son. Coach kept on moving as Al Westbrook stepped in and blocked the intruder. Here we were playing in front of sold-out crowds, winning, helping each other as teammates, and that still wasn't enough for this parent. He failed to see that his son was a part of something that was bigger than all of us. Ultimately, the only thing that parental outburst caused was his son's embarrassment. In the locker room, Jinx told us a story to get the focus off the young man, who was clearly shaken by the event.

"Don't worry. It's OK," Coach announced in the locker room. He went on to emphasize how important every player was to the success of our team. The Wizard of Western Mass continued, "From the starters to the kids coming off the bench, we are in this together and we are in this for each other."

I was the last player out of the locker room that night. Sandy always said I kept her waiting the longest after games. Coach O'Connor stopped me and began, "This is how it works with parents and basketball. First, they want their boy on the team. Second, they want him to start. Third, they want him to be the star. Fourth, they want him to take all of the shots he should take and all the ones he shouldn't. Fifth, and of course they want you to win."

We both had a good laugh.

"Don't worry, Coach, I will talk with Richie. He will be OK with his dad." I continued, "So Coach, let me get this straight. For the parents or family to be all good with you, their kid has to make the team, start the game, play all the time, become the star, take most shots, and win it all? Then will they be happy?

Coach replied, "Well, I wouldn't go that far."

Another reason I was drawn to the Nelson-Sanders Basketball Camp was the opportunity to work with Gary St. Jean from

Chicopee, MA. Gary had worked at the Nellie and Satch camp while coaching his Chicopee High School Pacers. Coach Nelson liked Gary's basketball IQ and passion for the game so much that he gave Gary his shot in the NBA. He started out as a scout for the Milwaukee Bucks, working his way up through the ranks from assistant coach, to head coach, then general manager in the world's best basketball league. Dave Godin, also from Chicopee and coach at Suffield Academy in Connecticut, was our western Mass contact to work the camp and get some of our players up to New Hampshire.

It was a lot of fun to see Nellie, Satch, and Saint work with the new draft picks or a free agent after the campers had gone to sleep for the night. These evaluation sessions occurred mostly in the late afternoons or late evenings. It was undoubtedly the best part of the camp experience to watch the professional coaches work out their players. The late evening sessions were closed to most of the campers and staff. However, Gary and Dave would sneak me in. It was in these practices that I could watch an NBA staff work their magic—Ralph Sampson, Chris Mullins, and Tim Hardaway, to name a few. Most memorable was Sarunas Marciulionis, drafted by the Warriors from Lithuania, scouted by Nellie's son Donnie, and one of the 2014 Naismith Hall of Fame inductees. Coach and the Warriors were ahead of the curve, looking to Europe and around the world for talent.

The Warriors' style of play was called small ball or Nellie ball on the Left Coast (as previously mentioned). The organization initiated a trending global talent hunt for the NBA. Don Nelson and his crew were innovators of the game. As I watched those workouts through the hot August nights in New Hampshire, it was easy to see the blend of genius and simple, basic teaching skill that they poured into each player. They knew Hardaway and Marciulionis were special talents.

One of my fondest memories is when our school's very own point guard, Ramon Cosme, who won the best player in the camp for successive summers, was able to duel it out with Hardaway during a camp lecture.

Hardaway had a fast one-two start off the dribble and became famous for his crossover move. Ramon could get by Tim; however, by step three, size and strength had won out and Hardaway would cut him off. Afterward I inquired, "OK Ramon, how was it?"

With a big smile on his face and a shake of his head, he stated, "He is pretty good, Coach. I think he might make their team."

This was yet another reason I loved working at the Nelson-Sanders Camp: the camp was an opportunity for my players and me to interact and observe excellence.

Note: Tim Hardaway was inducted into the Naismith Memorial Hall of Fame class of 2022.

Through the years, I met many incredible basketball players at Nelson-Sanders. One such player was Randy Breuer, a seven-foot-two center from the University of Minnesota. As he towered over the young campers, he would field questions during his lecture on postplay. Of course, many of the younger campers would ask him questions concerning his height. How could they resist? Breuer was always patient and kind with his responses, stating he liked being tall on the court but it had its challenges off court. He wasn't lying. A blessing from the basketball gods could be a complicated reality in the real world. Never was this more true than when one afternoon I witnessed Randy struggle with a simple daily task many of us take for granted.

Randy would come by the lower courts after dinner to watch the skill sessions. The former Gopher always drove his car down to the dreaded lower outdoor tar courts. This edition of the Nelson-Sanders Basketball Camp was being held at New England College in Henniker, NH. The courts were positioned at the bottom of a long hill well below the upper campus. It was a haul to walk up and down. It was there I realized what he had meant with some of his answers from the day before. Breuer had just finished talking about serenity away from the court and the challenges of doing everyday tasks. At the lower courts, I observed him getting into his vehicle. I watched him struggle with this simple maneuver that so many of us do without a mere thought. Indeed, some of life's simplest tasks were a challenge for this basketball giant.

Of course, height on the basketball court has its advantages. The tallest player my Purple Knights went up against was a young man named Neil Fingleton from Holy Name High School in Worcester, MA. Fingleton hailed from England. He was seven-foot-seven and gained some notoriety as "the Giant" in the Game of Thrones series. We faced Fingleton in a state semifinal game at the Mullins Center in Amherst.

I always wrote down in my game scorebook details and observations after each game. My notes ranged from comments about what we did well to areas we could improve on for the next game. I also included unusual things that took place on the court. It's not hard to imagine that a lot of my notes after this contest centered around the seven-foot-seven player. It is not every day you encounter a high school player that tall.

Looking back, it was not the center's incredible height but the sheer mass of his body that surprised me. If you were going to design a giant to be wandering around Westeros, Neil would be perfectly cast. Fingleton was stoic and kept his feelings inside on the court. I hope he was just concealing his joy concerning his play in the game. You could tell the Holy Name star was a smart player. He never tried to overplay on the court, and he was well coached. He was a driving force in getting his team to the D1 State Finals.

As in Randy's case, I am sure his size presented many challenges, including to his health. The Brit battled both foot and knee injuries throughout his playing career. These injuries most likely curtailed a chance for a lucrative NBA career, although he did have some stints with European clubs. After graduating from

Holy Name, Fingleton played collegiately at North Carolina and the College of the Holy Cross. Unfortunately, he passed away at the age of thirty-six in 2017 from heart failure in Gilesgate, UK.

Note: A documentary on Neil Fingleton entitled *Big Smooth* and directed by Paul Stainthorpe, was released on May 1, 2023. Fingleton's high school coach was Berkshire native JP Ricciardi. He knew his basketball and just how to use his wings to overplay the passing lanes. JP also had a passion for baseball that extended from scouting for the Oakland A's to serving as general manager for the Toronto Blue Jays and special advisor to the president of baseball operations for the San Francisco Giants.

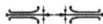

The lectures at the Nelson-Sanders camp were pure magic. There was always something to take away, something that hit home, for every coach. My favorite lecture was given by Jim Peterson with Sarunas Marciulionis. Jim Peterson was a combination of coach, sports psychologist, and ESL (English as a second language) instructor all rolled into one. He was basically attached to the Lithuanian player as his personal assistant and cultural inclusion ambassador. NBA life and the Bay Area of California were going to be a culture shock for someone who had grown up mostly behind the Iron Curtain.

In Sarunas's Hall of Fame induction speech reflecting on his rookie NBA campaign, he told a story about the strange and surprising things he saw in the Warriors locker room. "Ice! Yes, plenty of ice in the locker room." He noted as he started his speech, "I thought this is a good thing you know. In Lithuania of course we use ice for our drinks. Two cubes is too little and three is too much! I became very, how you say, concerned when I saw the players sticking their feet in the ice!" There was certainly a lot to learn about the American and professional athlete culture of the NBA for the Lithuanian with a lumberjack build.

Sarunas's mentor, Jim Peterson, was wearing many hats at this time. The future hall of fame member was married, and his wife and child were with him at the camp. Marciulionis's wife was also an exceptional player in her own right, playing for her national team. Jim Peterson lectured the campers and demonstrated the drills he put his rookie star pupil through. Sarunas was built like the mythical Paul Bunyan. His leg and arm strength were amazing. In the nightly camp games, opposing players would recoil off him on his drives to the basket. He had an effective midrange game, but it was his defense and passing that brought his teammates to a better level. Whether it was a camp pickup game or a showdown with the Lakers, the Lithuanian legend always played hard and played to win.

During his fifty-minute lecture, the mentor talked about the immense adjustment involved for Sarunas and his family in going from Lithuania to the Bay Area in California. He talked about the different strategies that he and the Warriors had in place for Sarunas and his family. The organization wanted to prevent as many problems as possible for the rookie and his family before they surfaced.

Teaching and coaching in a school system with many ESL students, I was very attentive when I heard Coach Peterson talk about the NBA rookie's challenge in learning English. Peterson did not speak Lithuanian or Russian, and Sarunas was just starting to learn English. Sarunas mentioned in his hall of fame speech that he finally mastered slow English. A translator would be added to the entourage in time for training camp. But now Jim had the groundwork to set up. He needed to establish a base of trust to steady his student to move forward. I was about to witness a master teacher at work. "These are the first words or phrases I go over with Sarunas each and every time we have a session: 1) intensity, 2) knowledge, 3) concentration, 4) try again, and 5) I can."

Marciulionis's adherence to these concepts was easily observed as his Warriors staff put him through sets of exhausting drills. He pushed through each task, never taking his eyes off of his mentor.

He repeated drills over and over again, going through hundreds of repetitions to improve upon his skills. A quick reset between drills, and they were off and running once again, always starting with Marciulionis stating, "I can" and Jim finishing with "Try again." It was a wonderful lesson for me as a young coach who would have players from different backgrounds and cultures throughout my coaching career.

I feel the years I spent teaching in a diverse community with various cultures, languages, and financial statuses helped me to be a better coach. The great tennis and humanitarian Arthur Ashe once said, "Start where you are. Use what you have. Do what you can." Good teachers never ignore any area that would prohibit development of a team or classroom.

A teacher or coach might be brilliant in their content area or specific sport, but if they cannot reach the students or players, then nothing will be learned. Teachers and coaches must develop structure, routines, and scaffolds to help their students and players acquire new knowledge and skills. Additionally, time needs to be set aside to practice and acquire ownership. Without these ingredients, not much of anything will be accomplished. Jim found a way to connect to his pupil. The result created a solid foundation for a magical NBA career that ultimately led to the Basketball Hall of Fame class of 2014.

Another great lecturer was given by shooting guru Dave Hopla, who worked with many NBA teams and players. The kids loved him. Who doesn't want to score more points when you are on the floor? This shot doctor broke down the physics of the ball going into the basket. He demonstrated the proper technique of shooting from head to toe. He would always tell the campers, "The road to success is always under construction." This is one of my all-time favorite quotes and a motto for pursuing any dream in life.

While I did not end up with Dave Hopla as a shooting coach guru for the Purple Knights, Chris Ferriter was an excellent alternative. Chris came to camp with us to work as a counselor. He was one of the smartest players to come out of the region. He played for Holyoke Catholic's Western Mass Championship team and Cushing Academy.

Chris was a great resource to bring in to go over our form shooting with the young Purple Knights. A forward by trade, Chris was like a point forward: pass first, create openings for your teammates, and take what the defense gives you. He really was the first player I came across who understood that offense didn't always have to be initiated by the point guard. Chris played the game the right way. I have always felt that if the best player on your team is willing to sacrifice for others and step up at big moments, that's the secret sauce for a winning team. Chris's game was based on precision and skill. It is no surprise, then, that he is also a champion golfer and an excellent tennis player.

Today he runs his own business and contributes to the local sports scene hosting a radio talk show that features high school sports.

Attending camps can bring you a lot of joy, laughter, and exhaustion from a hard instructional day. I loved that my longtime assistants at HHS Jim Hobert and Bob Lastowski were able to attend the Nelson-Sanders Camp with me. It was hard work, but those experiences made our program strong at every level: freshman, JV, and varsity. Additionally, I loved that I could share some of my camp experiences with my daughters, Kiely and Alexa. Alexa switched over to focus on swimming, where she trained with the YMCA Holyoke Vikings and HHS swim team, enjoying great success under coaches Randy Smith and Don Bergeron. Kiely stuck with basketball and played for Tom Brassil and Joe Dutsar. They were both so very lucky to have had these excellent coaches to help them along their high school journey. I feel strongly that their exposure to different camps and clinics helped them better navigate life's challenges. The lessons they received were not only relevant to the sport they played but also served as a blueprint for how to be successful in life.

Many times coaches and counselors complained about the low pay, long hours, and campers they got assigned, but these factors never concerned me. My time at the Nelson-Sanders Camp was invaluable, allowing me to focus on what I could learn and how I could use this knowledge to help our players improve.

CHAPTER 8

PURPLE KNIGHT CAMPS

I started the Purple Knight Basketball Camp to provide an inexpensive basketball experience for the youth in my community. Camps and daycare are expensive items for families, so one of my primary goals was affordability. Keeping this in mind, the local camp went through a number of designs and venues. I had my longtime assistant Jim Hobert at my side; he was a master at putting together a rewarding camp experience, with plenty of little tricks of the trade up his sleeve.

Jim organized the drill stations for skill work, but Coach also added plenty of fun activities throughout the day for the young campers. One of his more ingenious ideas was known as the "Play of the Day." At the end of each camp day, the coaches would sit the camp down to talk about the day and what was on the agenda for tomorrow. Then came the big announcement of which camper would be acknowledged for their triumphant play of skill, character, or teamwork. It was a great opportunity to give out an award to a camper who might not win a contest or team championship during the week.

Coach Hobbert and I worked a lot of camps together over the years. We picked up a lot from the Nelson-Sanders experience. We learned a lot from local camps led by exceptional high school and college coaches like Lou Conte, Mike Thompson, and Mike Martin. They were all excellent coaches and wonderful people to be around. Over the years, this trio of hall of fame coaches helped develop inner city and suburban players across western Mass. High school girls basketball had the bar set very high by Lou Conte at Agawam High School and Mike Thompson at Chicopee High School, while Mike Martin led his Commerce High School teams to multiple State Championships and later rebuilt the Agawam boys program to title-contending status.

Bob Lastowski, my good friend, classmate, teammate, and freshman basketball coach, was another member of the team helping to place the Purple Knights Camp on solid footing each summer. Coach Lastowski reached out to many different groups and organizations. He kept our camp enrollment high with the intent to keep the cost low to meet the needs of our city's socioeconomic structure.

The final element that helped ensure our camp's success was our partnership with the Holyoke Parks and Recreation Department, then headed by Pete Leclerc. The Purple Knights Basketball Camp was able to provide a positive experience in an air-conditioned gym from 8:30 a.m. to 2:00 p.m. a few weeks each summer. It also provided an opportunity to use the high school pool for a swim after lunch. Unfortunately, at this time the city's outdoor swimming pools remained closed due to budgetary constraints.

Another benefit for the community was that the camp provided a path to hire several student athletes from both the boys and girls basketball programs to work as counselors. This opportunity gave our young adults income, responsibility, and a chance to give back to their community. We made sure we hired a certified trainer and life guard, as well as cafeteria workers. We tried to share the income generated from the camp with as many people as possible.

The early years of the camp experience did not have the same fluidity as the latter years, when our camps started being run out of HHS. At the beginning, it was difficult to secure a consistent safe indoor site. The camps and clinics bounced back and forth from an eclectic group of beat-up outdoor courts in the city. We were subject to the whims of Mother Nature and neighborhood problems that might arise during hot summer days in the city.

The weather and tumultuous nature of our city were not the only challenges we faced during those early years. One July summer we were holding our camp at the outdoor courts of Holyoke Community College due to the school's lack of an indoor facility at this time. On the second day of our morning clinics, I arrived only to find the courts covered in graffiti with messages of racial hate and bigotry. Our small community camp had become the target of a hate crime. The basketball courts were covered with insults and hate speech directed at me, Coach Hobert, and the black players on our HHS boys basketball team. Our community has always been blessed with great black families and athletes. The Dotsons, Westbrooks, Jennings, and Moyes were important members of the Holyoke community. While Holyoke did not have a large African American community, it just so happened that at this time the best players moving through our high school basketball team were predominantly African American.

That upcoming season the Knights would have five African American players on its roster. This ruffled some people's feathers, and they often vented their frustration and insecurities through crank calls and hate mail to my home. That winter my jeep was the recipient of slashed tires and broken windows as it was parked in the school parking lot during an away game.

The messages of intense hate written all over the Holyoke Community College courts that summer morning were disturbing. Sadly, some community members believed our minority players were being given their positions on the team undeservedly. They thought starting positions should be held open for the white kids instead. Both black and white players quit the team that upcoming season. Although, I believe their decision to leave the team was more about playing time than race.

In the late '80s, as Holyoke continued to move away from its past glory days of manufacturing, the city would show her cracks in many forms. At times, it was poverty or unemployment. Other times it was the increase of drug use, gangs, crime, and arson. However, at its base was always the painful presence of prejudice and racial intolerance. Like in many cities across the changing landscape of America, rebuilding the community into a healthy place to live, raise a family, or work was an enormous challenge. It required the city and its people to embrace change and new experiences and seek alternative resources and solutions with drive, imagination, and tolerance.

Reflecting back on that morning at Holyoke Community College, I thought a lot about the concept of fairness. What part did I play in this display of anger scribbled out on the college courts? I never selected players or starters based on race, religion, language, or their neighborhood. Along with input from my coaching staff, I tried to put together the best Holyoke High team each season. There are many elements to consider in constructing a team each year, and it was never an easy decision. Selecting a team roster was done with great thought and care.

That July morning, we delayed the start of camp. I drove back to my house and got bleach and paint, and we erased or covered over the hateful messages. I did not want our campers or families to be exposed to such ignorance. They did not deserve that experience when they arrived at camp for the day. Next I followed up by notifying the campus police. They promised to look into it, but there were no surveillance cameras around the basketball courts and I was never notified if the security found anything.

When you teach and coach, you can always learn from the good and bad events that arise on a daily basis. I was glad we finished the camp, although I did spend some sleepless nights worrying if the hate would return. What helped me stay positive was reminding myself of all the good people I came across each day in my community. Those were the ones I needed to focus on, and hopefully I would earn their trust that our school's boys basketball program was a transparent, honest, and fair environment for all students. With that being said, I also learned once again that it's not my job to be liked by everyone but it is very important in leadership roles to believe in your convictions even when others do not. Coaching is never just about coaching a specific sport. Coaching is about working with others. It is about taking the lead and getting others to collaborate with each other for the greater good of the team while also challenging the individual to push beyond their own expectations. In order to lead, you need to know the values that matter to you. You need to know your own time and score, so that you can communicate that clearly to your team. That July was a lesson in time and score for me, but it was not so much about the hateful messages of a few; it was more so about the clarity of my convictions and the type of coach I wanted to be.

Last March I received a text message from Coach Lastowski. He mentioned to me that he always watches a couple of his favorite basketball movies to get ready for the NCAA playoffs and March Madness. He started talking about the movie *Glory Road*, based on the true story of the 1966 NCAA Champion Texas Western basketball team that upset Kentucky and started to change the face of college basketball forever. Western was coached by Hall of Famer Don Haskins, and Kentucky was coached by Aldolf Rupp from the SEC. Rupp was a hall of fame coach himself but did not recruit black players until his later years as a coach. On the other hand, Haskins started five African American players in that NCAA Championship game played at Cole Field House in Maryland. This was a monumental game in that it made people take notice of the discrimination against the black athlete. Coach Lastowski also mentioned in his text the many times Anglo parents of players in our program would ask him, "What's up with Coach? What's with his love affair with the minority players?"

Bob would always have our program's back. "Coach knows what he is doing. He just plays the best players, whether they are black, white, or brown."

Coach Lastowski went on to talk about how the world and our community were changing and the forces driving those changes. I believe the most important force driving these positive changes was people like Coach Lastowski. Like I said before, I was very lucky to have a wonderful coaching staff that shared my values about the time and score.

Camp notes: I came across a post on social media that Dave Hixon, longtime men's basketball coach at Amherst College, had retired. Coach Hixon was raised on basketball. His dad was a very successful high school coach in Massachusetts and member of the Massachusetts Basketball Coaches Hall of Fame. Dave Hixon would have been successful at any level of basketball from a rec league to the NBA. Coach's Amherst Basketball Camp was the first camp I attended as an instructor.

The Zieja family from Holyoke would religiously send their sons and members of the HHS boys basketball team, Nick, Tony, and Dave, to the Amherst College Camp. It was a family affair as their uncle Stan was a trainer at the college. They learned a lot of fundamental basketball from the Amherst staff.

Dave Hixon put together a great blend of coaches, counselors, and supporting characters each summer. Together they created a positive environment for staff and campers, with all staff subject to practical jokes and gags from a few of the coaching veterans. The staff included Rick Janes and Al Wolecko, both of whom were outstanding high school coaches who loved to compete, teach, and laugh. I can't be sure if they were always responsible for the hijinks and tomfoolery, but they were always at the top of the list as prime suspects.

The surprise attacks could be anything from a water soaking when you walked into a meeting to an elaborate hydro design rigged to the door, dowsing the poor soul with water once it was opened. Being assigned the camp team with the least amount of talent was also one test they put new coaches through.

The camp was so respected and in demand that the school stopped advertising altogether. Parents came calling on Amherst College and Coach Hixon to sign up. It is no wonder that the Zieja brothers were all part of Championship teams I coached at HHS. Each Zieja learned a lot of basketball knowledge and skill at Coach Hixon's camp. The Zieja children, including their sister Kate, were very good high school players for the Purple Knights and members of their school community. That is no surprise either, however, considering the abundance of guidance they received from their wonderful Polish family, led by Peter, Barbara, Babcia, and Dziadek (their grandparents).

Peter himself was a very good high school player, and Barbara was an excellent teacher for Holyoke Public Schools and taught many children who needed that extra attention and love. Peter and Barbara passed on to their children many important lessons about teamwork and the different roles that needed to be filled to make a family or team successful. Alexa, our youngest daughter, was friends with Nick and Tony, so Mrs. R and I were fortunate to be welcomed into many Zieja family celebrations. Over the years I saw numerous Holyoke families extend a sense of social equity to kids who had far less than they did. The Zieja family embodied the spirit of so many wonderful people in our community who through simple acts of respect and kindness helped improve the lives of others.

Coach Cal

CHAPTER 9
GO UMASS

I started going to UMass basketball games during Julius Erving's freshman year. I would listen to games on the radio, and I especially loved the Yankee Conference battles. Legendary coach Jack Leman led the Redmen-to-Minutemen at this time, and today the court in the Mullins Center is named in his honor.

During the time Dr. J played college basketball, freshmen were not eligible for varsity play and dunking was not allowed in games. How the game has changed! Many people feel this rule was implemented by the NCAA to negate the arrival of the great Lew Alcindor in the college scene. This rule change served no purpose except to rob players and fans of one of the most exciting plays in the game: the slam dunk.

Alcindor, the Power Memorial High School great, was coached by Jack Donahue. Donahue was hired by Holy Cross after Alcindor's senior year in high school. He was an excellent coach and ended up coaching the Canadian National Team for many years. However, he failed to deliver the future Naismith Memorial Hall of Fame center to the College on the Hill. When Sweet Lou "Sky Hook in Making" met the West Coast and the beauty of the LA campus on a recruiting visit, it was all over for the Crusaders. The Cross lost not only one of our all-time greatest players but also one of the most intelligent and thoughtful athletes of our time.

Together Leman and Erving brought an exciting game to the Amherst campus.

Fans started to flock to the Cage as word got out about this amazing high-flying freshman. You had to queue up early to get into those games. The highlight came in the warm-ups as the squads came out. Erving would circle to half court with a ball in each giant hand held out to each side of his enormous wingspan. He would then race unimpeded to the top of the key, elevate, and windmill slam dunk each ball. Boom—gasps and an explosion of noise followed as the Cage rocked.

After Coach Leman retired, UMass went through a number of coaches before the hire of John Calipari. Even before Coach Cal got things rolling again, I would try to send a few of my kids up to camp to support our local D1 NCAA team. Most summers the UMass basketball camp was conducted in Boyden Gym. Boyden was an aging multisport physical education building that housed its basketball courts on the top floor. By the afternoon it felt like 120 degrees Fahrenheit inside. UMass needed a lot of upgrades to their athletic facilities, and Boyden was just one glaring example.

One of my players who attended summer camp (pre Coach Cal) was Mike Stanley. Mike was a tall, thin lefty who weighed about 110 pounds soaking wet. In his senior year, Mike played an amazing all-around game when we almost upset a strong Central team. The southpaw could shoot and play smart defense; however, that summer those skills were not enough to lead Mike's UMass camp team to a single victory.

Before the camp director announced the weekly awards, he stated that we needed to uphold a universal camp tradition. That's funny. I was not aware of any universal camp traditions. That is when Mike and his teammates, with their consent and acknowledgment that they could swim, marched down to the pool in Boydan. There they walked the plank (otherwise known as the diving board) into the pool. No one seemed to mind. The kids got a kick out of it back then, but it does seem that somewhere between Redmen and Minutemen, this tradition of "walking the plank" for a winless week had run its camp course.

I first met John Vincent Calipari at his UMass camp. The university was again hoping that they had found the coach to turn the men's basketball program around. John is one of those coaches who gets your attention right from the start. At the beginning of his tenure, Cal was trying to build some community excitement for his season and get the fans back into the Cage. Any time they could, Coach Cal and his staff ran school programs and community days to build the UMass brand. The new Minutemen staff reached out to local high school coaches to work their camp, all part of Coach Cal's plan to get UMass basketball on the radar from the Berkshires to Boston and beyond.

So on a late summer afternoon, at the completion of the first John Calipari Basketball Camp, Coach Cal invited his staff out for some pizza. We met at Rafters, a local sports pub, located on Route 9 in Amherst. Opposite the sports bar was a giant strip mall, which did well when thirty-five thousand or more people were milling around on campus.

Coach was talking about getting the state behind the Minutemen. There were only five or six coaches who showed up for this get-together. "Let me get you guys some UMass stuff," he offered. "My treat."

Cal went on to explain, "I want to see coaches, kids, and fans decked out in UMass gear." Being summer and late in the afternoon, the campus bookstore was closed. Undaunted, Cal took us across the highway to the strip mall retailers, into the sports clothing section, which had professional sports attire and paraphernalia for the Celtics, Red Sox, Bruins, and Patriots, but there was no UMass gear to be found. Cal kept looking, and all he found was more pro sports team swag—the Jets, Giants, Yankees, Mets.

"What the hell?" Coach exclaimed. "Where is all the UMass stuff?"

We were less than a mile away from campus, and it was like we were looking for a North Dakota State hoodie instead of our very own Minutemen attire. It was then that Coach Cal realized what a challenge it would be to market the UMass brand into the state's consciousness. I mentioned to Coach Cal that for Massachusetts and New England, professional sports are king. We only have a few D1 schools who can compete in the NCAA but tons of smaller colleges.

Thus began Coach Cal's mission, with the help of his assistants, to be all in when it came to drumming up support for their program. Their agenda included talking to schools, as well as both civic and church groups. Name any place across the state, and Coach or one of his staff members had probably been there promoting that UMass brand! This new era of UMass basketball converged on all private, public, and nonprofit groups. Of course, to get people's attention, Cal and his staff needed to put a quality product on the court.

I attended many of Cal's practices. I loved to watch him and his staff coach at work, doing what they did best. I learned a lot from those practices, and I am grateful to Coach Cal, his staff, and the university for the graciousness they extended to me and other high school coaches. It didn't take long to see that Cal and the UMass basketball program would be a success.

Coach was a hands-on leader and teacher. He surrounded himself with a talented and energetic staff, which allowed him to delegate and develop his players. Assistant Coach Brusier Flint grew up in Philadelphia and played for Saint Joseph's College. He had a soft spot for the local city kids and always seemed to go out of his way to give them some extra time and attention at games or at a clinic where he was instructing.

Mike Mannix, an HHS graduate, was a team manager under Cal's tenure. I am sure he learned a lot about coaching and running a basketball program. Coach Mannix has worked at all levels of the game, including coaching at D1 Drexel University and D2 Western New Mexico University, along with a stint as an intern film coordinator for the NBA Indiana Pacers. Coach Mannix helped the Knights program out one time when he spliced together some defensive sequences that the Pacers would work on in practice. I have always said every little bit helps and it takes a village in the coaching world. Today Mike is the assistant director of athletics and head basketball coach at Wilbraham and Monson Academy in Massachusetts.

One outcome you always hope for as a coach is to have your players be better at the end of the season than they were at the beginning. The Calipari Minutemen teams individually and collectively improved each November to March. Coach Cal provided knowledge, passion, and reflection for his basketball program. He found a way to blend all three together seamlessly throughout his time at UMass. Cal could coach, resulting in his teams' effective effort, hard work, and collaboration.

Holyoke's own David Bartley, a former UMass player and high school coach, was a big booster of UMass and Coach Cal. David's service in the Massachusetts House of Representatives, which started in 1963, was nothing short of Parade All-American status. His commitment to public service with sound, fair, and thoughtful governance was his passion, along with basketball of course!

David served many roles as a member of the Massachusetts House of Representatives: majority leader, Speaker of the House,

Massachusetts secretary of administration and finance, and president of Holyoke Community College from 1975 to 2004. The Paper City native wielded political influence and was well liked from the Berkshires to Beacon Hill. Over the course of his life, President Bartley developed friendships and trust all across the state. The relationships he forged through his work and service made David an ideal candidate to help with Cal's master plan to bring forth a new era for the Minutemen basketball team. David's background in politics, combined with Coach Cal's vision and drive, was essential in cementing adequate funding for a much-needed new multipurpose arena at the Amherst campus.

In 1985 Ludlow's William D. Mullins, a state representative, suggested that the university needed a multipurpose arena and convocation center to help expand the athletic program and assist in the university's growth. Mullins passed away in 1986, but the state went ahead with the building of the complex, aptly name it after him (http://mullinscenter.com).

Cal and Bruiser were frequent visitors to HHS, sharing their time and wisdom to speak with students during several assemblies. The UMass Athletic Department strategically ran school community days as a way to build interest and fill seats. UMass would give local schools free tickets to Saturday matinee game during intersession. HHS would round up some teachers to chaperone and provide pizza money for lucky students.

It was always great fun taking the students to see some great Atlantic 10 basketball. One of my favorite memories from these trips was a contest at the infamous Cage between the Minutemen and Duquesne. There was a student section right behind the north end of the gym that was completely filled. Each time a Duquesne player would attempt a free throw facing the student section, the Minutemen fans would tip out a fishing pole with a distracting object tied to the end of it, shaking it violently in the opposing shooter's view. That particular section of fans would also look for an opportunity to help out on defense with deafening cries of support for the home team.

As UMass transitioned to offense, moving away from the student section, and the officials turned their backs to move down the court, a few Minutemen students went to work. Like clockwork, they popped up to shake the stanchion. When the Dukes players returned to their end to shoot, the rims were reverberating. It is no wonder the opponents field goal percentage always seemed a bit lower shooting at that end of the Cage. Home court advantage, indeed.

I can confidently say that it was a true learning experience watching the UMass Minutemen's basketball program grow and thrive under Coach Calipari. The opportunity to work with him and his elite coaching staff at camps and share the NCAA basketball game experience with so many high school students provided some insight into the importance that sports plays in the overall community. Coach Cal knew that while it was absolutely essential to provide a program that was top notch and strived for excellence, the role of a coach, his players, and a sport can have a powerful, unifying effect within a school or larger community. Sports can offer a chance for not only the team but also the fans to be a part of something bigger than themselves. It provides a chance for people to belong and perhaps through that belonging, develop a mindset that makes us all beholden to one another. Win or lose, as the old adage goes, "There is no *I* in the word 'team.'"

CHAPTER 10
WORLD SCHOLAR ATHLETE GAMES

I worked at the World Scholar Athlete Games (WSAG) for two summers. The camps were held at the University of Rhode Island (URI) in Kingston. The games were the brainchild of Dan Doyle, a coach, author, and lecturer. Coach Doyle was hailed as a visionary to bring scholar athletes from around the world together with the premise of friendship, understanding, and networking opportunities for our next generation of global leaders.

During the third week of June, the beautiful campus of URI was flooded with ambitious scholar athletes from around the globe. The camp took place at the end of the school year, also helping to ensure the best weather of a typical New England summer with long days, low humidity, and plenty of sunshine.

If Dan Doyle was the brainchild behind the games, Wally Halas, former star athlete for Clark University in Worcester, MA, was the boots-on-the-ground and go-to person who ran the show. I needed a recommendation from NBA general manager Gary Saint Jean to secure my coaching spot at this international event. One of the secretaries let me know how excited the administrative staff got when she told Mr. Halas, "The Golden State Warriors want to talk with you." A great start for any new job.

My first camp team included John from Uganda, four kids from the USA, and one player each from Italy, Spain, Germany, and France. Each day, the WSAG itinerary started with academic and cultural classes in the morning before moving on to sports in the afternoon and entertainment and guest lectures in the evening. The morning academic component entertained a multitude of pertinent topics based on the many global challenges the WSAG scholar might encounter back in his or her home country. The hope and objective was to encourage these campers to develop leadership skills and relationships within our global community to influence important policies in a positive way around the world. The courses covered writing, art, science, education, human rights, climate change, world health, the LGBT community, and pandemics to foster collaboration and solution-based thinking for the camp's future leaders.

Furthermore, there were amazing lectures each evening, including opening and closing ceremonies that were powered by big-time entertainers. Along with the campers and staff, I was able to listen to a global parade of people who intersected sports, culture, and politics. I ate dinner with Senator Bill Bradley and Sir Roger Bannister. I watched Kip Keino give a lecture about dreaming big and living small. Other guest lecturers included SJJ Byron, "Whizzer" White, Chi Cheng (named the greatest Asian athlete of the twentieth century), Israeli Prime Minister Shimon Peres, Bill Clinton, Ken Starr, and Mathew Shepard's mom. Throw in Elie Wiesel and Jane Goodall, and you get the picture. Students from around the world were able to watch and listen to some of the most important, influential leaders up close and personal.

Lectures were followed by an opportunity for play with low-key sports competitions, some form of entertainment, pizza, and ice cream. The WSAG also sprinkled in day trips off campus to Boston and Newport for the globetrotting teenagers. The WSAG went all out to make it a world-class experience for the campers. I was able to place five of our HHS students into this experience, including Max Perez (basketball), Julia Beaty (track and field), Andrea Lubold (tennis, future captain at Mount Holyoke College, where she played for one of my all-time favorite coaches and tennis mentors, Aldo Santiago), Antonia Kleinschmidt (tennis, German exchange student) and Carina Meisner (arts, also from Germany).

The Ryan Center, URI's multipurpose athletic facility, and a WSAG museum were under construction during my time working at the global camp. The Ryan Center and the WSAG Hall of Fame's construction had been delayed by the Rhode Island legislature, but eventually funds were granted to proceed with the projects. This delay provided a harbinger of trouble for our staff and campers.

The basketball facility we used was a nice indoor complex with four full-length courts, but it was very hot. As my American and Euro players sprinted up and down the court, transitioning between offense and defense, John from Uganda was relentless! He would exhaust himself in a few quick minutes. He only ran at one speed, 100 percent, full throttle. This was wonderful for defensive transition sequences but presented challenges when the team was trying to run sets on offense. John would invariably crash into one of his teammates, destroying any chance of running a play. Additionally, John ran so hard and sweated so much that he passed out from dehydration the first game we played. My exhausted small forward from Africa was carted off into the trainers room, where our medical staff pronounced his condition was due to dehydration, probably related to his long flight from home. The medical staff reassured John, "Don't worry, your body will adjust."

John looked a bit wobbly for our second game but got through it OK. Then came an unusually humid day with our game against the top camp team. Our kids wanted to pull the upset because we had not done too well the first few games. As the game started, my small forward from Africa was still red lining everywhere on court. I called time out when I saw John shaking. In the huddle I asked,

"John, what the hell is wrong with you? You need to slow down! Here, take this bottle of water and drink! When you are done, I will sub you back in."

"Fuck, Coach!" John shouted. "Do you not like me?"

Taking a deep breath to calm down, I responded, "John, you need to chill out."

"No! You are trying to kill me. It's the Americans and Europeans. You hate Africans!"

From that point on, John from Uganda wouldn't drink, so I had to make the choice and refused to sub him back in. There was water everywhere, but John refused to drink it. I could not understand his resistance until a bit later. In Uganda, it was standard practice: boil the water first or die.

John lived in an area of Uganda where most of the drinking water was contaminated. Families boiled all their water before drinking it. John and his family had grown up not trusting people in power, and that included me, his camp basketball coach. Fearing government leaders in the wake of the British Empire's protectorate from 1894 to 1962 was John's norm. He and his family believed their water was made dangerous by past European colonizers who wanted to kill off the native Africans. It took us another day to convince John that the water was OK to drink. He made it through camp without dehydrating again, but he never stopped running.

Note: Much of Uganda is open water and swampland, but the water is undrinkable. Meanwhile, high demand and poor management have led to shortages of clean groundwater. Facilities are under strain in towns and cities, and the springs and wells that rural communities rely on are mostly used up. It is hard to fathom that access to clean water is a challenge for so many people around the world. It should not be a luxury, but for many of us it is, and it should not be taken for granted (http://www/wateraid.org>Uganda).

Maxwell Perez was the starting point guard for all four seasons of his career with the Purple Knights. He played hard all the time. Max never missed practice or a game, and continued to fight through challenges regardless of the score. During his senior year, Max was being scouted by a number of college programs. They communicated to me how impressed they were by Max's sharp focus and ability to listen. This astute observation tapped into Max's true nature. He was not a vocal leader, but he led by example with his hustle and all-court play.

In his early years at HHS, the career 1,000-point scorer sacrificed his scoring to be a facilitator for the offense. He was a key component to our Western Mass Championship team his freshman year and led our team deep into the playoffs each year thereafter. The opposing point guard was always in for a long night with Max hounding full court and picking pockets for some easy scores. In the latter part of his high school career, Max was able to shine offensively and broke out as a team top scorer. His shot improved from beyond the arc, and he ended his career with 1,208 points. A very impressive feat for a high school player.

Invariably every high school or college coach would ask me, "Is he always like that? Does he always bring that energy?" My answer was always the same: "One hundred percent. All the time!"

One D1 school that was very interested in recruiting Max was Binghamton University. An assistant coach and former point guard for the school was very impressed with Max. I think he saw a lot of himself in the Purple Knight point guard. However, the assistant coach could not convince his head coach to offer Max a scholarship, so ultimately he settled on going to Lasell University in Newton, MA.

Attending the WSAG was great exposure for Max. By the end of the week, every coach there was salivating over him and his outstanding play.

"Who is this guy, and where does he play?" I was asked repeatedly.

Then it happened. I was approached from another coach hailing from Texas. "Coach, could I speak with you for a minute? I love the way you coach your kids, and your program's achievements speak volumes. I have a proposition for you. Our high school in Texas is deeply entrenched in basketball and soccer," he explained. Surprisingly, this upper-middle-class community had very much rejected football as religion. No *Friday Night Lights* for them!

The coach from Texas continued, "We would love to offer you a teaching and coaching position at our school. It would only pay about $55K, but our boosters will pay for your housing and a car. What do you think?"

Whoa! That was unexpected. I thanked him for the offer and his kind words but stated that I would need to talk it over with my family first. Before the Texas coach went back to watching the skill session we were attending, he turned to me with one final addendum to his offer: "One more thing, Massachusetts," he stated, using the common sobriquet of my origin instead of my last name, "if you take the job, you need to bring you point guard with you. We will find a place for him to stay. We do it all the time."

Ultimately I refused the offer, unwilling to uproot my family from our lives in Holyoke, but I must admit there was a slight temptation. Still, I knew I was very fortunate to coach kids like Max. He and players like him really gave their heart and soul to the game, and I respect that so much. While we didn't go to Texas, our time together at HHS was filled with many fond memories.

In fact, the first time I saw Max, he was climbing up the outside of his brick wall apartment building. Up the wall he went, Spider-Man with his spidey skills or Warren Harding on the ascent of El Capitan in Yosemite. I thought, *Well, if he can do that, basketball is not going to be that difficult.*

Another time, during our state semifinal game at the Worcester Centrum against Saint John's High School of Shrewsbury, the legendary central Mass program coached by Robert Foley, our team had just lost a tough battle. As we were going back to our locker room, out came a Mickey D cupful of orange drink right at Max. Splat! The drink hit Max straight on, covering his uniform. I thought Max was going to sprint into the crowd and go after the person who threw the drink at him, but to my surprise, he didn't. Instead, he stopped, looked down, and continued walking to our locker room. After congratulating our kids on a great season, I made it a point to commend Max for not taking the bait of an unruly, disrespectful "fan."

He replied, "It's OK, Coach. You always talked about not doing anything to embarrass yourself, your team, or your school. That guy was the jerk. He embarrassed himself. Why would I want to take away from both teams and the great game we just played?" I was so impressed by Max's composure and maturity. He continued, "If a fight breaks out, that's all the people will be talking about." And I knew he was right.

One by one, Max's teammates got up to congratulate him despite their broken hearts. Max's restraint had helped them realize what a special experience it was to participate in that game, together as a team, win or lose.

Memories like this make it easy to see that Max was a great example for aspiring high school players to follow. He continued to build his game every year. He came in with a great handle and defensive intensity. He continued his journey by adding a consistent three-point shot and became an excellent passer. The All Western Mass and All State baller finished up by becoming a great team leader, leading his teammates through an unrelenting work ethic. Max Perez pushed his teammates to be better by playing with maximum effort every single solitary moment he was engaged in the game he truly loved.

A Purple Knight Senior Night is a wonderful tradition that allows the community to celebrate the careers of our twelfth-grade students. It is always scheduled as the last regular season home game. It is an emotional event for our players and their families. Our coaching staff and the Rigali family liked to offer extra acknowledgements for the outgoing seniors. Mrs. Coach would help with signs and getting flowers from Jan's Florist Shop on South Street. I would order plaques from Dinn Brothers in West Springfield. Kiely would bake up some of her giant chocolate chip cookies, while Alexa would help me write my address to the seniors and family.

Additionally, several good friends and loyal fans of the team would add some special touches. English teacher and our meticulous scorekeeper Mike Mckenna would contribute wonderful congratulation cards with words of encouragement and a few greenbacks stuffed in them. Dave Hampson, a world-class photographer, would deliver action photos for the players. These generous members of our surrounding community provided support without being asked to do so. They simply wanted to contribute by creating a special night for the players. Parents, cheerleaders, faculty, and members of the community all contributed every year to make Senior Night a night to remember.

Senior Night celebrations always took place before the start of the game. It was an incredibly positive way to start the evening, and Max's Senior Night was no exception. Max was on fire during the game, and he lit up the court both on both offense and defense. He put on quite a show that game against Ludlow High School.

In fact, that was just one of many memorable games over the course of Max's career at HHS. I believe his very best overall game came in late January of his senior year against Amherst Regional High School, eventual D1 state champions. He dominated the game that night. Max pressured their excellent point guard into mistakes, led a showtime fast break, and scored thirty-two points on only thirteen field goal attempts. It was an impressive dismantling of a very good high school team, to say the least. But that was Max for you. He left everything on the court because he knew that every play and every possession mattered. Not all high school players acquire the skills of knowing the time and score, but Max always did. I am lucky to have been his coach.

CHAPTER 11

GAME TIME

During my tenure as head basketball coach at HHS, I held countless practices and coached many games. I always stressed the importance of focusing on the task at hand, encouraging my players to stay present and not get ahead of themselves. The game we were playing was the most important game of the season. However, looking back on my coaching career, there are several games that stand out to me as important and memorable.

D1 State Semifinals
March 15, 2000
Worcester Centrum
St John's 60, Holyoke 55

St John's: R. Hennigan 2-1-7-14, Avis 2-1-3-10, D. Kerr 1-0-2, D. Frew 0-1-1, T. Lahey 9-10-28, A. Newton 1-1-3, J. Plough 1-0-2. Totals: 16-2-22-60.

Holyoke: M. Athas 3-2-3-15, W. Cabrera 1-1-2-7, J. Pollard, 3-1-0-9, B. Griffin 3-1-3-12, N. Almodovar 4-2-10, M. Perez 1-0-2, M. Diaz 0-0-0, T. Zieja 0-0-0, A. Lynch 0-0-0, D. Shala 0-0-0, J. Ferreira 0-0-0. Totals: 15-5-10-55.

Note: T. Lahey 10-10 from the foul line was the difference in the contest.

As I typed in Dugajin Shala's name for the Saint John's box score, I thought about how sports can often place us at the confluence of politics and culture. To explain, first I need to go back to our team visits to the Shriners Hospital in Springfield as a result of participating in the Coca-Cola Holiday Classic at the Springfield Civic Center. The visits were arranged by the tournament committee to foster civic engagement among the players as they spent time with children at the hospital. During those visits, my players and I met many truly heroic people who worked at the Shriners Hospital. It was amazing to see all the good they did, as earthbound angels who treated the patients and their families with immense kindness and compassion.

My team and I visited the Shriners Hospital in December 1995. At the time Bosnia and Herzegovina had seen thousands of children injured by landmines. The Shriners mission was to help these children in an attempt to make them feel whole again. The wing we visited was filled with children from Yugoslavia whose lives had been ripped apart by the civil war. In both Bosnia and Herzegovina, children had been injured, having lost feet, legs, arms, and fingers. The land mines littered their communities, infecting places of play, school, home, and work.

This visit had a lasting impact on our players. They saw the brutal consequences of war and its unfathomable effects, which extended beyond soldiers engaged in combat. War's violence explodes into the everyday lives of civilians, changing lives forever. During our time at the hospital, my players asked questions:

"How did the war start?"

"What were the two sides fighting about?"

"Who won the war?"

They talked to the children who were being fitted for prosthetics and were learning how to use them. Our time at the Shriners Hospital was a humbling experience for our team as we witnessed a greater challenge than could ever take place in a sporting arena.

A few months later, I was checking with our returning players to see who was interested in playing in an upcoming summer league when I asked, "Carlos, have you seen Duga?"

"I haven't seen him in a while," Carlos responded. I was about to ask if he knew what was going on when he continued, "Coach, Duga left school last week. He was going back home to see if he could find his grandparents." It turns out his family had not had any contact with them for months. Carlos went on, "They are afraid they have been driven off their farm. Duga said the Milosevic government has been doing a lot of bad shit to Muslims."

I was confronted with stories like this many times during my teaching and coaching career. Another time, during D block, just before lunch. my students rolled into room 108, probably thinking more about the school menu than the oral reports scheduled for that day's class. I start by taking attendance when I notice that Danny is out. I look up, asking the class, "what's up with Danny? He never misses school and reports are due."

A voice from the back of the class rang out, "He had to go back to Columbia for his family." Danny Escobar was a good student in my senior English class. He was friendly, played soccer for the high school, and loved to talk about sports with me. After graduating high school he went on to serve in law enforcement for the city of Holyoke.

During the 1994 World Cup, the Colombian national team was placed under immense pressure to perform and to do well for their country. This pressure did not come from their manager, teammates, and their adoring fans, but from the drug cartels that controlled domestic football.

In the firing line was Andres Escobar, a defender that scored an own goal during the tournament and the uncle of Danny from my D block English class (Tito Football, December 8, 2022, The Athletic Internet). The World Cup game was in the US. This game between the US and Colombia eliminated the South American team from contention. Days after the elimination, Danny's uncle was murdered outside a nightclub in the city of Medellin. There are many accounts of this incident. ESPN's *30 for 30* is one, narrating the intersection of sport, culture, and society.

We all live in our own small circle, and these circles form our community. These small communities connect with a larger society. At times we may appear to be disconnected, but we are not. Sometimes the world shows up on your attendance sheet or athletic field and it catches you off guard, but you have to show up for the students and the players. During my teaching and coaching career, what I found notable was how the kids responded to being pulled into the chaos and disorder of our too-often dysfunctional world. The adaptability, resiliency, and generosity of these young people was truly inspiring. These selfless young adults would drop everything to be there for their family even if it meant turning their own personal life upside down.

Sometimes teenagers can be so very self-absorbed, but when the chips are down, they know the time and score. Duga and Danny dropped everything on a dime to go support their family in a time of need.

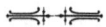

Two gems from Max Perez:

>January 30, 2003
>"Jinx" O'Connor Gym
>Holyoke High School
>Holyoke 87, Amherst 75

Holyoke: M. Perez 11-2-8-32, J. Almodovar 9-0-18, J. Galdon 1-0-2, E. Saurez 7-3-1-18, H. Perez 1-0-2, D. Falcetti, 2-1-0-5, J. Sarabaez 3-4-10. Totals: 26-7-12 87.
Amherst: K. Graves-Fulgram 2-4-4-18, J. Turcott 2-3-0-10, E. Robinson 0-1-1, M. Suprenant 1-0-2, J. Lewis 5-0-10, B. Coblyn 5-4-14, R. Jensen 1-0-2, D. Gonzalez-Kriesberg 8-0-16. Totals: 27-4-9-75.

Senior Night
February 25, 2003
"Jinx" O'Connor Gym
Holyoke High School
Holyoke 85, Ludlow 56

Holyoke: J. Colon 1-0-2, M. Perez 5-5-1-26, J. Almodovar 2-3-1-13, M. Porten 1-0-2, E. Almodovar 2-1-1-9, J. Galdon 1-0-2, E. Suarez 4-2-10, H. Perez 2-1-5, N. Todd 1-0-2, J. Sarabaez 6-2-14. Totals: 25-9-8-85.
Ludlow: D. Benoit 4-1-2-13, M. Kane 1-2-3-11, M. McGrath 4-1-2-13, Z. Miller 7-3-17, C. Regnier 0-2-2. Totals: 16-4-12-56.

Note: What made this game unusual was that Max either scored or assisted on fourteen of the fifteen baskets we scored in the first half, as well as five out of the first seven baskets we scored in the second half.

CHAPTER 12

JAMAL AND THE BOYS, A WONDERFUL COACH, AND "MAMA, THERE GOES THAT MAN"

Hall of Fame Invitational
January 18, 2002
Western New England College
Springfield, MA
Cathedral 78, Holyoke 72

Cathedral: K. Williams 3-1-2-11, T. Heaton 0-2-2, K. Harder 4-1-9, S. Rivera 1-4-1-15, P. Martin 2-1-3-11, D. Yvon 9-3-4-31. Totals: 19-9-13-78.

Holyoke: J. Warren 10-1-5-28, M. Perez 2-1-2-9, N. Almodovar 12-1-25, J. Sarabaez 4-2-10. Totals: 26-2-10-72

Jamal Warren came to us on his journey to become a D1 player at the University of Cincinnati. The prep school Jamal had been attending closed his sophomore year, so he and his mom had to figure out their next step. I only met Jamal's mom a few times, but you could feel the bond they had with each other. They decided to enroll Jamal at HHS as a school-of-choice student.

Jamal gave our good team a boost to compete with the top teams from western Mass. The future Cincinnati Bearcat dominated with his physical strength and speed, allowing him to score on drives, put backs, dunks, and fast breaks. Jamal was a great ball handler, much in the style of Kyrie Irvin, with a willingness to pass and set up many easy scores for his teammates. He also played solid defense and loved to compete. He got along well with his teammates, and I hope we played a small part in getting him to his dream of playing for a D1 school. Today, Jamal is living and working in the Berkshires in western Mass and raising his family.

Jamal only played with the Purple Knights for one year, but three games stand out during our time together. The first one took place in an event called the Basketball Hall of Fame Invitational, held at Western New England College (WNEC) in Springfield, MA. The Knights drew Valley League rival Springfield Cathedral in the opening round.

The matchup produced a back-and-forth contest, with the Panthers winning 76–72. Stepping back in time, that game reminded me of a great contest between one of my all-time favorite players, Ernie DiGregorio of the Providence Friars, in Pauley Pavilion versus the UCLA Bruins. There was Ernie D dribbling out, starting a fast break with Bruins all over him. The basketball world outside of New England was just starting to learn about this little Italian guy from North Providence. Few players could see the game like Ernie D! Number 15 was Beth Harmon (*The Queen's Gambit*) reading the game moves before they happened. Dave Gavitt, his college coach, said he was always five steps ahead of everyone else on the court. So in this instance of magical excellence, Ernie D decides to dribble behind his back and whip a seventy-five foot behind-the-back bounce pass through the entire retreating Bruin defense to a streaking Friar for a fast-break conversion. *Did he just do that? Yes he did!*

Three thousand miles and many years later, our game at WNEC showcases a similar performance from the one and only Max

Perez. Coming fast out of the pack, Max rebounds, one dribble, push, two dribble push. Max looks up. *Where the hell is he throwing that pass, and why aren't any of our guys near the hoop?* Then out of the right sideline, from nowhere, comes Jamal streaking down court, gliding up and up for the pass. Still nowhere near the hoop, Jamal adjusts in midair, grabbing the ball with his right hand and in the same motion slams it down into the hoop!

To the fans in attendance that day, nothing else mattered. Max's pass and Jamal's slam dunk were something beautiful to behold. Sure, it was a nice game (and it would have been even better if we had won), but it was at that moment I realized what a special talent Jamal Warren possessed. Max's pass wasn't exactly Ernie D in Pauley, but it was close, proving he was a pretty good chess player on the hardwood himself.

January 2, 2002
Pittsfield High School
Pittsfield 84, Holyoke 82 (2 OT)

Pittsfield: K. Dillon 5-3-4-23, B. Shove 8-3-9-34, D. Smith 4-2-2-16, M. Torra 1-0-2, G. Aloellie 1-0-2, J. Edgerton, 1-0-2. Totals: 19-8-16-84.

Holyoke: A. Lynch 1-1-1-6, E. Suarez 6-1-0-15, J. Warren 7-2-0-24, M. Perez 2-2-1-9, N. Almodovar 7-2-1-21, J. Sarabaez 5-2-12. Totals: 28-8-5-82.

Ron Wojcik is without a doubt one of the top basketball coaches and mentors in the high school game. A Worcester Polytechnic Institute (WPI) graduate and exceptional teacher, he is a gold mine for any school and community fortunate enough to employ his services. His background as college athlete and his career in education were a perfect combination to mentor high school student athletes. Ron could succeed in coaching at any level of basketball. The fact that he chose to craft his basketball talents in his beloved Berkshires was a big plus for the region. I met Ron on my basketball journey when he was coaching at Pittsfield High School (PHS). Last January, he sent me a note via Messenger.

"Hey, Coach!" Ron began. "Thought of you yesterday when some of my former players were over the house from our state championship team and we were watching some video tapes. They wanted to see when I coached the boys at Pittsfield. I pulled out our double OT game with you guys. Shove, Dillon, Warren, Perez, Almodovars were all a part of one of the best hoop games I was ever involved with." He continued talking about how the talent that night was absolutely amazing. The girls on his current Hoosac Valley team could not believe the skill of the players in that game. "Hope all is well," Ron concluded.

That particular night in the Berkshires, the Holyoke Knights and the Pittsfield Generals both played to their potential for the entire contest. Believe me, after coaching over eight hundred high school varsity games, I know that does not happen often. Both teams had several opportunities to win the game, but each group of players responded with winning plays, limiting their mistakes to keep the battle going.

Unfortunately, Coach Wojcik met with the same fate as I and many other dedicated professional high school coaches across America have with a new administration. Instructional, support, and extracurricular staff, including coaches, can be let go and replaced with little explanation. Despite countless years of dedication and success, coaches who are let go might receive no more explanation than a desire to "move in a different direction." Today this clichéd response simply is not good enough on so many levels. It is my hope this tired explanation from leadership positions can evolve.

A coach's classroom is constantly on display for the public to view and judge with praise or ridicule. It is impossible to please everyone, but it is usually clear from the majority of community members when a coach has an effective influence on young athletes and creates a positive team culture. When a coach's dismissal is unclear, people cry out for transparency. I hypothesize that our institutions take this stance of ambiguity to protect themselves and in certain instances, the coach. However, I feel that in many ways this generic response to a coach not being rehired hurts both the school community and dedicated coaches. People cannot help but question, What is the *real* reason the coach was let go?

Coach Wojcik had led the Hoosac Valley girls basketball program with class and dignity on and off the court. He led them to multiple sectional championships along with a state championship. His success as a coach was evident through the success of his team on the court. The manner in which Coach Wojcik, along with many other dedicated high school coaches, was let go is wrong and ultimately hurts the young athletes they work with both in school and on the playing field. At a time when our society is experiencing a teacher shortage, it is important to incentivize people to work with today's youth. The speed at which people are leaving the teaching profession is considered by some to be a modern-day crisis. If our institutions fail to improve their relationships with teachers, coaches, and the surrounding community, this problem will not go away. In fact, they will drive away quality candidates who are effectively skilled to work with the children in our schools. Fostering better relationships by communicating clear objectives and building a spirit of collaboration is a starting place for future leaders.

Of course there are many factors that influence administrators or school boards when deciding to let a coach go and move on to someone else. First, there is the common practice of community crowd refereeing. A new agenda is pushed by a group, parent, or institution to pressure school administrators or school councils to make a coaching change. Second is the growing power of technological and social media culture, which demands instant gratification and provides easy access to anonymous finger-pointing and bullying. Modern technology has many advantages, but fostering an attitude of impatience, blame, and harassment is not among them. Third is optics and analytics. It is necessary to look at the numbers, but simply using quantitative data as a driving force for the decision-making process without thoughtful analysis can be dangerous.

Sports analytics expert Bill James warned against failing to think purposefully about statistics during an interview on author Michael Lewis's podcast. He noted that people can just "look at the numbers without giving them much thought." Engaging in this single-minded thinking moves people further away from their own instincts and understanding of the game. A combination optics, context, and data analysis can provide a clearer picture for informed decisions both on and off the field.

With that being said, there are plenty of good reasons not to rehire a coach. Working with young people is a privilege and should only be given to those worthy of the position. However, the varied responsibilities of modern coaches, concerning educational, academic, and social aspects of the job, should afford the coach and the community they serve transparency when they are replaced.

The sad truth is that many people have lost the ability to talk to others about our differences and discuss issues face to face. Conducting business and important conversations through the technology made possible by smartphones, text messaging, email, and social media is quite frankly a cowardly shortcut. While it may be commonplace, that does not make it right. In fact, it is a practice of communication that is moving us away from our humanity. As a result, I fear that as a consequence, our high school athletic programs across the nation will be employing individuals who lack the skill, training, and experience to measure up to the important role of working with our children on the playing fields.

Western Mass D1 Quarterfinals
March 1, 2002
John "Jinx "O'Connor Gym
Holyoke High School
Longmeadow 73, Holyoke 68 (OT)

Longmeadow: J. Williams 5-6-13-41, A Weeks 3-1-1-10, M. Russo 3-0-6, A. Fortune 5-4-14, E. Hanney 0-2-2. Totals: 16-7-20-73.
Holyoke: A. Lynch 0-2-2, D. Falcetti 0-1-1, E. Almodovar 4-1-9, M. Perez 1-4-6, M. Koczocik 1-0-2, N. Almodovar 6-1-13, J. Warren 8-3-4-29, J. Sarabaez 3-0-6. Totals: 23-3-13-68.

Any high school coach can tell you just how important halftime is during a game. It can be used to motivate your players or make adjustments after the first half. Coaches look into our crystal ball, attempting to predict our opponents' moves for the second half. Other times our kids might just need to rest and take a breath from an intense game. I learned through coaching many high school practices and games that teenagers struggle with on-the-fly adjustments. That is why the key to a good halftime chat is to keep your instructions minimal and simple. In fact, the simpler the better. A few ideas will do just fine most of the time. Stick to what your kids know and what you have gone over during your practice sessions.

While halftime provides a great opportunity to adjust your game plan or your players' mindset, the narrative of a game does not always adhere to a strict time table. One of the biggest coaching challenges can occur after intermission when there is a radical change to the flow of the game by your team or the opponent. Thus strategically implemented timeouts, especially at the end of the game, are essential; however, there are a few factors to consider to maximize these short interruptions during a game.

The key thing to remember about time-outs is that they are short. The key thing to remember about most high school players is that they do not process big changes quickly. A big shift in the momentum, particularly in the second half, an injury, or a spectacular performance by an opposing player can throw a solid game plan and steady play from your team out the window. Time-outs can function as a Band-Aid, but many times they are not big enough to stop the hemorrhaging of a victory slipping away.

With these thoughts in mind, let us to turn to John Williams—not the Boston Symphony Orchestra composer who wrote scores for many major motion pictures, but the Longmeadow Lancer and future D2 All-American college basketball star. John was a key contributor to the 2005 Bryant College team that went all the way to the NCAA D2 College Championship.

Earlier in the season, we had handled the Longmeadow High School (LHS) Lancers in a comfortable victory. Keep in mind the balance of basketball teams is fragile, especially for high school teams. Entering the D1 quarterfinals, the Purple Knights had to make a big adjustment. Our big man Nelson Almodovar had sustained a stress fracture in our last regular season game. He was unable to practice leading up to the game, and his minutes had to be managed to avoid reinjury. In our early season win over the Lancers, Nelson had played a big part in cutting off Williams on his forays to the hoop. Without Nelson's full minutes, like Mark Jackson exclaims, "Mama, there goes that man!"

John Williams drove to the hoop time and again in the second half of our playoff game. He was practically unstoppable. We were able to hold Williams to three baskets during the first half, but when he came back out after halftime, it was a different story. Williams torched us, scoring thirty-three points in the last twenty minutes. The Lancers' upset of the Knights was fueled by Williams's spectacular one-man effort.

As the game unfolded, we attempted several adjustments. We tried different players on him. We tried to run a box and one zone game plan. None of it mattered to the future Bryant College star. His fellow Lancers deferred to John on the court. I remember during the last few time-outs imploring our defenders to double on every touch, to deny, but to no avail. Sometimes kids listen but don't hear you.

It was unfortunate that Nelson was injured for that game, but injuries are a part of sports. Sometimes they can be serious and untimely to the success of a team. Above all, though, they are disappointing and devastating to the athlete. A high school basketball season is short to begin with, and in Massachusetts twenty regular season games are all you are allowed to schedule. A good sprained ankle can cost a high school player a significant part of his season.

As a high school coach, I have witnessed injuries to players on my team. The two most serious were to Derek Brown and Joey Westcott. Both were on their way to exceptional high school careers. Both had a good chance of acquiring a college scholarship on the hardwood. In the case of both players, these injuries occurred relatively early in their junior years.

Derek fractured his femur going up for a dunk. Our trainer thought it was the sheer strength of his quad muscle, fully flexed, that snapped the bone. No one was around him. Derek was our mini Dr. J with enormous hands to palm and wave the ball around as he blew by defenders. I try to remember his wonderful big smile when I think about what he lost on that play. Derek played his senior year favoring his injury but still helped us to a state tournament appearance. That season we lost to Northampton High School (NHS) in the quarterfinals (more on that place later). I remember NHS coach Joe Mantegna being so gracious to Derek after the loss. He gave him a big hug and told him what an amazing job he did to come back from his injury. Derek played at the local Springfield Technical Community College (STCC) and did very well. He now lives and works in Atlanta.

The other injury was sustained by Joey Westcott. Our center crumbled to the floor in a heap of pain. I did not see the play as it happened in transition, and I had already shifted my eyes to the front court when the injury occurred. Tall and thin, Joey was just coming into his own. Big Joe was smart and friendly. He was the consummate big man, always looking out for others, always protecting the paint. As part of a good team with size (certainly rare for HHS), Joey clocked in at six-foot-six, while his teammate Julius Hobert was a strong six-foot-five. The team was abuzz as a pervasive feeling that we were on our way to a great season took hold.

Unfortunately for the team and player, Joey injured his knee so badly that he and his parents made the tough decision that he would not play basketball his senior year. He would continue his rehabilitation and focus on his baseball career. Joey Westcott was also an exceptional pitcher and would go on to pitch in college.

Derek and Joey were two of the nicest kids I had the opportunity to coach. The basketball gods dealt them a tough hand in high school, but that did not stop them from continuing on with their love for sports and becoming great adults.

CHAPTER 13

BACK TO THE WSAG

She was the equal to Max Perez in her intensity. I caught a few of the girls basketball games at the World Scholar Athlete Games in the late afternoons, and the skills of the young Sirocco quickly caught my attention. At night, she would always play pickup with the boy players. This fighter pilot of a point guard hailed from Palestine, but along with a number of athletes from Israel at the games, she was recognized under the latter nation's flag. The flashy baller had been enrolled under Israel as the Palestinian Territory was not recognized as an official nation. Some of the athletes attending the WSAG camp had even lost family members in the conflict between the two groups. Even today, Palestine is still fighting to be recognized as a sovereign state. I am sure the girl and her family had concerns about how she would be received by the Israeli athletes.

On the third day of camp, the WSAG would conduct an opening ceremony for the athletes. Family, friends, and community members were all invited to watch from the stands as an Olympic style ceremony unfolded. The URI football stadium was the hosting venue as athletes paraded into the arena. The parade was followed by a torch lighting and opening remarks from founder Dan

Doyle. Fireworks and a musical performance headlined by the Temptations completed the evening and celebrations.

For the parade, athletes were grouped by sport and nation. As I lined up with the basketball coaches and athletes, I noticed the Palestinian player sitting on the ground by a fence. She had her backpack and sneakers dropped over her shoulders, looking a bit lost.

"Let's go!" I shouted to her. "Line up. We are getting ready to go in!"

The noise from inside was getting louder and stronger.

"I'm not going into this fancy parade," she explained. "I can't go in. No flag. No march," she stated emphatically. She was correct. There was no Palestinian flag. The assumption was that she would march in with the Israeli athletes, represented by the Israeli flag. It was clear she was unwilling to support this action.

It struck me how little we know about people and the incredible struggles and loss they face on a daily basis.

Are they filled with anger and fear?

Are they traumatized by terrible memories?

Have they lost trust in humanity?

This player could have lost a family member or friend in the Middle East conflict. I felt compassion for this young girl, sitting alone among hundreds of young adults celebrating their accomplishments. I could not imagine the motions churning inside her.

Did she feel she would dishonor her family or friends if she walked under the Israeli flag?

War had ravaged her home. Many of the people in her community had become refugees. Later, I discovered that her family, who were concerned about a continuing Palestinian-Israeli conflict, had connections to American universities and decided to send her to the States for her senior year of high school. Their hope was for her to continue her postsecondary education here.

There are many other athletes around the globe that face the same challenges as this young lady. Like her, they too have families who are struggling to provide a better future that does not include the trauma and violence of war for their children. I was reminded of this scholar athlete during the COVID-19 lockdown. I watched the documentary *The Last Dance* centered around Phil Jackson, Michael Jordan, and the Chicago Bulls last championship season together.

One episode focused on Pippen and Jordan wanting to suffocate Tony Kukoc from Croatia and war-torn Yugoslavia during the 1992 Olympics. The two NBA stars were upset with the Chicago general manager Jerry Krause for failing to extend Pippen a big contract deal they thought he deserved. Krause had fawned over Kukoc and wanted to bring him aboard. In the Dream Team's initial matchup with Croatia, Jordan and Pippen smothered Kukoc, who only had four points and four rebounds. They were trying to embarrass him, and they did.

What the two hall of famers did not expect was Kukoc's reaction in the second meeting of the Barcelona games. They met in the gold medal game, and Kukoc played like the NBA star he would become. Jordan and Pippen had underestimated his toughness. Kukoc's grit was a byproduct of having had to make difficult decisions early in life concerning his family and basketball development. Some of these choices included leaving his family, watching the partition of his country, and losing friends and family to civil strife, all of which made Tony Kukuc ready to stand tall in the NBA.

Like Kukoc had in his context, the young Palestinian point guard stood solitary at the WSAG opening games. She was thousands of miles away from Palestine but still connected to her struggle. I think many would have just gone along with the proceedings, walked in, and enjoyed the night. Instead, she stood her ground and demonstrated a remarkable amount of integrity.

Suddenly, from her seat something appeared in her hand. There it was, a black and white fishnet pattern cloth that resembled a long scarf. The keffiyeh. The keffiyeh scarf was the traditional headdress worn by Palestinian men of rank, and it became a symbol of Palestinian nationalism during the Arab revolt in 1930 and the Palestinian resistance movement in the 1960s (Wikipedia). There was a quiet moment during which we all waited to see how the kids from Israel were going to respond. Adults are not always sure what is best to do, but sure enough the campers came through.

"Let's go, Jamila!" one of our players exclaimed, using the common phrase for "beautiful girl." When all else fails, flattery just might work. While she still did not move from the fence, players continued marching past into the opening ceremony.

Keffiyeh.

"Hey! Got any more of those in your backpack?" a male Israeli basketball player asked.

"Yes," she responded quietly.

"Well, give me one and get in line," the boy called out to her.

Into her backpack she reached, taking out another keffiyeh. The Palestinian and Israeli basketball players placed the scarves over their shoulders. There were several stares from the group and a few words spoken that I did not understand, but they walked in together under the Israeli flag and keffiyeh scarf.

No one wants to be perceived as weak, especially in a conflict. When considering the time and score, we all want to come out on top. Some attempt to achieve this through oppression and suppression of others. However, true progress can only be made when both parties in a conflict move together toward common goals that benefit each side. All that is required is a willingness to put down and step away from the hurt of past wrongs and toward a place of healing.

The young female basketball player from Palestine was tough. Kukoc was tough. Both had been through a lot at a very young age. Toughness and love come in many shapes and forms. This young man stepping out of line and extending compassion and understanding to a person standing alone is perhaps one of the simplest and most profound acts of kindness I have witnessed. To acknowledge another human being fully and offer them not only a way out but also a way forward is the work of a moment, but it can have lifelong effects.

With the keffiyeh being displayed by both an Israeli and a Palestinian, I hope that young girl no longer felt that she was letting her family, her friends, and her home down. At a critical moment, the young basketball player from Israel demonstrated empathy and concern for the Palestinian point guard. The young man did not know how his gesture would be received by the other Israeli athletes, but he bravely chose a wonderful act of humanity and courage that I will remember forever.

While researching the WSAG, I came across a very distressing story. It was about the founder of the games, Dan Doyle. He was accused of financial wrongdoings connected to WSAG funding (*Hartford Courant*), and in August 2017, the former boxing promoter, ex-college basketball coach, and founder of a Rhode Island based Sport Institute was convicted of embezzlement. A jury found Doyle guilty of eighteen counts, including embezzlement, forgery, filing false documents, and obtaining money under false pretenses in 2016. Prosecutors said Doyle, who lived in West Hartford, used the institute as a piggy bank, taking more than $1 million to pay for things including college tuition, wedding expenses for his children, and plastic surgery. The State Police of Rhode Island began investigating the institute, which received more than $7.3 million from the state between 1988 and 2011.

It was no secret that the WSAG spared no expense to get some amazing people to speak to the athletes from around the globe. The organization had a list of dazzling speakers, as I have mentioned, including Bill Clinton, Archbishop Desmond Tutu, Colin Powell, Jane Goodall, Elie Wiesel, and Matthew Shepard's mom. Insiders estimated that these speakers received upward of $100,000 to present at camp. Doyle's sentencing occurred in Kingston, RI, under Superior Court Judge Melanie Will Thunberg. According to the *Providence Journal*, Thunberg told Doyle exactly what she thought of his actions: "The number of people you let down with a lack of conscience and greed was shameful." She continued by admonishing Doyle for ruining a tremendous opportunity for generations of global youth. She concluded by stating, "In short, you played a dirty game." As of this writing, Dan Doyle is continuing his fight to clear his name and reputation. He maintains that he is innocent of the charges brought against him.

CHAPTER 14

DR. JAMES NAISMITH 2.0 AND THE EMOTION OF NO MOTION

It was the middle of May 2020, and the world was trying to stay healthy and avoid catching COVID-19. May has always been such a joyful month for our family. May brings with it the start of spring in New England, family birthdays, Mother's Day, and the anniversary of my wedding to my Irish bride. Additionally, high school tennis season is in full topspin flight and there are a multitude of school celebrations. In essence, May is motion, with plenty of movement and action!

The emotion that came from the shelter-in-place orders of May 2020 was a huge adjustment. Not being able to enjoy the many threads of society that connected us together and to movement was extremely emotional. With that being said, I was able to learn three new skills while confined in my home: 1) Zoom, 2) telemedicine visits, and 3) how to color Sandy's hair. When life throws us new challenges, it is important for us to adapt. May is the perfect month to look around to see how nature changes and adapts not only to survive but to thrive. The global pandemic of 2020 brought new rules and regulations to our world. It was a process, but we needed to find different ways to keep moving forward.

Like nature's changes, the evolution of sports has always been necessary to ensure the survival and relevancy of the game. Here is an example: Dr. Ed Steitz oftentimes is referred to as the father of the three-point field goal. The implementation of the three-point rule changed the game forever and hurtled basketball into a new era. Dr. Steitz, a professor at Springfield College in Massachusetts, was on the rules committee for NCAA men's basketball. As the story goes, Dr. Steitz started gathering data for the rule change on a court built in his suburban East Longmeadow home. Dr. Steitz would instruct his son Bob and the other neighborhood kids to shoot from different distances. He would have players shoot when guarded and unguarded. As the kids played, he would chart all the shots. He charted all kinds of players, ranging from little kids to high school players and college athletes.

During his research, Dr. Steitz took notice of those who felt comfortable shooting as well as those who did not. Dr Steitz was looking for the distance to plant the line and balance the risk-reward equation of the game. The NBA and even the top levels of college basketball had gotten away from the flow and beauty of the game. The rules committee recognized this and moved forward with the innovation. Watching *The Last Dance* documentary, I came to understand that the relentless physicality of the game plan in matchups like the Pistons versus the Bulls was brutal. Be physical, clobber MJ, and block off the space going to the hoop. I believe it became known as the "Jordan Rules."

The two biggest rule changes that occurred during my high school coaching experience were the addition of a shot clock and the three-point field goal. As is the case with changes, it took time to adapt to the new reality. How would players and coaches be expected to develop a three-point game?

Dr. Steitz and other members of the rules committee developed this new plan to bring back the true essence of the game. Their goal was to find a balance between skill and movement. Dr. Naismith often expressed concern that height would be too much of an advantage on the basketball court. I am sure this was also a consideration for the three-point rule change as a way of bringing the little man back into the game.

Looking at the present state of NBA and NCAA basketball, it is clear that the three-point rule has been incredibly successful. I wonder if these basketball innovators could have predicted the electrifying charge that runs through the fans, players, and coaches when a ball swishes through the net from behind the arc. From offensive design to defensive employment, the three-point shot has revolutionized and invigorated the game. From player development to managing a game from the sideline, the three-point shot has changed the game dramatically. No lead is ever safe.

The most important effect of this addition to the game of basketball was creating more opportunities in the offensive players' hands. Before the three-point shot, the best way a team could overcome a big deficit was from a defensive standpoint. Teams would use a full court press or traps to force quick turnovers and scores. But with the implementation of the shot clock and three pointers, teams had a greater probability of cutting a large lead if their opponent went on a run. Like I said, no lead is ever safe.

One game that comes to mind was a contest between the Holyoke Knights and the Chicopee Pacers. The Knights trailed by sixteen with just about three minutes left in the game. Holyoke responded with a barrage of three-point field goals, tied the game in regulation, and went on to win in overtime. Each three-point field goal built momentum and sent emotion through the players and the crowd.

While a thunderous big-time dunk is a spectacle of athletic beauty, it meets its match when a shot from behind the arc is attempted. The three-point shot has added an electric charge to the game of basketball. Players like Dr. J, Michael Jordan, LeBron James, Wilt Chamberlain, Bill Russell, Jerry West, Kareem Abdul Jabbar, and Oscar Robertson are all masters of the game; each player brought a unique quality to basketball, demonstrating both grace and power. But Steph Curry is without a doubt the father of the three-point shot. When Dr. Steitz and the rules committee introduced the new shot to the game, there is no doubt Curry's pacing, ability to create space, and deadly shooting precision exceeded their wildest expectations. Curry is the epitome of the delicate balance between movement and skill.

While players like Oscar Robertson, the big bully HOF guard who would back down his opponent to the baseline only to turn and shoot over him, used his size and strength to leverage the game, other players chose a more refined approach. Oskar Schmidt from the 1987 Pan American Games led Brazil to a 120-to-115 upset over the USA team. At this time, the USA was still only using college players, not professional players, from other nations. The International Basketball Federation (FIBA) had a rule against playing for your country and the NBA; players had to choose one or the other, if they were good enough. It was clear Schmidt had the skills but elected to play for his homeland.

Unfortunately, this meant NBA fans were deprived of watching the international version of Larry Bird. It is well documented that this defeat led the USA to develop the very first Dream Team and transition to this model. Additionally, Schmidt got American players and coaches thinking more about using the three-point shot on offense, in addition to defending it. Schmidt torched the US team by scoring forty-five points that day at the Indianapolis Market Square Arena, with thirty-five in the second half alone.

Kurt Russel, in his iconic performance as Herb Brooks in the movie *Miracle*, proclaims, "He doesn't know what to do!" referring to the Soviet coach when he fails to pull his goalie in the waning moments of the Lake Placid upset. Likewise, the coaches and players on team USA did not know what to do in their matchup against Brazil and Schmidt. American basketball's introduction to Dr. Steitz and his three-point game was painful as the Brazilian guards drove the paint with Schmidt following close behind. The penetrating guard would pitch back to Schmidt for an uncontested wide open three-pointer. At six-foot-nine, Schmidt made it look easy. The longtime practice on defense was to help from the wing to stop a drive and then recover out. Instead, Schmidt moved from the wing to filling in behind an aggressive drive to the basket. This pattern and style befuddled team USA. As each three-point shot was made by Schmidt (7-15) from beyond the arc, the dream, emotion, and belief in the Brazilian team's ability to defeat the kings of basketball grew.

The evolution of the three-point shot can be seen throughout basketball. Many games and contests have been decided from behind the arc. In episode IX of *The Last Dance*, Jalen Rose talks about a big three-point shot that Scottie Pippen made in an important playoff game against the Indiana Pacers. He recalls the play as "sucking the air out of the fans in Market Square." The Dr. Steitz three-ball risk-and-reward not only injected magic into the offensive team but instilled dread in opponents and fans, especially in the later stages of a contest.

December 28, 1987
Agawam High School
Agawam 103, Holyoke 101 (2 OT)

Agawam: J. Peterson 10-10-30, J. Patterson 1-2-4, J. Reece 2-0-4, E. Fogg 1-4-6, M. Dilillo 3-0-6, A. Vanderhoof 3 (2)-1-9, J. Lockwood 5-8-18, J. Wooley 2-1-5, C. Ollari 1-0-2, J. Serra 7 (5)-0-19. Totals: 35 (7)-26-103. Fouled out: Peterson, Lockwood, Wooley.
Holyoke: R. Thomas 10-2-22, D. Brown 7-5-19, J. King 7-4-18, T. Westbrook 2(1) 2-7, DJ Westbrook 6 1-16-29, B. Crowley 0-2-2, M. Wohlers 0-1-1, C. Hardrick 1-0-2, B. McDonough 1-0-2. Totals: 33 (2)-33-101. Fouled out: King, Wohlers.

Another game that stands out in my coaching career took place at Agawam High School (AHS) in December 1988. My grandson,

Syius, still has not figured out why the AHS mascot remains the Brownies. Gen Z does offer up some valid points.

The game was a matchup between two good high school teams who both had aspirations of a great season. This was already our second meeting of the year. During the first contest, the Brownies defeated us 76–61 at home, on December 13. Now, on December 28, we were playing at their gym. We came in 2-2, while the Brownies were 4-0 and playing great so early in the season.

It was a wild high school game. The contest featured drama on and off the court. In Australia they would refer to games like this as a "dog's breakfast" with both teams making and trying to defend three-point field goals. The Brownies were coached by MBCA Hall of Fame Coach Mike Martin. Coach Martin, who earlier in his coaching career led Commerce High of Springfield to a number of state championships, was a true coaching adversary.

The rosters for both teams were filled with excellent high school players. The Knights were led by JJ King, Roman Thomas, and DJ Westbrook, along with excellent role players Brian Crowley, Mark Wohlers (of the Atlanta Braves), Craig Hardrick, and Bill McDonough.

A brief side note about Wohlers, who was a great closer for the Braves and whose career was highlighted by getting the save in the deciding game of the World Series as his team defeated the Cleveland Indians. The cover of *Sports Illustrated* captured a wonderful photo of Mark leaping in the air after the last out. Mark only played basketball for the Knights his senior year. I had haunted him in the high school hallways to come out and give it a try. Mark's sister Cindy had threatened to kill me if he hurt his arm playing hoop. Luckily Mark made it through the season injury free and ready to play baseball in the spring. Mark provided rebounding, shot blocking, and team chemistry. He came off the bench to give JJ King, our starting center, a rest and proved to be a great asset to our team. As the season progressed, Mark played more and picked up the game so easily we could play both bigs at once.

There were two elements in this game against the Brownies that differentiated it from the many basketball games I coached for Holyoke. First, when I walked into my living room around eleven that night, my wife Sandy's voice came out from the back bedroom. "How did we do?" she asked.

"Great!" I responded. "We dropped 101 points on Coach Martin."

"Nice win!" she exclaimed.

"Well, not really.... we gave up 103."

"Who had a temperature of 103? You let him play?" Typically Sandy who had four careers: licensed nurse practitioner, schoolteacher, mother, and coach's wife. It's not necessary to ask her which one was the most difficult.

"No, we gave up 103 points."

Crickets.

Second, this was my coaching introduction to the emotion of Dr. Steitz's three-point field goal. At the start of the game, we were rolling. We got off to a 24-to-18 first quarter lead, closing out the quarter with a big three from Tony Westbrook. The Knights charged off the court to the bench for the quarter break. Agawam coach Mike Martin wasn't happy, to say the least. Mike was a great coach and competitor who poured his heart and soul into every game. Off the court, he was a gentle giant. He would give you the shirt off his back if you needed it. Mike always treated the kids from Holyoke with dignity and respect. Additionally, he provided many of them with opportunities in the basketball community they normally would not have had access to. Over our coach careers, we became basketball friends. When I coached against Mike, I pretended to draw a curtain at midcourt so I couldn't see him on his bench. His coaching box (when he was in it) was always energized. On the court, Mike was a fierce competitor. He demanded the exact same energy, drive, and excellence from his players (and the officials).

During the second quarter of that epic battle against Mike's Agawam Brownies, the Holyoke Knights started out with a blitz.

JJ King (career stats: 1,051 points, 843 rebounds, and 115 blocks) scored 11 points as the opposition could not find a way to stop him. The Agawam players were getting frustrated, and Coach Martin was starting to get on the refs. Wohlers was blocking shots, JJ was rebounding, and DJ Westbrook was running the show. We were on a roll!

As our bigs controlled the game and Ramon Thomas, our small forward, hit three consecutive baskets, the last one running over a Brownie who had stepped in for a charge with no call, Martin reached his limit. The Knights lead grew to sixteen points with only two minutes left in the half. Curtain or no curtain, Mike came charging right past our bench to have a conversation with the refs.

"That was a charge! A JV ref could make that call," Mike raged. "You know what? Here, take them!"

And just like that, Coach Martin began pulling his starting five from the floor. It is hard to say if he was more upset with the refs or his players for falling behind. After all, they had beaten us pretty good a short while back. In went the last five players on the Agawam bench. Still two minutes left to make hay. We pressed and took advantage, extending our lead to twenty-three points at halftime.

Agawam was led by an exceptional collection of all-around athletes and good basketball players. Jeff Reece, Eric Fogg, Mike Dilullo, Jim Lockwood, and Jason Wooley all had strong basketball skills, but it was their best player Jeff Peterson and sniper John Serra who were most instrumental in this memorable game. These two powerhouses, along with the exceptional leadership of Coach Martin, turned the game around. What happened in that Agawam locker room was pure genius on the part of Coach Martin, channeling Red Auerbach to get his team ready for the second half of the game.

Red was affiliated with sixteen Celtic Championship victories and is recognized as a master of basketball psychology. He is known for his ability to motivate the players on his team, especially in challenging gametime situations. *So what did coach Martin say to his team after a dreadful first half?*

He said everything and nothing simultaneously, understanding that sometimes less is more. Instead of ranting and raving at his players, he told Jeff Peterson, the future Lahovich winner, to talk to his team in the locker room. Maybe a different voice would get through to his players? It is small but significant decisions like this that can make a great coach. Coach Martin knew and recognized the time and score; he knew the best way to get his players out of their basketball funk. Unfortunately for us, that night it worked!

During the third quarter, Mike's starters came back into the game. DJ Westbrook buried a three for the Holyoke Knights right off the bat. Swish, and we are up by twenty-six. Now the ball started going to Peterson and Fogg every possession down the court. JJ King and Mark Wohlers got into foul trouble, leaving us with no bigs in the game by the fourth quarter. Peterson was killing us inside. Nevertheless we were still up by fourteen points, but the lead is dwindling.

Then the emotion of the three-point shot showed up for the Brownies. Vanderhoof scored two threes, and Serra made a remarkable five three-point shots. With each make in the second half, the flow of emotion percolated through the players and crowd. To my dismay, it seemed like each three was worth five points for our opponent. It also appeared to influence the officials' calls. The referees appeared caught up in the net of Dr. Steitz's "emotion of the three." No calls for the Knights. First JJ fouled out, and then Wohlers followed suit. Regulation ended in a tie. We responded by evening the score in the first overtime, once again on a powerful three-point shot. They outscored us nine to seven in the second OT, including another three by John Serra, the clear game changer. Time ran out, the buzzer went off, and the Agawam Brownies won an epic basketball game that I remember so clearly over thirty years later.

Looking back to that 103-to-101 double overtime loss, I cannot help but think of the role the three-point field goal played that night, and would continue to play in the future of the game of basketball. The emotion, the positionless player, the innovation of offensive and defensive schemes all were on the horizon. This was my epiphany to the great rule change by Dr. Steitz and the rules committee. As a coach and fan, the fascination with the three point shot started for me that cold December night in a steamy hot Agawam gym. It was not the number of threes made that evening. In fact, the count was nothing out of the ordinary by today's standards. However, it was clear that the work of Dr. Steitz and the little players firing up shots for him to chart in his East Longmeadow backyard so many years prior had forever changed the game.

Today, at all levels of basketball, the game plan is to maximize the number of three-point field goal attempts. The game between Agawam and Holyoke thus represented the dawn of a new era in basketball. As a coach, I witnessed firsthand the emotional avalanche that results from a deluge of successful three-point field goals on players, referees, and fans. It is a powerful force that can quickly change any game.

Modern basketball pundits would have had plenty to say about so many three point attempts being taken in a game. Some argue the game has lost its balance, while others worry about a lack of post play. They warn against too much dribbling and standing around on the three-point line and the decline of fast break basketball. Where are the days when players would finish by driving hard? While the latter still happens, the game has changed, leaning into Dr. Steitz's three-point game.

With that being said, basketball is a wonderful, thriving game that will continue to grow and evolve. I am sure there will be future adjustments to rules, spacing, and motion concerning the three, but for now the players, coaches, and fans seem to appreciate the genius of this innovation.

CHAPTER 15

BIGS AND BROTHERS

JJ King was one of the best high school players I had the opportunity to coach. The left-hander stood 6-foot-5, was pencil thin, and possessed a relentless passion for the game that gave the Purple Knights a great chance to win every night. As a coach, you cannot ask for more than that from your players. JJ rebounded the ball, blocked shots, and scored points. Essentially, he could command and control the game both offensively and defensively. He was a threat on both ends of the court.

JJ's family flocked to the games. They were so proud of his contributions to the team, and I believe his mom knew that basketball was a vehicle to help JJ in life and school. I remember one home game when JJ made an amazing LeBron James–like run down block from three-quarters down the court. To this day, I do not know how he got to the ball that fast. With a forceful swat, JJ crashed and rolled into the wall as his left hand and body straightened from the Euclidean geometry he used to reset the trajectory of the Spalding sphere. Quickly rising up, JJ sprinted back on offense through his family, who had spilled onto the court in a frenzied delirium celebrating the beautiful block. As JJ caught up to his teammates on offense, he crashed the boards, throwing down a dunk off a missed layup. The crowd went crazy, noise erupting from the stands as fans gave each other high fives, marveling at JJ's talent.

In Paper City, our boys basketball team was never known for our size. It just wasn't our thing. Most of my teams played small and fast. We did our best inside with whatever length we had. Over the years the Holyoke kids would rise to the challenge. I asked a lot of my players to play inside when they were undersized. Players like Billy and Matt Wresien, Mike Kennedy, Rafael Rodriguez, Eliezer Vazquez, and Chris Lachaplle got so much done for us playing against bigger players each night. They never complained because they were tough kids with grit who played their hearts out regardless of their competition.

Jenorow "JJ" King put up some amazing numbers during his career. He amassed 1,051 points and 843 rebounds. He was an All Western Mass selection his junior and senior seasons, and his teams qualified for the state playoffs three times. But beyond his talent and natural ability, JJ played the game with passion and joy. I loved him for that. He was a member of HHS's graduating class of '88, but unfortunately we lost JJ all too soon to cancer.

On November 5, 2022, Jenorow "JJ" King was inducted to the HHS Athletic Hall of Fame. In the program tribute at the induction ceremony, he was honored for "his friendly nature on the court," which was a "was a gift he passed down to his sons"; he "really instilled a love of all sports in his boys. His patience in teaching his sons the skills, tactics, fairness, honor, kindness, and humor was an inspiration for many others and a joy to witness" (HHS HOF program).

December 23, 1988
"Jinx" O'Connor Gym
Holyoke High School
Holyoke 106, Greenfield 69

Holyoke: JJ. King 13-9-35, B. McDonough 7-1-15, D. Brown 2-2-6, D. J. Westbrook 3-1-8-17, D. Bridgeforth 6-0-12, M. Fournier 2-4-8, R. Dowling 1-0-2, C. Delaney 1-0-2, M. Dunn 3-1-7, D. Quinn 0-2-2. Totals: 38-1-27-106.
Greenfield: S. Cassin 5-0-10, I. Tristan 4-1-9, B. Desautels 3-1-7, S. McDonald 2-4-1-17, K. Phelps 2-7-11, S. Wood 4-0-8, S. Sokoloski 1-0-2, K. McGahan 0-2-2, D. Gammpll 1-1-3. Totals: 22-4-13-69.

Ed Hart Chases Valley League Scoring Title
March 4, 1983
Cathedral High School
Springfield, MA
Holyoke 80, Putnam 78

Holyoke: E. Hart 10-12-32, J. Hart 3-0-6, C. Morales 3-4-10, M. Laplante 3-4-10, P. Fitzgibbons 5-3-13, P. Hobert 2-1-5, D. Gordan 1-0-2. Totals: 28-24-80.
Putnam: S. Addison 15-1-31, N Smith 6-0-12, R. Markham 6-2-14, J. Smilley 2-0-4, J. Huff 4-0-8, K. Sharif 2-1-5, S. Scott 1-0-2, R. Ramsey 1-0-2. Totals: 27-4-78.

There is an art to good post play. I hope that this part of the game can still flourish under the demands of the spread offense and three-point attempts. Players big and small who understand how to score and defend in the post area will develop a better understanding of the whole game. Angles, passing, footwork are all essential elements of a player's skill set. A player has to learn to pay attention to small details in order to excel near the basket. Teaching only perimeter skills is a missed opportunity to learn and utilize an important area of the court. Avoiding the teaching and mastering of the post area both offensively and defensively is not conducive to winning basketball games.

Today in tennis many lament the lack of the serve-and-volley game that tennis greats like Stefan Edberg, Rod Laver, Boris

Becker, Pete Sampras, and John McEnroe made look effortless. While it should be noted that many points are still won at the net, the players simply get there in a different progression. The same can be observed in basketball. The best coaches will incorporate post play and inside scoring through their offenses, making sure their players have down the fundamentals of guarding and attacking close to the rim.

Eddie Hart was one of the players on my first varsity team. I did not get to put Eddie on the 94-by-50 rectangle until our fifth game. He had sustained an injury playing for the Knights in the D1 Super Bowl championship earlier that fall. The high school football championship game was held the first Saturday after Thanksgiving, leaving only one week before the start of the winter sports season. As a result, Eddie missed all of the preseason for basketball and had to sit out at the beginning. Thus I started my coaching career 0–5.

Jim Hart, one of Eddie's brothers, was also on the team and filled our point guard slot during that time. The Hart siblings were one of many pairings of brothers I had the opportunity to work with over the years; nonetheless, coaching siblings provided plenty of challenges. If you could get through daily disputes between the brothers in practice, which most times had nothing to do with basketball, you were golden. On the other hand, brothers gave families a blueprint to what our coaching staff was all about. There were not a lot of surprises for them on how we were going to handle discipline, roster spots, or playing time. So any time we had a sibling come through who could make the team, we had already built up some social equity with the player and his family.

Eddie's strength was that he knew how to play on the inside. He could pass out of the post and understood how to effectively use his size and strength to get the better of taller defenders. He was a smart player. The All Western Mass center could see the ball and catch it with ease. This ability is made that much more difficult when a million things are swirling around you on the court. In post play, a player has split seconds to understand the best option. Eddie Hart had a soft touch that led to many points.

In fact, Big Ed was at or near the top of the Valley League scoring title in his senior year. To the best of my memory, only one or two other Purple Knights whom I coached finished in that rarefied air of leading the Valley League in scoring. Eddie was fortunate to play with an outstanding backcourt. His brother Jim and Carlos Morales were both exceptional post passers and balanced players. They kept the defense honest when they needed to score, preventing a lot of double-teaming in the post. Many times a coach will have a good big man but no one to get the ball inside to him.

Joey Hart (yes, yet another Hart brother, as well as my stats and score keeper) always kept track of how many touches Eddie had during a game. Our backcourt chalked up many assists, getting the ball to Eddie on the block, short corner, or high post. If Eddie touched the ball enough, we usually played well on offense. Playing through your post player to trigger your offense is often problematic for the defense because most teams are more accustomed to their opponents playing through a point guard or a motion offense.

It was great news for the team to get Eddie back into the starting lineup. The bad news was we needed to kick-start our team engine and get past our 0–5 record. With the big man we recovered to win eleven out of our final fifteen games. We just missed the playoffs as qualifying meant winning 60 percent of games played at the time. Our last two regular season games showcased how far our team had developed. We defeated both Putnam and Commerce, schools that would face off in the D1 Western Mass finals a few weeks later.

Note: Eddie Hart's football coach for that Super Bowl season was Jack Murdock. He was an excellent football coach. Coach Murdock was tough, hard-nosed, and very successful at HHS. Shortly after the Knights Super Bowl appearance, he moved on to coach in Pennsylvania. As a disturbing example of what dedicated high school coaches have to put up with at times, it was rumored that someone in the community set fire to his home. Needless to say, Coach Murdock did not stay around long to put up with that nonsense and rare, extreme example of community crowd refereeing.

Both Ed (posthumously) and Jim Hart were inducted into the HHS Athletic Hall of Fame on November 5, 2022. The program guide described them as "teammates, competitors…brothers. Together yet separate. The same yet different. Physically gifted yet strategically opposite" (HHS HOF program). Both together and individually, Eddie and Jim Hart were two of the all-time great three-sport athletes to grace the HHS sporting arenas.

CHAPTER 16

THOSE OTHER JOBS, THE GREAT ARTHUR ASHE, AND "I WILL BE BACK ON TUESDAY"

Summer Place at the University of Hartford was one of my favorite summer jobs during my teaching career. There is an ill-conceived notion out there that teachers just hang out and take an eight-week vacation. The truth is far different as most educators continue to work either at summer school or camps through July and August. Teachers, especially those starting out, paying off student loans, or supporting their families, are not paid well enough to be able to afford an eight-week unpaid vacation. Sometimes teachers might stay home with their young children to avoid the astronomical and growing costs of childcare, but as many found out during the COVID-19 pandemic, staying home with your kids all day is both a blessing and a ton of work. The inadequately low salaries of educators, the rising costs of home ownership and raising a family, and trying to save money for vacations and higher education are all challenges facing teachers today.

For "offseason" HHS teachers, Don Bergeron and Tom Brassil directed and organized the Summer Place camp at the University of Hartford. Don and Tom were organized and smart. They helped Summer Place provide a nice camp experience for children of all ages regardless of their socioeconomic situation. The Summer Place camp experience was a blend of academics, athletics, and the arts. During my time at camp, I coached tennis and basketball. Summer Place was located in affluent West Hartford. The camp drew children from surrounding suburbs, rural areas, and inner-city neighborhoods of Harford through Insurance Industry Charitable Foundation grants. Most campers were from the Nutmeg State.

It was at Summer Place that I was granted the opportunity to listen to tennis great and humanitarian Arthur Ashe. The news spread fast around camp that the Great Arthur Ashe was coming to Summer Place to promote the National Junior Tennis League (NJTL). The NJTL was the brainchild of Arthur and the United States Tennis Association (USTA) with the goal of getting more inner-city kids playing the wonderful game of tennis.

Ashe was in the first group of professional players I followed when I started to play a bit of tennis myself. Through the writings of Bud Collins and the *Boston Globe*, I was introduced to the wonderful game and my love affair with tennis was ignited. I would eagerly await Bud's columns and thoroughly enjoyed his entertaining and informative writing, always enchanted by the names I read: Bjorn, Ilie, Guillermo, and Adriano. Most of the guys I grew up with were named Bob, Jim, and Tim. *Who were these guys with such different names?*

During my teaching and coaching career, I put to good use two quotes from Arthur when I found myself out of my comfort zone and needed to push forward. The first was "Start where you are. Use what you have. Do what you can." And the second was "From what we get, we make a living. From what we give, we make a life."

The world of tennis was new to me as I had grown up playing baseball, basketball, and football. My interest in tennis only began in my adult life, but the opportunity to see Arthur Ashe in action, patrolling the University of Hartford courts on a very humid July morning, added fuel to my newfound fire. He was scheduled to arrive in the afternoon, but the threat of late-day thunderstorms pushed his clinic into the early morning. Some might have canceled, but Arthur kept his word and stayed longer than expected on the courts with the kids. He was kind and soft spoken with the children. They flocked around him like they knew something the world did not yet know.

Children are often the best judges of character. It is difficult to fool them, so it was clear that they sensed what a special gift this tremendous athlete and human rights activist truly was. The tragedy was losing such an incredible person far too soon, but it was clear he did not waste a minute of his life. For Arthur, the story was always about the kids and the work and not him. It was true that day and many other days. He shied away from any extra attention and simply did the work and shared his vision.

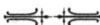

At Summer Place I had the opportunity to work with kids from various backgrounds. Many of the campers came from families of extreme wealth and privilege. This was a very different experience from teaching and coaching at HHS. But I find that despite our differences, we have more in common than we think. For starters, when all is said and done, kids are kids regardless of where they come from. Ultimately, they all want the same things: a chance to discover who they are and an opportunity to fulfill their dreams. From adults, they simply want time and attention. They want to know they are seen and that they matter. That is their barometer for time and score.

One afternoon, while I was finishing a tennis session, Eric (one of my campers) approached me. Eric was a promising player who had just completed the seventh grade in West Hartford.

"Hi, Coach!" he bellowed. "I won't be here on Monday." It was a Thursday before the long Fourth of July weekend and many families had travel plans.

"OK," I responded. "What's up?"

"Going skiing!" he quipped.

"All right, I'll see you when you get back!"

When Tuesday arrived, Eric had returned, pounding forehands like usual. I meandered through the courts talking a bit to each camper. When I got to Eric, he shot me a smile and I asked, "Eric, how was the water?" It had been a pretty raw and rainy weekend for most of New England. Not the best weather for the water or jet skiers. Eric suddenly cast me a strange gaze from under his hat, three times too big for him.

"What, Coach? I'm not sure about the water, Coach, but the snowpack was amazing!" Eric the little jet-setter had gone to the Andes in Chile. "There is plenty of snow this time of year!" he explained. And of course he was right.

Kids! They never cease to amaze me, and I am sure adults never cease to amaze them. The great Arthur Ashe understood the tremendous importance of and need to work with kids. He knew how sports and being involved in a team can empower children on their journey to becoming who they were meant to be. While some kids, like Eric, start off with a great advantages in life, all kids benefit most from our time and attention. Sure, adults and kids sometimes misunderstand one another, but the work is always interesting and definitely worth it.

CHAPTER 17

HOOPS AND INVITATIONS, CINDY, AND FATHER JACK

It is always gratifying to be recognized for a job well done. Throughout my life as a student, athlete, teacher, and coach, I have been blessed with several honors for my hard work and service in the Holyoke community. Each award and acknowledgment is connected to a particular moment in time, connected to the faces who helped make these honors possible. Like basketball, life is a team sport. Sure, isolation ball is a new trend in the modern game, but each player is able to achieve more when the team collaborates. I know this is true of my life, when I consider my family, friends, mentors, teammates, colleagues, students, and players. I have been able to achieve many good things because of these important relationships in my life.

For example, the five times I was honored by the Massachusetts Basketball Coaches Association (MBCA) as Coach of the Year, which included winning the award two of the last three seasons I coached despite not being rehired due to the receivership, was a great honor. And the Purple Knight teams winning the Sportsmanship Award, given out by our local officials board, five times is an acknowledgment that fills my heart with pride.

Away from the court and all its accolades, the invitations from former players to special occasions like graduations, weddings, and career accomplishments will always have special meaning to me. I am forever thankful to be included in their journeys to building a successful life. Educators and coaches do not always get to see the fruits of their labor, so an opportunity to see past students and players achieving happiness and success in their present lives it is a very joyous occasion.

The first time I can remember being recognized publicly was during my junior year at HHS. It was not an award given out by the school but rather an honor given to me down at an old building on Race Street in downtown Holyoke. This small three-story structure with a compacted basketball court and oval track above it was my second home during the fall and winter months. The Holyoke Boys Club was small, but her heart was immense and it pumped hope, discipline, and opportunity every day into our community.

It was at the Boys Club that learned to travel outside my immediate community with respect, dignity, and honor. The following mantras were drilled into us with consistency and clarity: "Treat all competitors with respect," "Stand up for yourself, and "Take off your hat when you walk into the building."

I made friends and played ball with kids from all races and nationalities. I was coached by two of the toughest and most gracious people to walk this planet: Nick Cosmos and Wey Dotson. Nick's dedication to our community is legendary, and Dot was one of the Knight's all-time great basketball players. Having them in my ear day after day helped me grow up.

So when Nick called my home to talk with my parents, Chick and Pego, to let them know that I had been selected as the club's Boy of the Year, it was a proud day for me and my family. Being a part of the Boys Club community is something that shaped who I was from an early age. It was a partnership that continued into my career as a coach. Winning that award, learning from two amazing mentors, forging relationships with my teammates, and helping my own players build that same sense of community and belonging has been a true gift.

Places like the Holyoke Boys Club are essential in every community. During the pandemic a lot was taken away from us. We all missed out on things both big and small. Lockdowns caused us to reimagine celebrations, acknowledgments, and social/community gatherings. Schools and parents did an amazing job with putting together graduation car parades and other unique forms of celebration for graduating seniors. People did their best, but it was not the same as the real-time, face-to-face meetings of prepandemic conditions. Now that life has gone back to its regular rhythm, I try not to take these opportunities and gatherings for granted.

One such gathering I was always fond of was Class Day at HHS, held for the graduating seniors the week leading up to the commencement ceremony. It was a day that filled both students and faculty with pride. For us teachers, it is very rewarding to look out at the graduating class and recall how collectively we helped get this class of students through. Whew!

During Class Day the final class rank is acknowledged with the announcement of the valedictorian and salutatorian. The results of the class celebrities vote are shared, scholarships of all kinds are awarded, and the school yearbook is dedicated to a faculty member. On one occasion, I was fortunate to receive this honor. It was special because the dedication is voted on by the graduating class. I have always felt like kids can figure you out better than adults can, so I was truly honored and humbled by the HHS students' appreciation and gratitude.

One of the most joyous honors I have received is having my name on the basketball court in John "Jinx" O'Connor Gymnasium. The thick purple sideline block that encases the court spells out "William C. Rigali." This dedication was a surprise and an honor. Truly, I really do not feel I deserve it, but all I can say is it was a very proud day for the Rigali family. In truth, it is my family, in so many ways, who deserves the credit along, with my assistant coaches and of course the wonderful kids I got to coach over the years.

For an educator, seeing the success of the young people you work with can be the greatest of rewards. While each individual's triumphs are a result of their own choices, it is a wonderful feeling to know you have made a contribution to their success. In particular, graduation day is a source of pride for all. Teachers are just as proud of the students and families who have struggled to get to that special day as we are of our truly exceptional students. It is good for a community to see someone from your school step out into the world and achieve great success.

JOHN F. KENNEDY SCHOOL OF GOVERNMENT
HARVARD UNIVERSITY
Class of 2002 Graduation

Cynthia Medina
Master in Public Policy

Thursday, June 6 2002

8:30 AM
Morning Exercises
viewed at Sanders Theatre

12:00 NOON
Diploma Ceremony & Lunche
JFK Park at Kennedy School of Gov

4:00 PM
Cynthia Medina Graduation Fiesta
Cynthia's House
19 Caldwell Avenue
Somerville, Massachusetts

Harvard invitation from Cindy Medina-Carson.

Cindy Medina was one such exceptional student I had the privilege of teaching and coaching at HHS. Several years she graduated from high school, my wife and I were sitting at a table in Cambridge, MA, for the John F. Kennedy School of Government graduation ceremony. We were listening to the speakers address the graduates about their role and obligation to serve others. Many talked about the need for the public, private, and nonprofit sectors of our society to work collaboratively.

Sandy and I were there because we had received an invitation from Cindy, a former student and tennis player. On this cool, rainy spring day, Cindy Medina Carson, a Purple Knight, Georgetown Hoya, and soon-to-be Harvard Kennedy School graduate, was beaming. Making the day even more special was the fact that Cindy was the class marshal. It did not surprise me that she had achieved such great success after leaving high school. Her Harvard graduation day has always been at the top of my list of special moments because not only was Cindy's achievement a remarkable one but her happiness was evidence of a fulfilling life.

Cindy had plenty of ability to do well in any career path she chose. She was representative of the many girls who play high school tennis. The HHS tennis landscape was not typically filled with many Grand Slam champions. However, it was filled to the rim with community leaders, future CEOs, and well-rounded young women. The group of players who came through with Cindy were mature, sharp, and focused. In fact, they probably had the ability to run the school if no adults showed up (though that never happened).

During Cindy's senior year, the seven starters went on to pursue degrees of higher education from elite schools such as Smith, University of Connecticut, University of Oregon, Georgetown University, University of Massachusetts, Amherst College, and Providence College. That year the team was brimming with leadership.

As both basketball and tennis coach, I always make it part of my responsibility to check in on my seniors and their future plans after graduation. In basketball, I had a bit more time to help students, with the longer season occurring earlier in the school year. Due to the shorter tennis season in spring, usually the players only needed a few reminders about deadlines for work, military applications, or school choices.

One day at practice, I asked Cindy if she had decided on a school. Had she visited any campuses? Was she leaning toward any particular school?

"I really haven't seen any yet, but there are two or three at the top of my list," Cindy responded.

Having been the first person to graduate from college in my family, I knew some of the steps Cindy might miss. I felt that visiting campus and getting a feel of what it actually looked and felt like was an important part of trying to make the best decision. What energy, either negative or positive, could be found on campus among the students? How did the environment make one feel? How long was the drive from home?

Sandy and I decided to take Cindy to one of the schools she had applied to previously in the fall. Additionally, she made arrangements to visit her other top choices. She just needed a touch of social equity, such as people and experiences, to help her make an informed decision about her future. Today, through her career ventures, Cindy has paid the opportunities provided to her forward time and again.

Cindy is now a Georgetown and Harvard graduate, wife, mom, community leader, tennis player, and conqueror of Mount Kilimanjaro. She is a social advocate for women in the workplace as her own career path has been a blueprint for women to achieve their professional goals and dreams. Cindy's focus is offering advice and leadership on ways for women to navigate through the glass ceiling and take on consequential roles both in the national and global community. She is passionate about how women can find ways to succeed and give back, helping others climb the ladder of success. My family and I are avid believers that growing up in a diverse community like Holyoke has always been an advantage in our professional and personal lives. I am sure Cindy feels the same.

In the spring of 1973, I was playing baseball for Coach O'Brien and the Assumption College Greyhounds. The weather was cold and gray. I was experiencing a hitting slump and had been in and out of the starting nine. We were playing a doubleheader, and I had been benched in the first game. However, during the second game, Coach put me in to pinch hit in a big situation. I answered with a well-timed home run to win the game.

"Let's hear it for Rigs!" Coach exclaimed as my teammates broke into applause.

Coach O'Brien was always the last person out of our locker room at the end of the day. He grabbed my arm as I was heading out. "Rigs, sometimes you have to do something big to really feel a part of something."

I had heard him say this many times before, but that day the meaning of his words hit home. As I watched Cindy graduate from Harvard University, Coach O'Brien's words came back to me. Sometimes you are the star and sometimes you are the observer, but either way, seeing the brightness of one shine is a wonderful feeling. To teach and coach is to do something that not only connects you to others but helps others connect to each other and the world around them.

I have been honored for my lifelong work in teaching and coaching through various awards and celebrations, but there was one acknowledgment that was truly unexpected. Usually when I get a letter from a religious organization, I expect to be reprimanded for not putting enough money into our weekly church envelope, so when I received an invitation to attend Father Jack Fagan's celebration of fifty years in the Jesuit Order, I was ecstatic. The event was to be held at Boston College High School (BCHS). The breadth and scope of the people who attended Father Jack's celebration were impressive. From Chile to Carnegie Hall, people came from all over the world to be there and honor Father Jack. It was like attending a United Nations Assembly. People from all walks of life gathered to celebrate his lifetime of work because regardless of who you were or where you came from, Father Jack treated everyone he encountered as truly unique and special.

I got to know Father Jack while he was assigned to Sacred Heart Parish in Holyoke. This Jesuit, fluent in Spanish and armed with a great ability to connect to young people, was a perfect fit for the neighborhood community. Sacred Heart sat in a tough section of town. At the time Holyoke could be described quite similarly to how Mark Twain had described Montreal: "Throw a rock,

Father Jack Fagan, pictured far right, at his 50-year celebration as a Jesuit priest.

you'll hit a church." The same was true of the Paper City as every section of Holyoke had its own church. Catholic, Baptist, Jewish, Protestant, Pentecostal, and Muslim people worshipped throughout the churches, temples, and synagogues across our city.

At the time Father Jack was assigned to the Church on the Hill, our city was overrun with poverty, crime, drugs, and gang violence. The parish was an anchoring institution attempting to help the surrounding community in more ways than just a weekend mass schedule. The surrounding neighborhood was dotted with corner stores and small businesses. Families with their homes downtown lived in block apartment buildings, many in need of serious upgrades. The section of our city known as Churchill had stood tall during Holyoke's industrial days with beautiful architecture but had suffered years of neglect.

Today the neighborhood is home to many Hispanic families along with elderly of different European ethnicities who have watched the neighborhood change over time. Many of the kids in the basketball program lived in the blocks on Sergeant, Walnut, Oak, Pine, and Chestnut streets. I think Father Jack got to know every family in the area many kids called the "hood" even if they were not regular church attendees. The reason was that Father Jack was everywhere in the community. You could find him at basketball games or in the streets greeting kids on the corners as they walked to school. Father Jack also helped with community homework centers located throughout the city. One was the Homework House, run by Sister Jane Morressy. Sister Jane, a saint in the making, had a special place in Father Jack's heart.

In fact, I served as Sister Jane's Uber driver to Father Jack's fifty-year celebration. On our journey to BCHS, Sister Jane talked a lot, and I listened, learning a lot about their work together at the Homework House, which provided a quiet, safe place for local children after school. They provided students with some tutoring to improve academic skills and performance at school.

Father Jack understood the importance of positive relationships for kids, whether in church, at school, or on the athletic field. He did not wait for the kids to come to church; he went out to where they were instead. He came to HHS basketball games and was also a regular at the Rigali home for our pasta team dinners and end-of-season pizza party. The ubiquitous Father Jack. What an amazing difference he made for the young adults and families he came across.

Jesuits are particularly known for taking to the streets, fighting for the betterment of their communities. They refuse to give up on anyone, following in Jesus's path to help those who are most in need. Father Jack fought for everyone. He mentored families on how to get loans or seek employment. He informed families how to obtain legal services or health care. He worked with gang members to move them in a more positive direction. All were welcomed by Father Jack.

Wilfredo Cabrera calls out a play.

One day one of my players approached me before practice.

"Coach, I need your help," Wilfredo Cabrera started. "There's this crazy white dude all dressed up, and I see him on the corner walking to school. Do you think he is trying to get us to buy or sell for him?"

Wilfredo was one of the toughest and most talented Purple Knights I coached. I thought for a minute, then remembered Father Jack.

"Wilfredo, don't worry about that dude. You are correct. He is part of a gang," I responded. "The gang of Jesuits."

CHAPTER 18

GARANIMALS TO ARMANI, "WHAT IS THAT?" AND "HIRE THAT MAN"

At the end of my first year teaching at Lynch Junior High School, I was ready for a break. Teaching is a lot more challenging than most people understand. The job requires you to constantly be on your toes, to adapt to each day's new challenges, and to learn from both your successes and failures on a daily basis. However, I did not think one of the challenges to becoming a successful educator would have to do with fashion.

As I listened to the will being read at the ninth grade graduation, I realized that my first year teacher's wardrobe had received less than stellar marks from the graduates. The students had bequeathed me a year's supply of Garanimals. Yes, those Garanimals. For those of you who are unfamiliar with Garanimals, they are a clothing line that makes baby and kids clothes that are "adorable, affordable and mix matchable!" I got the message, and I do think I improved my wardrobe over the years. I also made darn sure that I looked my best when I showed up to coach at practice or a game. I wanted my players to know they were important, the event was important, and one way to respectfully represent my community in the best light was to dress appropriately for the task at hand. It was important to model for my students and players that our personal appearance should not be an afterthought.

Whether I was traveling with my team to away games or walking into "Jinx" O'Connor Gym for a home game, I tried to influence my teams to put their best selves forward as well. Some years, we had money in the budget to purchase travel warm-ups, and that worked well. But most years that line item was cut, so I would ask our kids to dress up and wear a tie. At times, this was problematic as many of our players did not own a dress shirt or a tie. In fact, some did not even own winter coats for the cold bus ride home.

Cue the Purple Knights guardian angels, Judy Falcetti, a Spanish teacher at HHS, and Norma Lee, aide to Vice Principal Chet Dudley. Every winter at the start of basketball season, I could count on these two women to provide for the team. Shortly before the start of the basketball season, I would arrive in room 108, coffee in hand and open my closet to put my coat away, only to find it filled with dress shirts, ties, and winter coats of all sizes. Our freshman, junior varsity, and varsity teams were able to keep a dress code for the season because of Judy and Norma's generosity. I have always felt it was important to have our teams dressed appropriately. It helped instill a sense of responsibility and respect for self, others, and community for our players. As a program and school community, we invested time to make it happen, and I will always be grateful for the support we received from our surrounding community members.

Judy and Norma were two of the many people at our school who would step up behind the scenes to help. The HHS Art Department, Paula Marcotte, Bill Greany, and Darlene Henshaw are among the many school and city community members who contributed to the support the success of our team. From banners to posters, painted basketballs for 1,000-point scorers, and caricatures, people offered what they could through their own unique talents. Laurie Marvel in Home Economics would host a breakfast for our championship teams to make them feel special. Kathy

O'Neill, our resource teacher, was wonderful at keeping so many of our kids on task with their school assignments. Jim Barrett, industrial arts teacher and artist, made wood carvings for the players, including his classic of Ramon Cosme winning the Lahovich Award! The HHS staff stepped up for the team and showed their support, helping our players have the best possible high school basketball experience we could provide.

Many things have gone away from the world since I was a kid growing up in the Elmwood section of Holyoke. From typewriters to toll collectors, things have passed away through the sands of time. Gone. The internet, smartphones, and computers have us all swirling to find balance in a hectic, fast-paced culture that demands instant gratification. Throw in a global pandemic with COVID-19 in 2020, and things have gotten very complex for our society.

I was particularly struck by this several years ago, when I was out for a walk with my grandson Syius. He stopped suddenly and asked, "What's that?"

I looked around to see what he was looking at, and I saw him staring at the square phone booth across the street. I explained what it was, and he replied, "So it's like a static cell phone?"

Pretty close.

My grandchildren will see a world that experiences change like rapid fire, coming at them almost instantaneously. Our communication through technology is ever present. As I reflect on our ever-changing world, one of my previous students comes to mind: Jeff Stieger, a seventh-grade student in my homeroom at Lynch Jr. High School. Students reported to homeroom to start the school day, and attendance was taken there. Each day begins with the ringing of the bell, signifying the start and end of classes. The first bell lets the students know they should get to homeroom and clear the halls.

On this day I looked around Mrs. Hoey's sewing room and noticed it was just Jeff and me.

The second bell sounded to tell students they were late, but still it was just Jeff and me.

The third bell went off to send the students off to period one. The only two people in the room were Jeff and me.

"Where is everyone?" I inquired.

Honestly, this could never happen again anywhere on this planet.

Jeff and I had both gotten up and walked to school on that brisk December morning without having received one text, email, phone call, instant message, tweet, DM, or alert that school had been canceled that day. Sure, our technology today has its advantages, like being informed of a cancellation due to impending weather. Still, it is important for us to continue to develop the necessary social skills that help with the everyday interactions of daily life.

Eventually, Jeff and I figured it out and both got home safely. That being said, I like kids and people who show up, who are both physically and mentally present; there are two necessary ingredients for getting anything accomplished. In a world where our attention is constantly being pulled in a multitude of directions, remaining grounded in the here and now requires practice and persistence. We need to show up for our family, our friends, and our community. Wherever you are, Jeff Steiger, I hope life has treated you well. I have no doubt that if you ever had any children, they made it to school each day.

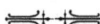

Reflecting on those first years of teaching, I can still recall what a daunting task it is to embark on a career in education. There are so many challenges to figure out. At times you wonder if you are ever getting anything across to your students.

Are they listening?
Are they learning?

A while back, I ran across one of my first students, Joe Sweeney, from Lynch Jr. High School. He mentioned he was a few years from retirement as a public school teacher. We talked about a number of things. Most of our conversation centered around the COVID-19 crisis and how it had turned everything upside down around the globe. He was proud of his work and friends within the Holyoke circle.

"Mr. R, we had so much fun and learned a lot," he explained about his time in my classroom. "You always seemed happy and upbeat. You looked like you loved your job."

Joe, who is finishing up his own wonderful career as an educator in the Longmeadow Public Schools, was exactly right.

I have always felt that being a classroom teacher and a coach is an incredible honor. Every day you have the chance to help someone and provide young people with opportunities to grow as individuals and members of a community. Teachers, in many ways, are our nation's first responders. Kids come to us from many different circumstances, and we help them embark on a lifelong journey of learning and self-discovery.

CHAPTER 19

GEORGE FLOYD

The world watched over and over again as George Floyd lost his life while being arrested in Minneapolis. For over nine minutes, Derek Chauvin knelt on Floyd's neck while several other officers assisted in restraining him and preventing bystanders from intervening. All were charged with varying degrees of murder. Chauvin was convicted of second-degree murder, third-degree murder, and second-degree manslaughter. All officers were found guilty of violating Floyd's civil rights. The videos shared of Floyd's murder by bystanders and surveillance cameras went viral the next day, sending shock waves across America and around the world.

While Americans were wrestling with the death of George Floyd, they were also confronted with a fundamental lack of humanity toward each other that was brought to the surface during the Trump administration. Trump certainly did not create a society ruled by inequities and hostility, but his presidency, unfortunately, emboldened people to act out on their feelings of hatred and fear.

The new challenges facing Americans today are many. First, we must prevent deaths like George Floyd's from happening. Floyd was neither the first nor the last victim of police brutality.

The best we can do is, hopefully, put systems in place to ensure that all organizations have measures of proper training and accountability. Second, Americans need to develop better communication and collaboration skills in order to reach a middle ground on fundamental issues and problems. George Floyd's death, which happened in the middle of the pandemic as we all sat at home on our couches in social isolation, exposed our flaws as a nation. America received harsh reminders concerning the problems we face in our daily lives in housing, health care, and education. Families are struggling to maintain a middle class lifestyle, and for the first time in our history, children will find it difficult to achieve the American Dream of exceeding their parents' success.

I am so very proud of the work my daughters do as teachers. I am proud of the work both Sandy and I provided as educators. As I noted before, teachers are our nation's initial responders. America's teaching force is often the first to see and interact with children on some of their very worst days. Every time our nation's educators step into a classroom, they are confronted with children affected by poverty, food insecurity, abuse, and learning deficits, among other immense challenges.

Aside from teaching content knowledge and skills, teachers attempt to provide students with a safe, dependable social structure when the pieces of their lives outside of school are cracked and broken. All four of the Rigali teachers have worked with many different academic, economic, and ethnic groups in education. We are better educators and people because of our exposure to a diverse world.

Kiely helped organize a response to George Floyd's death on Martha's Vineyard within a few days of his passing. The event was a well-attended, peaceful, socially distanced, and powerful demonstration of community members who wished to make their voices heard. Alexa has gone the extra mile for her students at Randolph High School. She made sure in the time of distance learning that the senior class was able to access meaningful scholarship opportunities for their futures. Great educators pass on social equity to their students each day through the classroom environments and lessons they lead. More now than ever, a good teacher is a priceless commodity.

CHAPTER 20

WE WANT JORGE!

Western Mass Quarterfinals
February 28, 1986
Taconic High School
Holyoke 86, Taconic 72

Holyoke: M. Tully 6-10-22, D. Brown 5-9-19, C. Montemayor 2-7-11, D. Pratt 4-2-10, T. Cavanaugh 7-0-14, G. Doulette 2-0-4, R. Thomas 1-0-2, J. Neves 1-0-2. Totals: 28-28-84.
Taconic: P. Brindle 5-2-12, M. Carnevale 0-2-2, S. Austin 5-0-10, J. Gamberoni 3-3-9, C. Murphy 9-2-20, S. Cusson 0-6-6, S. White 2-0-4, M. Walford 1-1-3, D. Bair 3-0-6. Totals: 28-16-72.

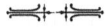

Western Mass Semifinals
March 4, 1986
Springfield Civic Center
Chicopee Comp 65, Holyoke 55

Chicopee Comp: M. Drabinski 10-1-21, D. Francis 5-1-11, M. Kijak 2-5-9, E. Medina 4-0-8, S. Sawa 2-6-10, S. Malone 0-1-1, M. Nadeau 0-1-1, G. Beauregard 2-0-4. Totals: 25-15-65.

Holyoke: M. Tully 8-2-18, D. Brown 3-0-6, C. Montemayor 5-0-10, D. Pratt 2-3-7, T. Cavanaugh 2-2-6, G. Doulette 4-0-8. Totals: 24-7-55.

I found something to like about every player and team I coached at HHS. As a coach, you always want to feel like you are making a difference for your team. It is your job to maintain hope that your team and the players can improve and act collaboratively as a group that your school and community can look to with pride.

The Purple Knights team led by All Western Mass player Mike Tully in the '85–'86 season was one of those special teams that stands out and you never forget. This group of players holds a special place in my heart for a number of reasons. No, they did not win a Western Mass Championship, but they did come close. That season we lost in the tournament semifinals against eventual champion Chicopee Comprehensive High School.

What stood out about this group was their quiet toughness. They learned from their mistakes, handled adversity well, and always presented themselves as first class to the rest of the Pioneer Valley. This was my first team to advance to a big stage game at the Springfield Civic Center. These Knights did so by making a late season run and defeating a good Taconic High School team from Pittsfield, MA, on the road in the quarterfinals of the state sectionals. That win had a bit of everything in it. Our victory was fueled by a great defensive effort that frustrated the Braves' leading scorers and some clutch scoring from Mike Tully down the stretch.

Taconic was coached by Al Belanger, brother of major league gold glove winner Mark Belanger, who himself was a great high school hoop player. The great Baltimore Oriole once scored thirty-two points in the New England Championships. Coach Belanger and his kids battled to the end of that game, but Mike Tully carried us home to victory.

Tully, tall and thin, could shoot and score from anywhere on the court. He scored over eight hundred points in only two years of varsity play, and that was without the benefit of the three-point field goal rule.

Tully and his teammates got off to a slow start that season. We were giving up a ton of second chance points, while our team captain was being assaulted by the other team's bigs each game.

One night after dinner, I heard a knock on our front door. It was Tully.

"Coach, can we talk for a minute? I am getting killed inside," he said.

Tully was not wrong. The opposing teams would always put their biggest and strongest player on him, leaving Mike in the unfortunate position of getting pretty beat up by the end of the night.

"OK, what can we do differently?" I inquired. A bit to my surprise, Tully was prepared with a few ideas of his own.

"Well, Coach, I was thinking that if we start Cav, it will force the other guys to put their big guy on him." Tom Cavanaugh was my sixth man Kevin McHale, and I loved to bring him in off the bench.

"I will think about it and run things by our assistant coaches to see what they think."

After I discussed the suggestion with my coaching staff, we went with the lineup change and our team started to perform better. Tully's shooting percentage skyrocketed, and we were on our way to a very good high school season. Additionally, Tully's success helped elevate the play of other players. In Tom Cavanaugh's first game as a starting center for the Knights, he put up sixteen points and pulled down sixteen rebounds against Putnam High School.

There were so many things to like about this group of players. They were coachable, possessed a willingness to sacrifice individual stats for the greater good of the team, and championed each other. Early in the season, we had a disappointing loss against Commerce High School when we committed a disconcerting number of turnovers. Our point guard Chris Montemayor had a tough night, and the team could see he was losing confidence. The next few days of practice were going to be critical to get him back on track. The coaches explained to the team what had happened down at Kiely Jr. High and how we could fix it to beat Commerce next time.

During the rematch against the Red Raiders, we were able to reverse the tables and take the other team down after losing to them by thirteen points in our previous contest. The big reason for the turnaround was Chris's play at point guard. He had gained his confidence back, which was the key to winning the game.

Another part of this team and their story was a Purple Knight who did not play a lot in the games but worked as hard in practice as any of our starters. His name was Jorge Neves. He took it on himself to harass and push Chris in practice and during drills. He made it so hard for Chris that the games became easy. We let Jorge attack him, never calling fouls. Jorge haunted him on the court and made Chris a better player.

Jorge Neves is in the middle row third from left.

What makes Jorge Neves's story so interesting to me is that he did not get a roster spot with the Purple Knights until his senior year. Now most people, especially teenagers, do not actively seek out situations that could lead to disappointment. At this time, we only had a junior varsity and varsity team, so it was difficult for kids like Jorge to make one of the two teams. I was amazed and proud of Jorge for continuing to try out. The crafty little guard was determined to earn a spot on the varsity team. To his credit and our benefit, he earned his spot in his senior year, and he was a big reason for our success.

This team loved basketball. They loved being together and being members of our school community. They prepared so they could be successful in life well beyond their high school glory days. In addition to his tenacious spirit, Jorge was a school leader. He was a class officer and was always involved in school activities. The son of an immigrant Portuguese family, he was chasing down his American Dream. It is no wonder that Jorge Neves was much loved by his classmates. Without fail, at the end of games when the Knights had a victory in hand, the chant would rise up from the stands: "We want Jorge! We want Jorge!"

Each member of that team gave everything they had to each other and their community. Their good work did not end on the basketball court or in high school. It extended beyond into their adulthood. Currently Mike Tully is the head men's basketball coach at Roger Williams University and has administrative duties too. Mike played four years of varsity basketball at Clark University in Worcester, MA. Mike and his family live in Rhode Island. Dave Pratt currently serves as the chief of the police in Holyoke. Chris Montemayor has been the men's basketball coach at Holyoke Community College for many years. Derek Brown worked at the Brightside Orphanage in West Springfield. Glenn Doulette is the athletic director at West Springfield High School.

Sadly, Tom Cavanaugh and Jorge Neves have passed on. Both young men were contributing members of their community, helping to make it better and stronger. Tom was a fireman, and Jorge was a practicing attorney. Both were actively involved in Holyoke's youth sports programs, designed to help instill children with knowledge, skills, confidence, and teamwork. There are many days when I would love to talk with Cav and Jorge. I would let them know what a difference they made for me as a coach.

In a recent conversation I had with Coach Tully over the phone, I asked him what he remembered most prominently about Jorge.

"Everyone loved him and wanted to be around him. He made you feel good about yourself and absolutely loved the game of basketball."

City councilman and Saint Patrick's Day Parade guru Attorney James Leahy related a story to my wife Sandy over social media not long ago when reminiscing about Jorge Neves. Leahy wrote, "I would go by a man standing at an intersection on my way to work asking for money. He looked in rough shape. He held a sign reading 'Homeless.' I stopped and spoke with him once in a while and learned this story." He continued, "One time, I noticed he was wearing a very nice golf jacket with a DiNapoli Golf Tournament insignia on it."

This was an event held to honor Ralph DiNapoli, a Holyoke police officer who died in the line of duty.

"Where did you get that coat?" Leahy asked.

"My friend gave it to me," the man responded. "My friend Jorge Neves. I like him. He doesn't judge me. He respects me. He is a good man."

Yes, Jorge Neves was a good teammate and a good man. I have found over my coaching career that it is rather difficult to be one without being the other.

CHAPTER 21

THE STREAK IS OVER!

Once Travis Best showed up at Central High School (CHS), everyone in the western Mass basketball scene was put on red alert. The solid NBA player of ten-plus seasons relegated all of the locals to competing for silver medals. Travis played in the NBA finals versus the Los Angeles Lakers. He was an all Atlantic Coast Conference (ACC) selection three times at Georgia Tech University and a two time Parade All-American while playing for CHS's Golden Eagles, where he led his team to a D1 State Championship.

Travis demonstrated his ability each season against the elite basketball players from around the globe competing in the NBA. The local great finished his professional career playing overseas. Whether he was playing for CHS, Georgia Tech, the NBA, or a European country, Travis was always a winner and played the game the right way. His legendary eighty-one point game against Putnam in high school is basketball folklore, but I really wasn't surprised Travis scored that many points in a game. If he wanted to, he could get fifty or more points in any game he played.

While Travis was an elite talent, he was also surrounded by excellent talent at CHS. He wasn't afraid to share the ball as he trusted his teammates, which made the Golden Eagles invincible.

Bobby Cremins, his college coach, was asked by local writers what impressed him the most about his five star recruit.

He responded, "He can get anywhere he wants on the court at any time."

At one contest at a sold-out "Jinx" O'Connor Gym, as he signed autographs before the game, including one for my daughter Kiely, the stage was set for Travis to score his one thousandth career point. We were determined to not let it happen in our gym. Our game plan was to double-and triple-team him, trap him, forcing him to give up the ball. The first quarter of the game went as planned. We slowed Travis down and were in the game. You could sense some nerves coming from the Central fans. At the start of the second quarter, they started to urge Travis to shoot. Even his teammates seemed a bit on edge. They all wanted him to do it.

It should be noted that at this time in Massachusetts, high school athletes were only allowed to play for the school their principal presided over. Travis surely would have passed the thousand-point milestone long before this night in Holyoke had he been eligible as a ninth-grader.

When the horn sounded to start the second quarter, Travis went to work. In the next twenty-four minutes, he got whatever he wanted, and his entourage went home happy. I think he finished with 40, but it felt like 140. It didn't matter what we did. We could not find him or stop him. We could not even get close enough to foul him! This great player, prophetically named Best, had made up his mind that he was not going to send his family and faithful home without getting to that 1,000 point bucket. He succeeded, and the rest is history. It is no contest. Travis Best was the most complete and skilled player I came up against in my coaching career.

January 22, 1993
"Jinx" O'Connor Gymnasium
Holyoke High School
Holyoke 65, Central 50

Holyoke: R. Cosme 8, R. Sisson 16, Chatman 5, W. Cabrera 12, M. Gubala 18, M. Gubala 6,
Totals: 32-1-65.
Central: Denson 14, S. Smith 16, Dickerson 5, Goetzendanner 9, Clark 2, Williams 4
Totals: 20-7-50. Three-point FG: S. Smith.

The Travis Best era of high school basketball represented many things. First, Best captured the imagination of the entire region. Everyone wanted to be part of the excitement he brought to the hardwood. It also represented one of the last great periods of quality high school competition, which included Derek Kellogg (Cathedral-UMass) and Damon Franklin (Chicopee Comp-Yale). The high quality of players and teams from this time still leaves me a bit speechless. There was an abundance of talent at the high school level, and there were some epic battles to be sure.

So what happened? Where are the great high school teams now?

The dilution of strength and skill on high school rosters is the result of several factors. First, the privatization of public education has led to an increase in the number of schools competing for students and athletes. This means the quality high school players are spread out over more venues. Second, the proliferation of Amateur Athletic Union (AAU) basketball and the pay-to-play organizations has affected high school play. AAU ball places an emphasis on play, not teaching the player how to play. The number of games crammed into weekend tournaments often leads to a devaluation of the sound fundamentals of the game. Third, the recent mentality of "everyone gets a trophy" has fostered unskilled, unmotivated play beyond the basketball courts, in all areas of life and competition. Organizations have created so many divisions for high school sports that it is hard to keep track of all the champions crowned. The hard truth that many young people are missing is that you do not get a trophy or reward every day in life, but we seem to be sending this message on playing fields across the country today.

When Travis Best, thankfully, left western Mass for Georgia Tech, the Central Golden Eagles had amassed a long winning streak against their opponents. They had lost to an East Longmeadow squad coached by Bill Ross when one of Central's key players missed the bus, but losses were few and far between the wins. High school coaches could write volumes about the learning and teaching process of working with teenage boys. Nevertheless, it was a great victory for the East Longmeadow team and Coach Ross.

On January 22, 1993, the Purple Knights were ready to take down the Central Eagles. In front of a sold-out gym with 1,600 fans packed into a raucous O'Connor Gymnasium (the gym has a much smaller capacity today), the Knights showcased a showstopping fast break offense, running the Eagles off of their 83-game winning streak. Led by Lahovich winner Ramon Cosme, all 5-foot-3 of him, the Knights relentlessly pushed the ball up the floor and beat Central at their own game. Somewhere John McClendon is smiling down when he sees the game orchestrated this way.

The Knights scored every single point from inside the paint or from the foul line. The victory gave the team enormous confidence, propelling them to an electric season. The 65-to-50 victory pushed our record to 10–1, while dropping the Eagles to 10–1. Holyoke and Central were two very good high school teams that year. The stage was set for two more delicious battles between the teams during the upcoming months. Sportswriter Bill Wells, who covered the game for the *Union-News*, spoke with Ramon Cosme after the game and quoted him as follows:

"This is the greatest win ever in my career at Holyoke." Cosme, a first team All Western Mass selection that season, continued, "I thought I had to have my best game, control the tempo, get the ball to my teammates, break the press. But I wasn't the only one who played well. The whole team had to play well, and we did."

There it is in a nutshell, the secret sauce to any successful player and teammate. Downplay your roll and extend grace and accolades to your teammates. When you lose, say little; when you win, say less. No smack talk directed at the Central team. A first-class response from a first-class player and extraordinary human being. Classic Ramon Cosme.

CHAPTER 22

SPORTS REPORTERS

My coaching and teaching journey granted me the opportunity to work with various groups: fellow educators and coaches, students, athletes, parents, administrators, referees, and fans. However, by far the most eclectic group that crossed my path was the sports reporters. Reflecting on the evolution of how the Purple Knights were covered during my coaching career tells the story of the changing forces pushing our society and culture into the future.

Reporters can be quite a group. Most knew that they were writing about teenagers playing a game. It was not a life-and-death situation, and they portrayed the participants they covered in a good, positive light. It was high school basketball, not the NBA. The media and sports writers I encountered as a coach each had their own style and slant while covering high school sports across the happy Pioneer Valley.

At the beginning of my career, Holyoke's daily newspaper, *The Transcript Telegram*, was graced with writers like Joe LaRose and Jack Curtain. Springfield boasted reporters like Gary Brown, Paul Donahue, and the ubiquitous Ron Chemiles, both in print and on WREB radio. Ron was everywhere covering Holyoke and sports news. Excellent coverage from Larry Silber, Bill Zajac, Bill Wells, and Paul Taylor depicted the stories that played out on the court each night. WWLP's Rich Tettemer, TV and media personality, and the extraordinary Scott Cohen spun tales of high school triumphs and losses.

Toward the end of my coaching stint, Rick Lajoie and Greg Scibelli from the *Holyoke Sun* and Meredith Perri and Gage Nutter from *Mass Live* continued to report on the local high school sports landscape when the bigger papers started disappearing. I was lucky that so many talented and fair people covered my basketball journey.

One scribe who I got to know at the start of my career and toward the end of his was Jim Reagan. Reagan reported for the Springfield papers. He was a Holyoke native, Notre Dame graduate, coeditor of the *Daily News,* longtime golf writer, and sports reporter. Jim received many awards in journalism, including the New England Sports Writer of the Year award. I got to know him through my nephew Anthony Dulude, who is also an excellent hoop official. Jim loved many things, with his top passions being golf, writing, and Holyoke sports. He had a particular love for Holyoke's basketball teams, who were right at the top of his list.

The grace and good will Jim Reagan handed out to me was special, talking to me about everything from what officials look for in games to how far coaches could go in hand-to-hand combat with the zebras! In March 1993, the day after our miracle win over Central with Robert Sission's three-point shot at the buzzer, Jim and Tony Dulude drove me down to scout Saint John's in the central Mass finals games. I remember being exhausted from our emotional Western Mass Championship win the night before. I did not get any sleep at all that evening.

"Don't worry, Coach," Jim stated, "Tony and I will drive. When we get there, you just check out size and speed. We will write down some stuff to help out."

So down we went to the WPI Auditorium to scout—Jim Reagen, whose love for his community was second to none; Tony Dulude; and one elated but exhausted coach.

Even though Saint John's Murphy and Coach Foley took us down, we played a very competitive, close game. The scouting mission had helped keep us in the game, giving us a chance to win until the very end.

The best writers always look past the sport to uncover the essence and truth about the players, coaches, and community they are writing about. Scott Cohen had a gift for making both the kids and coaches feel at ease. Ron Chimelis was the conscience of western Mass and brought forth his wisdom with each line. Ron, of Puerto Rican heritage, had his pulse on what influences were driving our Hispanic community. Bill Wells had our game analytics down to a science and never asked dumb questions.

Today, if you coach in a town or city that reports daily and still has a print edition, you are lucky. The daily reports allow the paper's readership to receive a better perspective on the kids, coaches, and community. The internet and advancement of digital content have given all of us instant results, statistics, scores, and images. There is no going back, for better or worse. Online media is here to stay. Hopefully with a skilled personal touch like that of *Mass Live*'s Meridith Peri and Gage Nutter, good, insightful reporting can still be accomplished for the high school sport scene. Both have shown through their work that fair and unbiased reporting is still possible. For all that, it is the on-site insight that makes game reporting stand out. Good reporting requires boots on the ground and in the trenches.

I once read, "Writers write to tell the world what they need to know." Sometimes it's not just that Wey Dotson scored twenty points for Holyoke last night. Although that is an important detail, it is not the whole story. The how and why behind Dotson earning his twenty points is actually the real, more interesting story. The best sports writers understand this. They know the time and score, which ironically is not just about the scoreboard.

Recently, the Martha's Vineyard (MV) girls tennis team, which I have coached the past four seasons, lost a tenacious battle to Foxborough in the D2 state south semifinals. The joy present all spring long from my ten Vineyard tennis players was a special gift to me. We were all happy to get back to the courts after missing the previous spring season due to the COVID-19 global pandemic. It had been a fantastic season, and now we were confronted by another tremendous team.

Both teams were undefeated; the match was tied 2–2. Third singles would decide the victor. The MV and Foxborough teams battled for over two and a half hours to determine the outcome. A digital report would read something like, "Foxborough wins 3–2" and a line score of the five matches. However, the real story was the reaction from our team. Seconds after MV player Karinne Nivala's forehand landed just inches long over the baseline, our perfect season was gone, or so I thought. As Karinne walked to the net to tap racquets (COVID protocol) and congratulate her opponent, MV captain Cali Giglio yelled to her teammates, "Let's go get her!"

The nine other girls from MV poured onto the court to celebrate their teammate. Huddled around Karinne, they hugged and applauded her heroic effort on the court that day. For me, that is the beauty of sports. Even in our defeat, the human spirit can achieve perfection. Was this story covered? Unfortunately, no. A story missed in the digital age.

CHAPTER 23

SECOND CHANCES

We all deserve second chances in life; some form of a safety net should be in place to help families, students, and athletes move forward when that first foray to the basket turns into a charging call. Second chances take place every day in life, and I always tried to make the mulligan a part of my playbook when working with young adults. The waiver process from the MIAA is a good example of providing deserving athletes a second chance. In this scenario, a regional committee can look at an individual's unique set of circumstances and grant eligibility to participate in sports for a local team. In my experience, a high percentage of the high school athletes who were granted such an exemption took advantage of it, representing themselves and their school very well.

On a number of occasions, I was asked to write a letter in support of a student athlete from an opposing school. I looked beyond Holyoke and our collective community of western Mass. We were not just in the business of teaching and coaching the students in our school; we were a part of a larger group dedicated to the development of all youth. If the opportunity arose to help a student and the student's family to get his or her eligibility, I always tried to look at the bigger picture. What would it mean to that athlete and their family, school, and community?

Shaka Rivera was a very good player for Cathedral High School (CHH). He needed a waiver to play his senior year. Over the years, we had some great battles with the Panthers. Outside of a win over Central, a victory against the purple-and-gold-clad Panthers was next in line. Today, CHH is known as Pope Francis High School (PFHS) and is a much smaller school than it was in its team's glory days.

CHS had a great tradition of high school basketball. Gene Ryzewicz, Syriac, Joe McDowell, Gene Eggelston, Kevin Kennedy, Mike Juilian, Justin Delessio, the Yvon brothers, Earl Sherman, Shaka, and the late Kamari Williams all represented the Panthers with pride. Not to mention the Martins—Mike Jr., Billy, and Pat—who were relentless on the court. The Panthers were renowned for having really tough, smart, and exceptional players.

Shaka's coach at this time was Gene Eggelston. He approached me about writing a letter in support of his player so that he would be eligible for his fourth and senior year of high school. I was happy to do this for him, along with many others. Today, Shaka is the head coach for the boys varsity basketball team at the High School of Science and Technology in Springfield. They are lucky to have him.

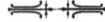

Jose Ortiz, who played for the Purple Knights, was another kid who needed a second chance during the '91–'92 season. This time it was not about needing a waiver but about an opportunity to get back on our roster. During the previous season of his junior year, Jose had left the team. Some things had been bothering him, and I believe he felt he was better off not finishing the season. Nowhere is it written down in any coach's playbook how to figure out the correct way to handle the many different feelings teenagers go through. I wish it were, but that is the challenge and joy of working with adolescents.

Get on the Purple Line

Jose's last game for us that season was up at Northampton High School (NHS), which is a notoriously tough place to play. I was disappointed in myself for not being able to coach Jose to a better place where he saw his importance on the team. One of my coaching goals every season is to help my players finish the year in good standing both athletically and academically. Teenagers face many struggles as growing up can be difficult. They are juggling grades, relationships, family responsibilities, parental expectations, work, and ego all the time. Throw in the pressure of competing in sports, and that is a lot on their plate. When you are a coach, part of the job is helping your players develop the skills and a game plan for their problems and conflicts off the court as well as on it.

On top of the tumultuous life of teens, the gym at NHS was not an ideal environment, with the heat turned up like a pressure cooker, triggering teenage angst and stress. Just ask any western Mass coach their least favorite gym to play in, and believe me most will say NHS. The Blue Devils played in a small rat gym with bad lighting, narrow sidelines, and fans seated right on top of you with an actual fire escape at one end. I once witnessed a ref tumble out of the gym by route of that escape opening; unfortunately he came back in. Fire alarms were pulled a few times during games, and the teams were forced to wait outside until the all clear was given. A slippery court, rabid fans, and the killer Northampton teams, who always had excellent players and great coaching, made NHS a formidable place. With players like Joe Mantegna, Al Wolecko, and Ray Herp, a team was in for a tough night against the Blue Devils.

One memorable game, we finished an overtime contest with just four players on the court. It was a power play for the Blue Devils in the last few minutes. One by one the horn sounded to signal five fouls on a Purple Knight and disqualification. One, two, three, four players fouled out in the second half and overtime. Another Knight smacked his head against a NHS player, and both were sent off to the emergency room for stitches.

Over the years, I did not come home with many victories up there. Was it the gym? Was it the fans? Hometown referees? Or just excellent high school players and coaches? Blue Devil Jake Ross poured in so many points against us that by the time he was a junior, I only played a box and one defense against him! Ross went on to All American status at Springfield College and plays professionally in Europe. As the old commercial jokes, "Must have been the shoes!" Regardless, playing at NHS against their team and coaches was always fierce competition.

February 17, 1992
Peck Junior High School
Holyoke 50, Catholic 48

Holyoke: W. Cabrera 6-1-15, L. Rios 0-0-0, R. Cosme 2-0-4, S. Chatman 2-0-4, J. Ortiz 3-0-6, C. Sears 1-1-5, T. Neves 0-0-0, M. Gubala 0-0-0, M. Wresien 0-0-0, R. Miranda 3-0-6, M. Gubala 4-2-10. Totals: 21-2-2-50.
Catholic: Jacobson 4-4-12, Stanek 1-1-3, O'Brien 8-1-17, Weslowski 2-0-4, Zedonis 4-4-12. Totals: 19-10-48.

In the spring of Jose's junior year, he came to speak to me with his good friend Richie Miranda. Richie had been lobbying for a second chance for his friend in the upcoming season. Of course, Jose would have to do what everyone else did: try out, keep his grades up, and be a good citizen in and out of school. Richie Miranda was the consummate team player. He did whatever you asked him to do. Richie's assignments changed from game to game, but he never complained. We could ask him to cover anyone, big or small, and he was always ready to accept the challenge. Richie came up big for us on a number of occasions in his senior year. He even produced a game-winning shot right before the buzzer to defeat an excellent Holyoke Catholic team coached by Bob Prattico.

The game between the once archrivals was played at Peck Middle School.

Jose could not have had a better advocate for his second chance than Richie. After a number of conversations and the setting of a few ground rules, Jose was welcomed back on the team, having earned his spot and second chance. Richie was a good friend to Jose and the Purple Knights. He knew we would be a better team with Jose Ortiz.

Note: This Gael team came in 16–2 and went on to become a D3 state finalist. Our victory that year was a good win for the Knights. Lenny Jacobson, who played for Holyoke Catholic that season, was the 2023 Saint Patrick's Day Parade JFK Award winner for his work in the media and movie industry in Hollywood, CA. The Gaels were coached by Bobby Practico, who led his teams to many successful seasons and always handled himself with dignity, class, and competitiveness.

February 29, 1992
D1 Western Mass Quarterfinals
"Jinx" O'Connor Gymnasium
Northampton 75, Holyoke 72 (2 OT)

Northampton: B. Cicharski 3-2-1-9, J. Johnson 2-2-6, J. Moulton 1-0-2, D. Lapage 6-1-6-19, B. O'Brien 3-0-6, T. Michalowski 3-12-18, J. Kelly 7-3-17. Totals: 22-3-23 75.
Holyoke: W. Cabrera 1-1-2-7, R. Cosme 3-4-10, S. Chatman 1-2-5, J. Ortiz 8-5-21, C. Sears 1-3-2-13, M. Gubala 6-4-16. Totals: 19-5-19-72.

As for what happened during Jose's senior year and second chance, the young man did everything that was asked of him and more. He was an exceptional teammate, coachable, and on a tournament team that helped create the building blocks for the championship teams that were just around the corner. Jose played very well throughout his season of redemption. Ironically, his last game as a Purple Knight was once again a contest against NHS. It was the quarterfinal matchup in the D1 State Western Mass tournament in "Jinx" O'Connor Gym. It was an amazing game, with NHS taking down the Knights in double OT 75–72. The best player on the floor that night for either team was Jose Ortiz, with 21 points, 7 rebounds, 6 assists, and 3 steals.

As previously stated, when your high school team loses in the tournament, it is like running into a wall. All the emotion, hard work, and sacrifice hits hard. No more practices, no more games, and no more seniors. I liked this team a lot, and I loved that Jose took advantage of his second chance so he could be a part of what we all built together. Today, it is wonderful to see both Jose and Richie raise their families and give back to their communities. In the '20–'21 high school hoop season, Jose Ortiz's son was selected to the All Western Mass team by *The Republican Mass Live* sports department as a player for Longmeadow High School. I am sure that Jose was extremely proud of his son's accomplishment.

In many ways, we look at the kids on our team as part of our extended families. We are proud and happy when things go well for them; we are disappointed and saddened when they do not. It is what we hope for when a player steps onto our court and into our lives as a kid. Every good teacher and coach knows the extreme privilege it is to see the young men and women they work with grow into individuals who can provide for their families and help make the world a bit better each day.

CHAPTER 24

TROY BASKETBALL, THE FRIAR, AN APOLOGY, AND A SHOOT-OUT!

The Jack Troy Summer League for high school basketball teams was the brainchild of four exceptional western Mass coaches: Mike Martin (Commerce, Agawam), Alec Vyce (Chicopee Comp), Mike Labrie (Chicopee High, Central, Chicopee Comp), and Kevin Kennedy (Cathedral). The four coaches put together a well-organized summer league for high school ballers in the early '80s. The league was named after a Springfield coaching legend: Jack Troy was the basketball coach at Commerce High School and is credited with starting a wonderful tradition of coaching excellence at that school. Included in that exceptional list are Gary Mindell, who was the school's first coach to reach 300 career wins; Henry Payne, who won two Western Mass titles for the school; Jerry Wrobleski, who won one; Mike Martin, who won five Western Mass titles and three state championships; and Tom Russo, who coached, served as an athletic director, and was a power broker for the local area with the MIAA. These coaches led teams and demonstrated leadership at the highest level.

The Troy League rules were put together to emphasize player development, discipline, and sportsmanship. If a player committed a technical foul, they were out for the rest of the game and the next one. Man-to-man defense was encouraged as zone defense could only be played the last six minutes of the contest. The league founders built in rules that would foster individual player development and skill, as well as team-building concepts. The league was a welcomed addition to the high school basketball summer scene.

But the question remained: Who would drive the Jack Troy Summer League high school bus?

Billy Eason was the man chosen to run the high school summer league. He was the perfect choice to drive the bus and get the players where they needed to go. Billy propelled the Jack Troy League to early success and popularity. The games were always packed as people flocked to the courts on a nice summer evening at Dana Park in Chicopee.

Sir William, as Billy was often called, was also one heck of a basketball player in his own right. Additionally, he was smart, loved the game, and cared about the kids who played in the league. Commissioner Eason took on many roles in addition to directing the summer league. He would talk with the kids and demonstrate a skill to improve their game. It was not uncommon to see Billy stop a player after the game for a quick word.

"Son, can I speak with you for a minute?" he would begin. He would talk to them about the game of life and how to use basketball to help achieve success both on and off the court.

Before his work with the Jack Troy League, Commissioner Eason had a great college career playing for the Providence College Friars and legendary coach Dave Gavitt. His Providence team even took down National Champions Louisville and Denny Crum three years in a row. Billy likes to tell the story of how that streak ended in his senior year.

"We had to go to Freedom Hall and play against the Cardinals. Most of us fouled out. They shot forty-four free throws; we shot only two!"

The story of how Billy ended up playing for the Providence Friars is a fascinating one. Before entering college, Billy finished up his scholastic basketball career at a prep school in New England where a number of their players moved on to Providence College. Billy was up in air about where he wanted to go to school and play ball. He was torn between playing for the Providence Friars or the North Carolina Tar Heels.

Like many growing teenage boys, especially those burning up thousands of calories a day on the basketball courts, he was perpetually hungry. One evening while helping at the scorer's table, I learned how Billy made his choice while munching on one of Kiely's famous chocolate chip cookies.

Kiely's chocolate chip cookies.

"Hey, give me half," Billy chided. After taking a bite, he exclaimed, "Whoa! Where did you get these?" Thus started a tradition of triple cookie delivery to summer games. He called them "hot chip cookies." By the commissioner I was directed to bring three giant-size freshly baked "hot chip cookies" to every game the Purple Knights played in the summer league.

Billy, presiding over his scorer's table like a justice in a courtroom, continued to talk as he enjoyed a cookie. "You know, I was always starving at school. I wish I had had these cookies back at school to snack on. All we had at the end of the day were our secret night excursions into the cafeteria to make some peanut butter and jelly sandwiches."

Billy explained that he and his teammates didn't have any pizza money hanging around. Most of the kids and families in the hoop program were balancing on a precipitous tightrope to pay for schooling. Many families managed to scrounge money together with the help of their extended families, scholarship awards, and booster club contributions. Billy and many of his teammates resorted to nightly visits to the school's cafeteria after hours to ease their hunger.

Billy continued, "A week before the signing letter for D1 school deadline, I was called in to talk with a school official. 'William,' he says to me, 'it has been brought to my attention that you have been trespassing on school property.'"

Billy thought for a second, then asked, "I live on campus. How can I be trespassing?"

The official responded, "Well William, you and a few of your teammates have been going into the cafeteria after hours to dine."

Billy responded incredulously, "I wouldn't call P and J sandwiches dining!"

"No matter, William. I am afraid this adds to your balance sheet of school infractions and this could possibly place your graduation in peril."

This was not what Billy wanted to hear. The official went on, "I will speak on your behalf to get you across the stage. I know that such issues can be complex. And William, one more thing..." The man trailed off. "Have you made a choice on school for next year?"

Billy knew that in the past many players from his school had matriculated to Providence College and how happy the board would be about his prospects playing for Coach Gavitt. Notably, at this time it was necessary to graduate with a high school diploma to receive an NCAA D1 Scholarship.

Billy paused for a moment to think, looked up smiling, and said just two simple words that changed the course of his life: "Go Friars!"

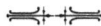

Billy Eason went on to have a wonderful college career. At Providence College, his Friars won eighty-nine games. They played in two NCAA tournaments with one matchup against Michigan State University and the great Magic Johnson and two NIT tournaments. By the time he finished his college basketball career, the slender forward was among Providence's career leaders in points and rebounds. A Friar or a Tar Heel? The basketball Gods roll the dice and determine your fate.

One of Billy's greatest nights as a Friar happened on February 6, 1978, during an iconic blizzard that hit the Northeast. Snow fell at a rate of four inches an hour, and winds gusted up to the eighty miles per hour. Yet the weather did not stop the North Carolina Tar Heels and the Providence College Friars from playing before nearly seven thousand fans at the Providence Civic Center. A few days later, the Hartford Civic Center roof collapsed due to the weight of the snow. Probably not the safest of conditions for players and fans alike, but that did not deter people from attending the epic game.

Dean Smith with his vaunted and at times despised four-corners offense took on the Friars led by Billy Eason, Soup Cambell, and Bob Misevicius. In the final minute of the game, with the score tied at fifty-nine, Coach Smith instructed his team to go into their four corners offense and play for the last shot. Coach Gavitt would have none of this and instructed his team to foul. The Tar Heels went to the line and missed! The Friars brang the ball down the court with Soup Campbell spinning on the baseline, drawing a crowd, only to find Billy for a short corner floater. The Friars won 61–59. Was it the blizzard? Was it the basketball gods? To be sure, it was Billy and those darn peanut butter and jelly sandwiches. Go Friars, indeed.

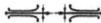

The Jack Troy Summer League was a wonderful program that focused on providing local high school players an opportunity to work on their skills both on and off the court. Kids need the support of their communities all year long, and these games helped continue the work that educators and coaches tried to instill during the school year. That is not to say that the occasional misstep didn't happen.

One evening at the end of a victory, Billy Eason approached me. "Coach, can I speak with you for a second?"

"Sure! What's up?"

"We didn't mean to embarrass anyone, but I had to grab someone at the last minute to coach your kids."

Our Purple Knights had just finished pummeling Palmer High School in a Jack Troy Summer League game at Blunt Park. It was the summer of '94, and the Purple Knights had a loaded roster. This group was on its way to play in the D1 State Final against South Boston. Our team was stockpiled with size, speed, skill, and team chemistry. The Purple Knights were hungry to excel. They looked for any chance to play: pickup games, scrimmages, and summer league games were all opportunities to be ready for the basketball season. If you stepped on the court against this group, you needed to be prepared to work hard and play smart. These Knights were ready to rock from the get-go. Robert, Wilfredo, Joey, Larry, Cedric, and Eddie—they were the core of a talented and driven team.

On this summer night, the power of the Purple Tsunami found Dave Gowan, an MBCA Hall of Fame coach, and his developing players. Coach won multiple sectional and state championships. As an educator and coach, he understood what high school sports were all about. He understood the importance of the Jack Troy Summer League and helping young players develop their skills, self-esteem, and sense of community. That night he was coaching the Palmer team because his son was in their program.

After the game, I approached Dave to offer an apology. "We should have stopped pressing early."

Dave responded like the class act he was. "Hey, Coach! No worries, we want to play against the city teams." Dave felt the best way to get better was to play against better competition. He wanted his kids to face speed, athleticism, and presses. Dave continued, "I would have been more upset if your coach had called off the dogs." So even with the Jack Troy mercy rule in effect, the Knights still put up ninety-seven points. Kids very seldom realize when enough is enough. It's up to the coach to step up and lead their team.

Driving home from the game, I had the opportunity to speak with our interim coach.

"Well, nice win. Your record is officially 1–0. However, ESPN is reporting that you have been removed from consideration for the Sportsmanship Award. You just embarrassed one of the best coaches in the region and a true gentleman."

"I didn't mean to," our interim coach protested, "but the team plays like someone is stealing their dinner and they haven't eaten in days."

I went on to console our coach, my wife Sandy, who had been roped into coaching that night's game because our regular coach could not make it. Instead of forfeiting the game, Sandy stepped in, but the players took over.

"No worries. I smoothed it over and apologized to Coach Gowan. Just don't let it happen again," I said firmly, then smiled. "So. What's for dinner?"

Not all the games in the summer league were blowout victories. Most were epic battles against strong teams. The Jack Troy Summer League saw much of the area's best basketball talent. In fact, two western Mass elite players dueled it out one evening in the Jack Troy Summer League. These two were part of an excellent wave of local high school talent during the late '80s and early '90s that included Central's Travis Best. At any other time competing on this high school landscape, Franklin and Kellogg would have been considered top candidates for player of the year honors. Damon Franklin from Chicopee Comp High School went on to play at Yale, and Derek Kellogg of Cathedral High went on to play for Coach Cal at UMass. After his own career as a player, Derek went on to coach at the D1 level for both UMass and Long Island University.

One early August night, with a big crowd smothering Dana Park in Chicopee, the two exceptional high school players went back and forth battling it out on the court. I am not sure who actually won this Troy playoff game, but I believe their combined score neared one hundred points. The crowd was entertained by some excellent high school basketball.

The irony of this game was that both Franklin and Kellogg played in the flow of the game. Neither player seemed to overshoot or overplay. They were outstanding players with a tremendous amount of skill, but they were also great teammates. Without a doubt, they were two of the smartest and most respected players I came across in my coaching journey. The way they handled themselves on and off the court made it easy to project the success they would achieve in life.

The beauty of sports is that you never know when and where something wonderful and unexpected is going to occur. It can be an unexpected outcome in a youth game or a magic Carlton Fisk moment as he leaps and jumps to keep the ball fair in the World Series. Sports brings magical moments into our lives, many times when they are least anticipated. The outcome is not always what we wish for, but that is part of her alluring charm to the masses. The Jack Troy Summer League helped keep that magic alive during those months when too many of our students and players were without purpose or positive connections.

CHAPTER 25

THREE CATHEDRALS, CHASING THE VALLEY LEAGUE TITLE, AS THE CLOCK WOUND UP, AND BALDO VERSUS YVON

During my coaching career, I coached against the Cathedral Panthers more than against any other high school program. The Panthers were always fierce competitors, whether we faced them at home or away. Our victories were hard earned and our defeats tough losses. There are three stories that stand out to me when I recall our battles against this stellar high school basketball program, which helped me in my journey as a teacher and coach.

February 24, 1994
Cathedral High School
Holyoke 58, Cathedral 57

Holyoke: C. Washington 3-3-9, J. Reyes 0-0-0, R. Sisson 10-5-25, T. Lawson 0-0-0, A. Lunardini, 2-1-2-9, R. Diaz 1-1-3, J. Quinn 0-0-0, M. Gubala 5-3-13. Totals: 21-1-14-58.

Cathedral: K. Canty 4-2-2-14, T. Pare1-0-2, B. Martin 10-0-20, J. D'allessio 5-1-11, T. Shuer 2-2-6, P. Brown 1-0-2, R. Neal 0-2-2. Totals: 23-2-5-57.

"Great win, guys!" I told my team. "Monday night we play for the Valley league Championship down at Cathedral." Knowing this would be a tough battle, I encouraged my players. "Let's go take it!" I exclaimed as they looked up at me with smiling faces, exuding happiness in the Knights locker room.

Of course, winning the Valley League Championship in boys basketball is easier said than done. It is no small accomplishment and hard earned. Case in point, in my career as head varsity coach, we won four Valley League titles. In comparison, our teams reached seven Western Mass D1 sectional championship games. As the old saying goes, "You can't win them all!"

Why was winning the Valley League title so difficult?

It was the philosophy of the Pioneer Valley Interscholastic Athletic Conference (PVIAC) athletic directors to place school programs in groups based on the strength of a given school's program. The PVIAC leagues were called by names honoring people or places, but basically it was as A, B, C flighted competition.

For example, the HHS boys hoop program played out of the VL, which represented the strongest teams in the PVIAC. Other Holyoke athletic programs were placed in the B or C flighted league based on their strength. In boys basketball, other Pioneer Valley schools floated in and out competing against Holyoke and the Springfield teams. Many schools wanted nothing to do with playing 60 to 70 percent of their schedule against top competition. The VL had as many as ten schools and as few as five over the years.

The redesigned VL came about because many area schools were reluctant to compete against the Springfield teams. At one point in time, the city schools were down to a twelve-game schedule because they did not have enough teams to play against. Few schools in the valley were willing to compete against them. Subsequently, the Springfield high schools (Tech, Classical, Commerce, Trade/Putnam, and Cathedral) would go against each other three times each for a twelve-game season. If a school's program dropped in talent, organization, leadership, or the will to build a program that could sustain playing at the best level, they could request to be "realigned." It did not take much for many schools to leap at this opportunity to move away from the top teams.

Holyoke, however, remained a staple of the VL group. And now we were facing the Cathedral Panthers for the Valley League title. This would be a real challenge with the Purple Knights being down some key players.

The first half of the game was virtually a rugby match, complete with scrum-like action all over the court. The officials were letting the boys play with minimal calls, and the Purple Knights rose to the challenge. At the half, we were in the game, but down by 5 (34–29). The inside play of Robert Sisson and Matt Gubala kept us close. It was clear both teams were hungry for the win and were willing to give everything they had to make it happen, earning a Valley League title!

Raul Diaz, our all-court defensive phenom, drove us to victory in the second half. Some might know Raul for his viral moment of fame on *SportsCenter*, namely his reaction to his son's first major league home run, which occurred while he was being interviewed.

"Isan! Isan!" he yelled as his son, Isan Diaz of the Florida Marlins, sent the ball flying.

That night in the game against the Panthers, Isan's dad came up with every loose ball. He covered for his teammates with his amazing defense. He took charges, and he exhorted his teammates to keep on pushing. We were in a fight that Raul was not going to allow us to lose. Raul recognized the time and score. He understood the DNA of victory, what it would take for us to earn the Valley League title. Offense was not enough; it would require defense. Raul Diaz knew who had to be stopped on Cathedral and who should be getting the shots down the stretch for the Knights.

Most high school players when placed in this situation would try to do too much by themselves. Raul took on a more mature and effective role by recognizing that our strength was in the five Purple Knights stepping up their defensive game.

In the end, the Knights prevailed 58–57! On the way back to the locker room, Joe Pantuosco, hall of fame soccer coach for the Panthers, grabbed me by the arm. "That is one of the toughest groups of kids I have seen play in a long time. If it was a fight in the alley, your guys would win."

On a side note, a few of our fans walked out at the start of the game when they realized we had key players out of the lineup. They must have been surprised when they picked up the paper in the morning to see we had won. If there is one thing I have learned about sports, it is to never count out fearless effort and drive. Most of the time, talent trumps all. But the great thing about sports is that during any given game, anything can happen.

February 2, 1993
Cathedral High School
Holyoke 70, Cathedral 68 (OT)

Holyoke: W. Cabrera 8-4-0-20, R. Cosme 2-1-0-7, J. Reyes 0-0-0, R. Sisson 7-7-21, S. Chatman 1-0-2, A. Lunardini 0-0-0, T. Neves 0-0-0, M. Gubala 9-2-20, C. Washington 0-0-0. Totals: 23-5-9-70.
Cathedral: J. McMahon 1-2-4, A. Chase 3-0-6, K. Burns 2-1-5, S. Dean 2-0-4, B. Martin 7-1-4-21,T. Pare 8-5-21, S. Jones 1-0-2, F. Murray 1-1-0-5. Totals: 25-2-12-68.

Often, you will hear the sports broadcaster announce that "time is winding down on this contest" or something like that refrain. However, another memorable matchup against the Panthers at Cathedral High school would have baffled the very best of sports media personalities. It was a game for the ages!

The Knights came in led by Ramon Cosme, front-runner for the Lahovich Award (signifying the top player in the region). Panther coach Kevin Kennedy was an exceptional leader who would go on to lead the Panthers to a state championship in later years. A wonderful high school and college player himself, Kevin always had his team ready to play. Coach had been a member of the Panthers team that knocked out the Purple Knights in my senior year of the western Mass tournament at the Pittsfield Boys Club. Kevin Kennedy, along with Mike Julian and Billy Moge, did a number on us and ended what was a very good season. In fact, it was an undefeated Valley League season that featured two victories over archrival Holyoke Catholic. The Gaels, at that time, were led by John Grochowalski, Assumption College All-American, NBA draftee, and pro player in Italy for many seasons. Needless to say, Coach Kennedy and I went way back in our basketball battles.

Kennedy stood up for his players, and I think he sensed Ramon and the Purple Knights were getting a bit too much attention. Going into this late season contest, Cathedral stood at 11–3 and Holyoke 11–2. It was a pretty even matchup, and what resulted was a flaming barn burner.

The momentum flowed back and forth between the rivals. With regulation ending in a tie score, the game stretched into overtime. With a few seconds left in extra time, the Knights were in possession, inbounding the ball from the right corner of their own basket. The score was noted at 68, and less than 3 seconds remained on the clock. It was a tough spot for both squads. I called time-out and drew up a play with a couple of options.

The plan was to hit Cabrera on a curl for a jump shot or a direct pass into the post to Sisson. I didn't think there would be enough time to enter the ball to Ramon with a drive to the hoop. Also, I thought the Panthers would try to trap or deny him the ball, making it hard for us to get a shot off. The horn sounded, signaling the end of the time-out. I reminded the kids before they took the court in the huddle, "Remember in your head, a second for each dribble. So if you get no more than two dribbles, we want to get a shot up!"

The Panthers and Coach Kennedy were ready for us, though, and had figured out our plan of attack. Our inbounder looked for option one and two but settled on handing the ball off to Ramon as he raced to the sideline.

Well, this isn't going to work, I thought to myself.

As Ramon got the ball in his hands, he was immediately trapped in the corner.

Looks like another overtime.

Then Ramon performed his magic, spinning away from the double team and escaping along the baseline to our basket. One, two dribbles, but no shot. Ramon dribbled on, going to the other side of the basket.

Shoot now! I was screaming in my head.

The clock was ticking, but when I looked, it read four seconds.

Where is the horn?

Finally coming back to the side of the hoop where it all started, Ramon fired up a hook shot high off the glass and into the basket. The Knights' bench flooded the court, while the Panthers' bench, distraught and puzzled, crumpled to the floor in defeat. Coach Kennedy flew into a frenzy. First he was on the officials and next the clock operator.

That's when I saw it. The scoreboard clock had ticked up, not down. After we had called our time-out, which is timed at the scorers table, somehow the scoreboard had been reset to count up and not down. The officials conferenced but concluded that the game was over. A victory for the Purple Knights.

Coach K continued to have a chat with his clock operator. Just another reason to always know the time and score, even if a tad bit is added.

Note: Recently Kevin Kennedy passed away. I know he loved his family, he loved basketball, and he loved Springfield. I was lucky to compete against Kevin Kennedy both as a player and a coach.

February 11, 2000
"Jinx" O'Connor Gym
Holyoke 86, Cathedral 83

Holyoke: M. Athas 1-0-3, M. Vasquez 2-1-0-7, W. Cabrera 14-4-5-45, B. Griffin 2-1-1-8, J. Ferreira 0-0-0, M. Diaz 0-0-0, T. Zieja 1-0-2, M. Perez 4-3-11, N. Almodovar 3-4-10, J. Pollard 0-0-0. Totals: 26-7-13-86.

Cathedral: S. Neal 2-4-8, M. Martin 3-1-7-16, M. Yvon 12-2-7-37, D. Yvon 3-1-0-9, B. Berthiaume 6-1-13, K. Williams 0-0-0, J. Warren 0-0-0. Totals: 26-4-19-83.

Wilvaldo Cabrera scored a game-high 21 points as Holyoke High School came from behind to beat Central 56-48 Sunday night in the Western Massachusetts Division I final at the Mullins Center

Wilvaldo Cabrera took the Purple Knights to two state sectional championships.

The most points scored by one of my players in a single game is credited to Wilvaldo Cabrera. The younger brother of Wilfredo, "Baldo Could Ball" Cabrera was on fire that night against the Panthers. He put on quite a show, dueling Matt Yvon in a classic Larry Bird versus Dominique Wilkins scoring frenzy. Baldo had an amazing senior year and was in contention to win the Lahovich Award. Since 1946, this honor has been given to a tremendous basketball talent in western Mass. The award's namesake was a Springfield Trade High School star who was killed during World War II.

That year, Cabrera spearheaded our run to a Western Mass Championship, which included upsets against Chicopee and Cathedral in the semifinals and title games. Combined, the opposing squads had an impressive record of 40–3 entering our playoff meetings held at American International College (AIC).

Outside the weather was cold; inside the gym was an inferno. The battle raged from the first jump ball. Baseline line drives, Earl Monroe spin moves in the paint, three pointers from the left corner. Baldo was *en fuego*! Four made three-pointers in less than two minutes, as well as high fives to the fans in the front row while dashing back to play defense. Baldo drained shot after shot, scoring twenty-four points in the first half. Meanwhile, Yvon was doing his best to keep his team in the game, scoring sixteen points by halftime.

Now, most high school players with these stats would have been satisfied with their initial effort and coasted when they reentered the game. This was not the case for either of these two sharpshooters. In the second half, Cabrera poured in another 23 and Yvon added 21. The final totals were 45 for the Purple Knight, 37 for the Panther. It was an impressive effort for both players and a truly remarkable accomplishment to watch. Ultimately, the Knights won 86–83 in a classic high school battle that left the sellout crowd talking for days.

Note: The son of Wilvaldo and his wife Kathy, Jael Cabrera, was a star player in both basketball and football for the Knights. He did his dad one step better, winning the Lahovich Award his senior year. Although, Dad can always counter with two Western Mass Championship titles.

CHAPTER 26

LUNCH—THE TREE HOUSE

Teachers and students are given very little time to have their lunch break during the school day. Scheduling and cafeteria services are programmed to get food out and into people as quickly as possible. Where your classroom was located in the high school during the lunch block determined if you could get down to the cafeteria with enough time to grab a hot lunch and eat. The scenario was simple: race down to the cafeteria, wait in line for your food, shove it down your gullet as fast as possible, only to race back to your classroom before the signaling bell. This applied for both students and teachers.

As a result of this crazy school lunch block dynamic, complete with rushing crowds (especially on chicken nugget Thursday) and sprint eating, the Tree House was formed by a group of teachers in an attempt to avoid the cafeteria chaos. Room 108 in the English wing at HHS was where my best teaching friends and I would gather for lunch in an attempt to save both time and a bout of indigestion. Along with partaking in a more relaxed form of eating, we would tackle global crises and any local and school conundrums that presented themselves. If only the powers that be had listened to us, we could have solved so many problems!

However, the greatest benefit of the Tree House was it allowed plenty of time for us to focus on our favorite pastime: sports. Once again, we had all the answers. Occasionally, a female member of our faculty would venture into this abyss, but they did not stay for long or return very often. They were much smarter than their male cohorts.

Over at Chicopee Comp, Alec Vyce referred to their version of the Tree House as the Bunker. In the English wing of HHS, four to five days a week, the house friends covered it all. The Tree House roster of HHS teachers included Bob Lastowski, Mike Mckenna, Roger Cook, Dave Cavanaugh, and Hank O'Rorke (who is sadly no longer with us), with the occasional cameo by Jim Hobert. I was so very lucky to teach in the Holyoke Public Schools with so many great students and staff. This group, dubbed "The Tree House 7" by Hank O'Rorke, was just what I needed to sustain my spirit through the various trials and tribulations of teaching. They were friends whom I ate lunch with for many seasons. They knew both the time and score of teaching because they also knew the importance of supporting their colleagues. I am forever grateful for their time and friendship.

Those daily twenty-minute Tree House meetings during lunch block were brief but meaningful. They brought joy and true connection to my career as an educator, which is a profession known for its isolation. In those few brief minutes, we engaged in inconsequential arguments, reflection, jokes, and easy conversation that often led back to our families. A lot got packed into the lunchtime meetings. And while the Tree House members no longer meet daily as we are all retired (and can now eat lunch at our leisure and discretion), our friendships remain strong today.

CHAPTER 27

THE RIP!

"Why is that man standing on his desk?" my student teacher asked as I was giving her a tour of the high school.

As we walked through the third floor history wing at HHS, she noticed a teacher standing on the top of a student's desk, smack in the middle of the classroom. The man was teaching, pontificating, cracking jokes, and encouraging his class.

"Abby, take attendance! Searsee is killing me on this stuff."

"Kiely, go make fifteen copies down at the teachers room."

"Leahy, what do the Puerto Rican people think of statehood? Oh yes! Cedric, you are lucky you have that big Irish lad blocking for you like a madman!" Cedric Washington at one time held the Massachusetts state rushing record in football, and a lot of those yards were gained behind Pat Leahy.

Mr. Ripa ran his classroom like a general, shouting information and orders at his class with gusto. Questions and directions came streaming out of his mouth before the fast-paced internet was available. James Ripa was hotwired with an incredible exuberance for life and endless stores of energy. He was a smart, knowledgeable history teacher, but his real strength lay in his ability to form positive connections with all types of students. He was a man of deep faith who believed in the importance of family and community. He came to work each and every day with a clear mission: to help his students and colleagues feel important. Everyone knew, as it was plain to see, that he really cared about his students' academic, social, and emotional growth and development. He supported students in the classroom and on the playing field. He rooted hard for the kids I coached. In fact, Mr. Ripa was an equal-opportunity supporter of the HHS community. He was an outstanding colleague. He understood the challenges teachers and coaches faced on a daily basis. He spent his career placing his entire heart and soul into championing his students and coworkers, wishing for nothing but their happiness and success.

Problems in Democracy teacher Jim Ripa.

Contract builder extraordinaire Drew O'Brien loved to tell stories of kids actually sneaking back into school so they could attend Jim Ripa's class.

"Who does that?" Drew questioned incredulously. Recalling a fond memory from his days at HHS, he continued, "I mean, these kids would be MIA all day, except for James Ripa's Problems in Democracy class."

In addition to loving his job and students, Jim Ripa loved the Boston Red Sox. Legend has it that Jim wandered his neighborhood endlessly for hours after Buckner's infamous error that cost the team game six back in '86. Mr. James Ripa was a passionate man who cared deeply about the people in his life. He did not do anything in half measures. He was all in, and we were all lucky that Jim Ripa loved HHS and its kids so much. Countless students' lives and high school experiences were enriched by his presence.

"Murph, who wrote the Federalist Papers? Hamilton, Madison, and…"

"Hey, Jason, pick up that map and bring it over to me please. *Jay*-son! Hurry up!"

"Right answer! Kaboom! Seven points on your test!"

Jim Ripa always knew the time and score in both the classroom and life.

CHAPTER 28

FIVE CHAMPIONSHIPS

While Springfield, MA, is credited as the birthplace of the great game of basketball, HHS by many accounts was the first school in the USA to have their own organized high school basketball team. Springfield is also in the running for that distinction; however, I believe their team was a combination of players from all of their schools. I will leave the conclusions of that debate up to the historians.

At the inception of Dr. Naismith's glorious game, HHS competed against private prep schools, Ivy League institutions, and semipro teams. The Purple Knights also competed in national championship events held for a number of years in Buffalo, NY. Any way you cut it, HHS has been playing boys basketball games for a very long time. In fact, their journey mirrors the journey of the game and its rich history in this country and around the world.

In 2007 the Knights defeated Central 58–52 at Curry Hicks Cage on the campus of UMass Amherst. It was our school's ninth sectional title and my fifth as head coach of the Purple Knights.

CHAPTER 29
THE TWIN TOWERS, A GIFT FROM CHARLESTOWN, AND HALFTIME SPEECH FROM JIM HOBERT

March 10, 2007
Western Mass D1 Championship
Curry Hicks Cage
University of Massachusetts Amherst
Holyoke 58, Central 52

Holyoke: P. Zayas 2-4-8, I. Robinson 4-3-11, F. Valentine 1-1-2-7, D. Zieja 4-1-9, N. Pollard 4-1-4 15, I. Linton 0-0-0, T. Dunn 4-0-8. Totals: 19-2-14-58.

Central: J. Nijiai 3-1-7, V. Delrosario 5-1-3-16, B. Barber 1-0-2, G. Alvarez 1-0-3, E. Jones 1-0-2, T. Belton 5-1-11, P. Preyboye 2-1-4-11, J. Roy 0-0-0. Totals: 17-3-9-52.

Playing in a championship game is a dream come true for anyone involved in sports. It is the culmination of everyone's hard work, hopes, and dreams. The players, coaches, and community rally together in camaraderie and spirit. The building excitement is electric as you get closer to game time and tip-off. During this contest, the Purple Knights were truly up against it, competing against the beast, otherwise known as Springfield Central High School (CHS). Other schools in our sectional division would take turns having a run at the title, but many a year, CHS found themselves in the title game. Now it was our turn to face the Golden Eagles for the championship. To make matters worse, the Golden Eagles were led by longtime rival and friend Mike Labrie, who was regarded by many as one the top high school coaches in the state.

Our success during this championship was delivered in three parts. First, there were the Twin Towers, Tim Dunn and Dave Zieja. These two players were top-notch big men in the history of HHS hoops. Tim was a career 1,000-point scorer, and both were highly skilled in blocking shots and rebounding. Historically, these were two areas in which the undersized Purple Knights fell short in competition against the Springfield schools. Central had very good bigs led by Preye Preboye, a powerful left-handed forward. Tim and Dave had a knack for bottling up the inside game for opposing teams, and this night was no different. As Tim and Dave took to the court in the Cage, they controlled the paint and glass for a good portion of the thirty-two minutes.

Both Tim and Dave arrived on the scene from families that had a lot of success in high school sports. Tim's dad Chris played for Holyoke when they challenged Cambridge Rindge and Latin's Patrick Ewing in state championships games. Dave's dad Peter played on excellent high school teams, while his uncle Stan was also the longtime trainer for Amherst College. Growing up, both of our Twin Towers were surrounded by athletic and academic success. They were taught the importance of team first, individual second. Tim and Dave benefited from the family lessons preached to them each day, so by the time these two embarked on their careers at HHS, they were well versed in knowing the time and score in both sport and life.

My youngest daughter, Alexandra, was friends with Nick and Anthony Zieja, Dave's older brothers and members of previous championship HHS basketball teams. On several occasions, the entire Rigali family attended birthday parties and family gatherings at the Zieja home. I even learned to sing "Happy Birthday" in Polish as a result: "Stolat! Stolat!" The Zieja clan is one of many special families I have encountered over the course of my coaching career. In fact, a common thread to all five of my Western Mass Championship teams was as follows: good big men and either a Zieja or a Cabrera on the roster.

Throughout the season, Tim and Dave connected on the court. They helped each other on defense, covered for our perimeter players so they could pressure the ball, and when they got beat on a drive, they were there to contest. On championship night at the Cage, the Twin Towers hit each other with passes. Tim and Dave defended and rebounded for the full thirty-two minutes to keep Central at bay.

As we were closing out the game, Central started fouling to stop the clock. Our lead was always around three to five points in the last few minutes. The Golden Eagles were still in it, and Coach Labrie was not going to let his kids give up. We struggled to hit our foul shots at the end, with Dave only making one out of several attempts. On his one make, he raised his hands in jubilation. Central could not score and take advantage of the misses. The Towers limited our opponents to one shot, with Pollard, Robinson, and Zayas playing smart on the perimeter and closing off the three-point line. This elite defense led to our victory, 58–52, and clinched championship number five for Coach Rigali and crew—number nine for HHS boys basketball.

Another important member of that championship team was Isiah Robinson, who came to us from Charleston High School. He had been a member of a dominant program in Charlestown under coach Jack O'Brien. Coach O'Brien had won five state championships and garnered plenty of college scholarships for his players. His team was the pride of a tough Boston neighborhood.

Isiah had moved out to western Mass to stay with his father. The smooth lefty was an enormous boost to our program. Isiah was a smart, fast player. He could take you off the dribble and shoot from the perimeter. His greatest strength was his defense. Isiah had a great defensive stance with balance and lightning-quick feet. He had this uncanny ability to stay in front of any opponent he was assigned to guard. He was the final piece to the puzzle needed to win a title.

A few years later, Coach O'Brien took over the helm at CHS but only stayed one year. The commute from western Mass to Boston invariably took its toll. You can read about Jack O'Brien's success in Neil Swidey's book *The Assist*. The book provides excellent insight into the passionate coach and the kids from Charlestown.

As the game was winding down, that sound started to reverberate through the Cage. During the COVID-19 pandemic, I often found myself missing that sound when confronted with the silence of sports not being played before their adoring fans. It is the sound produced at the precise moment when your fans truly realize and believe that your team is going to do it and win the game. I know the exact moment and play in every championship game when that sound erupts from the stands. In this battle at the Cage against CHS, it was our Heat set 1-3-1.

Pety Zayas feeds Tim Dunn in the high post, and Isiah Robinson slashes to the rim from the left wing. A no-look bounce pass from the Irish Twin Tower, a Central defender left flat footed, and Isiah lays the ball in softly for two more points. The Purple Knights go up by eight with three minutes to go, and suddenly that sound rises from the stands, with Holyoke fans going crazy in their seats.

While Holyoke ultimately won the game, it was a constant battle and hard-earned victory. Central led at halftime 27–21. They were controlling the game, keeping our point guard Pety Zayas rattled. Guillermo was off his reliable and steady game, and it was clear from the start that he wanted the win badly, affecting his play. Our floor leader was impatient and not getting us into our sets. It was a rough first half, and we all knew as a team we were capable of much more.

During halftime, we trudged into the locker room for our ten-minute intermission. As stated previously, it is a coach's job to know the right way to motivate their team during these brief pauses in play. That night it was Assistant Coach Jim Hobert who found the perfect words for the perfect halftime speech.

The speech was textbook and clearly directed toward Pety. Jim's words got straight to the point about what the hell was going on with our team on the court and more importantly, what the hell Pety was going to do about it in the second half! Coach delivered his talk without crushing his confidence. Coach Hobert knew our players were capable of better play, and our players knew it too. But instead of ranting and raving about playing poorly, Coach Hobert threw his players a lifeline. It was masterful motivation.

"OK! That's over," he began. "You are much better than you played, and *you* are the reason we are playing in this damn championship game."

Coach continued (and this was the absolute genius of the moment) by doing more than telling Pety to simply do better. He went on with clear, concise directives on how Pety could improve his performance and what his teammates could do to help him. These purposeful words took all the pressure off of our point guard.

"Play direct...get into sets...avoid traps...don't try to do it alone, and use your teammates first before stepping up." Coach Hobert left no one off the hook, holding our core players accountable, while at the same time driving the message home that if Pety played ball, we could still win this freaking championship.

After Coach Hobert's rousing speech, Pety and the team did not disappoint. Pety's skill, toughness, and character shined through the nerves and anxiety. He began to play the game the way we all knew he could and played a hellacious second half of basketball. Pety protected the ball, worked it inside, hounded the CHS offense from the top of our Ameba Zone, and finally broke the

Golden Eagles press, breaking their hearts in the process. Frank Valentine and Nathaniel Pollard gave us just enough outside shooting to complement our point guard's great second half. Frank and Nathaniel were exceptional teammates who never stepped away from any challenge.

The Twin Towers, Isiah, and Coach Hobert's halftime fireside chat, along with Pety's willingness to stand tall, brought us home to victory. The win raised my record to 3-0 against CHS in the Western Mass finals, something I am extremely proud of to this day. It also evened the score against my friend and rival Mike Labrie, with a record of 1-1 in championship contests: in '94 his Chicopee Pacers defeated us 50–46 in OT at the Springfield Civic Center.

CHAPTER 30

FRIEND AND RIVAL

Mike Labrie was one of the first people to reach out to me after I was let go as the boys basketball coach at HHS. Mike was upset about me not being rehired as he truly understood what my coaching career had meant to me and my family. He knew as well as anyone the demands, expectations, and pressure that high school coaches are under, including the sacrifices their families make throughout the season.

Mike is undoubtedly one of the top basketball coaches in the state. He chose not to coach in 2020 but has not ruled out returning to the sideline in the future. What is certain is that Mike will be taking his place in the MBCA Hall of Fame this fall, a well-deserved honor.

Throughout my thirty-six year career, I coached more games against Mike than against any other high school coach. We would play twice a year when Mike coached at Chicopee High School and Central. We would play once a year during his time at the helm of Chicopee Comp's basketball team. Add in several playoff game contests, and the result was a lot of matchups against three of the Purple Knights biggest rivalries: the Pacers, Colts, and Eagles. I am not sure who won more games overall in these contests, but each game was a battle against Mike's well-prepared teams.

There is one statistic, however, on which I know Coach Labrie had me beat: technical fouls. As a coach, Mike was prepared, passionate, and demonstrative during games. He coached in the style of Gary Saint Jean, Chicopee's gift to the NBA coaching elite. A practicing attorney by trade, Coach Labrie was famous for prowling the sidelines. It took only a few minutes after the opening tap for Mike to rip off his suit coat and dishevel his tie. He was always ready for action. I used to love looking down toward his bench when he felt one of his players had been subjected to a questionable call. Mike would put on a good performance for the crowd. It did not matter whether he was working with the Pacers, Eagles, or Colts. His teams (and the referees) always knew the temperature of the game just by peering over to the sideline where Mike was doing his best to keep within the confines of the coaching box. In or out of the box, Coach Labrie knew where the line was to avoid getting ejected from a game.

Mike's approach to the madness of high school basketball was quite different from the mine. That is the beauty of sports. There are lots of different approaches to and styles in any given game. People participate in a manner that is unique to their DNA. Whether they are a player, coach, official, or fan, each brings their strengths and weaknesses to the competition. This is not to say there were not times when the Purple Knights would call out a questionable call and I would take the mantle in order to stand up for our players. It was just my personality and style to focus on the emotion of my team first and interact with the officials later. Through my friendship and rivalry with Mike Labrie, I have learned that there are many pathways to success but they all require one to be true to oneself. Authenticity is essential in the secret sauce of collaboration, especially when you are coaching a group of young people.

Coach Labrie has proven himself to be a wonderful coach and friend over the years. Any time I led our team against one of Mike's, I knew we were in for a battle. Our rivalry pushed me to always keep learning about my players and the great game of basketball. As a couple of Assumption College (University) Greyhounds, Mike and I went around the track quite a few times as we led our teams. Like any worthy adversary, he pushed me to be a better coach and leader for my team.

CHAPTER 31
A PUNT AND A TECH

I was assessed one technical foul as a head coach in my career. In truth, it had nothing to do with a perceived bad call. The technical foul was given out by Mr. Tom O'Neill, professor of business and economics at AIC. Tom is one of the nicest people to ever walk this planet. He is a very good official in both basketball and football. What I loved about Mr. O'Neill's officiating was that he would always talk to the players, having a calming effect on them. He had great confidence in his abilities and did not feel the need to muscle players around on the court. He understood his power as a ref and did not lord it over the student athletes. Tom O'Neill exhibited respect for the game and the kids. He called the game as an educator, with his patient style helping generations of high school players enjoy their experience. I believe Tom wanted the game to be played well and fairly. Through his interaction with players, he believed in the opportunity for each young adult to showcase their skill, hard work, and talent to the best of their ability.

So how did it happen that this kind man and excellent official earned the distinction of handing me my only technical foul in thirty-six seasons?

The events unfolded one night during my early years coaching for the Purple Knights. I had started off with a number of winning seasons, and I had naively thought that I would coach winning teams every year. I learned quickly that is not the reality for 90 percent of high school coaches, including me. There are some schools and communities that have a built-in advantage and resources to produce winning teams every year. A coach in that position does not have to worry about the dreaded rebuilding season.

Transition seasons can be rough for players and coaches. At the start of this campaign, practices went OK, but we were only playing ourselves. A couple of preseason scrimmages were nothing spectacular, but it was still early in the season and I had not taken off my blinders yet. My expectations were unreasonable high for the team I had before me.

In this early season contest against Chicopee Comp, reality was about to set in and take a seat right on the bench. We were away playing in a very small junior high school gym due to the Colts' regular venue being refurbished. At the start of the game, we looked pretty bad. As my coaching career moved forward, I came to an epiphany and was better equipped in judging a team's talent and chances for success. This would prove very helpful in upcoming seasons but was no help during this contest. What I came to discover was quite simple, so prepare yourself—if your team is passing the ball to your opponents more often than to their own teammates, then you are in for a long season.

During my first few years as a coach, I learned that passing and decision-making were the analytics to focus on early in the season. Your teams can be coached out of many weaknesses, and you can cover up a lack of talent by playing a certain way. But bad passing and terrible shot selection will bring instant chaos (and many losses) to your season.

This late Saturday afternoon, set to ruin the remainder of my weekend, showcased a barrage of passes that went to everyone except the guys in the purple shirts. Comp started the contest with a sneaky half court trap and built a double digit lead by halftime. Colts and Coach Vyce started the second half with what I call the Four Minute Kill, which entails them pressing us again but this time full court. This strategy is the finishing push that coaches do to put the contest away early in the second half. They can then call off the dogs and enjoy a good portion of the game coaching fairly relaxed with an opportunity to play everyone on the bench.

I remember calling a time-out to mention to my team what color shirts we were wearing. Halfway into the third quarter, with about twenty-five turnovers, one of my guards found himself trapped in the coffin corner while being pressed. He was stuck on the opposite sideline from our team's bench. Suddenly, Reynaldo spotted an open teammate down court. My Purple Knight executed a perfect step through of the trap, sending a splendid pass right to me on the bench. I was open, but since I had already used up my high school eligibility, I probably was not his intended target.

Spaulding in hand, I did the only thing I could think of at the moment: in a bout of frustration, I drop-kicked the ball all the way up into the gym rafters on the other side of the court.

Mr. O'Neill calmly walked over to me, saying, "Sorry, Coach. I will have to administer a technical foul for that." After taking two steps away from me, he turned back and continued, "But Coach, that was a really good punt. Great hang time."

Tom O'Neill always knew the time and score.

CHAPTER 32

THE CHARGE AND PUNCH

Dr. Naismith's beautiful game of basketball has been entertaining fans for over one hundred years. It is a team sport that allows for individual acts of athleticism and grace. The slam dunk, three-point field goal, and smooth crossover past an opposing offender all have the power to captivate the crowd and invigorate a team.

But what play has the most emotional effect on a gym full of fans?

My vote goes to a basketball classic: the charge and punch. No, not the famous punch Kermit Washington hit Rudy Tomjanovich with during an NBA contest. This punch is handed out by the basketball official. It signals when a player with the ball runs into or charges upon the defensive player who has purportedly established his defensive position. The charge is one of the toughest calls to make in real time for any ref, from high school to the pros. Most high school refs do not have access to Secaucus, NJ, and replay to verify this hit-and-run call. They need to rely on their eyes and instincts to get it right. The emotional charge that occurs with a player control foul can change the entire momentum of a game.

I have always found "player control" an interesting moniker for that tort. Most of the time when this infraction happens, it does so because the player is totally out of control. The chain of events that unfolds during the charge and punch is electric. The player runs into the defender, who falls back, and the referee blows the whistle to stop play. The official then puts one hand to the back of their head and punches the air with the other hand in the direction of the opposite end of the court. On the other hand, this is a painful call for both the coach and offensive player. It is always hard to absorb the abrupt sequence of events that does not end up going your way.

The very best at squeezing the most emotion out of the "player control foul" was Bernie Cohen. Bernie was an excellent referee who officiated many of my games at the start of my coaching career. I referred to him as Zorro, his primary weapon being his

The charge call is always full of drama!

whistle. Immediately, after one of my players had run over someone, Bernie would blow his whistle to stop play. He would always hesitate slightly before making the call, building up the drama and anticipation of the players, coaches, and crowd.

Was it a block on defense?

Was it a charge of offense?

The crowd waited with bated breath for the moment of truth. Bernie delivered the verdict. Hand behind his head, he pirouetted down the sideline. The crowd would go wild, jumping around as if in a mosh pit. Bernie's movements were showmanship at its finest. He would gracefully slide across the hardwood, mixing in a tango step or two, and then deliver the dramatic punch with power. The sword of Zorro flashed and cut into the gym air, slicing the soul of the offensive player in two. The call sent the fans into a tailspin. Most times it was hard to tell if they were cheering for a good defensive play or the swashbuckling official. Alas, Bernie was not done yet. He would spin out of his punch like Mikhail Baryshnikov, sprinting full tilt like Rafa Nadal to the baseline after the coin toss, awaiting his next curtain call.

CHAPTER 33

MIKE, GRIFF, AND "MY DAD IS THE COACH"

March 11, 2000
Western Mass D1 Championship
American International College
Butova Gym
Holyoke 62, Cathedral 59

Holyoke: M. Athas 4-4-12, M. Vasquez 0-0-0, W. Cabrera 2-4-3-17, J. Pollard 3-0-6, B. Griffin 2-3-7, T. Zieja 1-0-2, N. Almodovar 5-8-18. Totals: 19-2-18-62.
Cathedral: M. Martin 1-1-4-9, M. Yvon 5-1-11, B. Berthiaume 1-4-6, S. Neal 4-2-10, D. Yvon 2-3-13, K. Williams 3-0-6, J. Warren 2-0-4. Totals: 17-4-13-59.

If there is one thing you can count on while coaching high school sports, it is that something will not go according to plan. In the rest of life, you have to adapt to unexpected circumstances, and so must every coach and player who bravely steps into the sporting arena. Adaptability is key to survival and success. This was certainly true when the Knights approached their Western Mass Championship game against Cathedral in March of 2000.

The final was to be played on a Saturday at Butova Gym on the AIC campus. Thursday night's practice went off without a hitch. The team was in sync and working hard to prepare for the upcoming contest. It was almost too good to be true. The kids paid attention to detail. We went over our game plan repeatedly. The coaching staff collectively agreed that the key to victory was to play a box and one against their best player, Mike Martin. Our belief was that by playing box defense against Mike, we could keep the ball out of his hands and force the other Panthers to make plays. We believed minimizing the impact of their best player would give us the best chance to win the game.

Mike would go on to win the Lahovich Award that season and go on to have an excellent career at Brown University. Today, Mike is in his tenth season as head coach of the Brown Bears. The other day I watched his team play on ESPN against Michigan State, and Coach Izzo had some great things to say about the young coach.

The box and one is an excellent defensive strategy. I am often surprised that it is not deployed more often, especially in high school settings where many teams' good fortune is constructed around a key player. This player takes the lead, allowing his teammate to perform with less pressure.

So why is the box and one defense not used more frequently?

Perhaps the reason is it is rare that a coach has a player who is capable of and willing to focus his entire game on playing defense. The goal is simple: do not let him touch the ball! Sounds easy enough, but it requires several key components from an individual player. First, the player needs to be in great shape. Second, the player cannot be concerned about their own offensive statistics. This requires a lot of sacrifice on the part of the adolescent mind, which is often more focused on scoring points than preventing them. And finally, it is essential this individual does not get frustrated when their assigned player has success. Good players are going to find ways to make plays, and Mike Martin was a good player.

It would be an unreasonable expectation to think a player of this caliber could be completely shut down.

Did the Purple Knights have a player on their roster that met the criteria for a box and one defense?

Yes, we did.

Mike Athas, raised by Jim Jr. and Nancy Grumoli-Athas, was the ultimate team player. Both Dad and Mom came from families where sports played a big role in their daily lives. Nancy's brothers, Mark and Gary, were members of elite HHS teams in baseball and basketball, winning a state title in baseball and coming very close in basketball, losing twice to Cambridge Rindge and Latin, led by Patrick Ewing. Mike's brother Jamie was one of the best all-around athletes to come through HHS, going on to sign a professional baseball contract with the San Francisco Giants. Sisters Kate and Kristen were also all-around athletes for the Purple Knights.

The Athas family was highly regarded in our community for their dedication to coaching youth sports. In fact, they were the first coaches I encountered in organized sports as a youth. I was extremely fortunate to have them in my corner growing up. The family patriarch was Jim Sr. Mr. Athas worked full time for Table Talk Pies but always found time to give back to his community, with his sons following suit. Jim Jr., Chuck, and Teddy were always involved and influential in the Holyoke sports ethos. The Athas family mentored our Paper City youths, laying the groundwork for coachable and competitive athletes both in sports and in life. They championed sportsmanship, discipline, practice, and accountability for the youth of the city and their own children.

It was from this background that Mike Athas emerged as the clear candidate to take on Mike Martin. We had a plan, and we had the player to do it. Mike was destined to take on this kind of challenge. That is, until all hell broke loose.

Friday morning, the day before our scheduled championship matchup with the Panthers, the absent report rolled into room 108. I was teaching English to a very sleepy bunch of seniors.

Scrolling down the list, my heart skipped a beat as I read, *Grade 9: Maxwell Perez.*

Max was our starting point guard, and he had come down with a virus. He quite literally could not get out of bed. There was no way he could make an appearance in school to be eligible to play in the championship game on Saturday. It was our school policy, not MIAA rules, that required the student athlete to be in attendance on Friday if they were to be eligible to play on the weekend.

OK! No problem.

The championship game was a little more than twenty-four hours away. We had one practice left. Time enough? We had a plan in place to cut the head off the snake, as Al McGuire often called the box and one defense.

Would it even matter now?

Would we be too vulnerable to the press without our starting point guard?

Could we get into our sets?

The questions came at me in a barrage. Max was not scoring a lot as a ninth-grader, but he would defend the opposing point, placing pressure on the ball. Then he pushed it on the break, creating our sets and getting the ball to our scorers.

Brian Griffin, son of Joe and Linda, was also raised in a household where sports played an important role. Brian's brother Joe was a western Mass champion in golf and lettered in soccer, swimming, and basketball. Brian and Joe's sister Laura was a fine three-sport athlete, lettering in soccer, swimming, and tennis! Brian was the quintessential three-sport throwback high-school athlete. He could play any position in any sport, and now he was going to be the new starting point guard for the Purple Knights on Championship Saturday. Brian Griffin had one day to figure it out.

Both Mike Athas and Brian Griffin were exceptional athletes and competitors. Their families expected them to do well in school and athletics, and both were raised not to back down from any challenge. Now Brian was just as much a key to a championship as Mike.

As I've mentioned, the game was scheduled to take place at Butova Gym on the AIC campus for the first time, with both boys and girls D1 Championships being held at this venue. The change came with a few unexpected problems. First, Butova Gym was a much smaller venue than the Cage at UMass and the Mass Mutual Center in Springfield. The size limited the number of fans who could attend the game. Additionally, adequate parking was a problem. There were not enough parking spots, and there was little turnover time between games for people to leave as the final games were scheduled so close together. The overlapping crowds created issues both in and out of the gym. But the final difficulty came in the form of a March Nor'easter. Needless to say, it was not easy for the loyal, devoted fan base to navigate to and from the game to support their team. Even my own daughter struggled to make it into the gym for game time.

"Let her in!" someone shouted from inside the gym. "She's the coach's daughter!"

The line of people queuing up to get into the gym stretched through the ticket lobby and out into the pouring rain flooding the parking lot. There was no guarantee that these brave souls would get into the game as many fans from the previous game refused to leave. They were not going to pass up a D1 Boys Championship Game. Among the many fans in line was my oldest daughter Kiely Elizabeth, who was currently faced with a challenging dilemma: stay in line, patiently waiting it out, or try to find another way in. Kiely chose the latter, going out into the parking lot with the rain pouring down in buckets. With a hopeful heart, she had made her way around the building when she suddenly came across a security guard.

"My dad is the Holyoke coach," my daughter pleaded. "I'll sit on the bench. I won't take anyone's seat."

The guard, looking unconvinced, responded, "Sure, lady! And

the Celts and Lakers are playing tonight. It's a sellout, but I'll let 'em know I'll just sit on the bench. Sorry, no room at the inn!"

Kiely had just finished her weekend shift as a social worker. She had a ticket but was shut out by the site directors, who were waiting for some fans to leave from the previous game and getting very nervous about overcrowding. I wasn't sure if we could beat the Panthers on this day, especially without Max, but I was 100 percent sure that all of my family would get to the game and root us on. Your family and very few others truly understand what goes into coaching. They understand that most high school coaches only get a handful of chances to play in special games like the Western Mass Championship game. I would always take a peek around the court to see where my family was sitting.

I had faith Kiely would find a way into the game. Having been thwarted by the first security guard, she refused to give up, morphing into Natasha Romanova and pressing on to find another way. Having made her choice to leave the line, she braved the windswept rain and frantically looked for a crack in the fortress. Nothing was going to keep her from missing this championship contest. To avoid getting saturated by the Nor'easter, Kiely hugged the outside perimeter of Butova Gym, checking each and every window, door, and fire escape. Nothing was unlocked.

Finally, in the rear parking lot, she spied a glimmer of hope: a second security guard opened a door for a staff member, an AIC trainer assigned that day to work the event. Seizing the opportunity, Kiely sprinted to the door before it closed. And just like that, she was in the building. The entrance led down a long hallway with offices and the trainer's room. Beyond, she could see the gym. She was almost there.

Suddenly, from behind her a guard yelled, "Hey! Where are you going?"

Thinking fast, Kiely replied, "Working the game! Had to park in the back."

Quickly, Kiely flashed her yellow badge from work, which luckily resembled the AIC Yellow Jackets badge.

"I am working game two tonight!" she continued. Without waiting for a response, she moved fast to the end of the hall, through the trainer's room, past MIAA site people, and into the gym. Go Knights!

On the heels of upsetting the number 1 seed—Coach Labrie's Chicopee High Pacers, with an amazing record of 20–1—in the semifinals, the Purple Knights were now facing the Cathedral Panthers once again. The Panthers were the number-two seed, with an equally impressive record of 20–2. This was going to be a challenging matchup without our starting point guard Max. Of course, there are always doubts when you find yourself on such an important stage.

Was the terrible weather outside that afternoon a portent to our fate inside?

Were the basketball gods trying to tell me something?

Did the team have what it took to deliver a victory?

I can honestly say I did not have a good feeling going in, but I knew I could not show my true feelings to the team. Now was the time to stay calm, focus, and coach the kids in front of me.

Per my pregame ritual, I said a little prayer. People are a bit surprised when I tell them what I thought about during this time. I prayed to coach my best; I prayed that both teams would play their best and that it would be a good experience for both teams and their families. I prayed that I could control my emotions and would not act out in any way that would embarrass my team, school, community, or family.

As the game was about to begin, center Nelson Almodovar sauntered into the jump ball circle. My biggest concern was that the Panthers would go after us early with a press. Their assistant coach went directly to head coach Gene Eggelston when they found out Max was out. I was sure a reporter would soon come by to inquire what had happened.

In anticipation of Cathedral's game plan, the last thirty minutes of Friday's practice was devoted to breaking a press. No one pressed us with Max because it was basketball suicide. Ramon Cosme and Max Perez were two athletes on a very short list of players I coached who could break a press all by themselves. Slash, drive, spin, through the legs, behind the back, head up (always head up), right hand, left hand, layup, and two points. Their ball-handling skills were often so discouraging for other teams it resulted in the opposition backing off from the two elite point guards.

Right from the opening tip, the fans went crazy. It is hard to describe how much fun being a part of games like this is. To my surprise, there was no press. Mike Athas covered Martin and forced the ball away from him. Meanwhile, Brian Griffin was running the show on offense, getting us good shots. Nelson Almodovar was playing like Wes Unseld and pulled down every rebound. The Purple Knights were off to a good start.

In fact, Mike Martin only scored six points in the first half, while Wilvaldo Cabrera poured in fourteen to give us a 30-to-28 halftime advantage. Heading into the locker room, I knew what was to come during the second half. My team needed to be ready for the press, so it was the focus of our halftime talk.

The second half of the game was a back-and-forth slug fest. Neither team could shake the other as the two longtime rivals were evenly matched and hung on for dear life. Mike Athas was exhausted but was doing his best to limit the touches for a future Ivy League player and Brown Bears coach. In the second half, Mike Martin did his best to get his teammates some great looks, but on this night, there seemed to be a lid on the hoop for the Panthers. Despite this, about halfway into the last quarter we were still even.

Cathedral called a time-out, and when they came back onto the court, they were in full press mode.

Press offense requires spacing, as well as heads-up, look-first, don't-dribble, and flash-to-the-middle plays.

"Nelson! Nelson! Where are you?"

Turnover. Cathedral scored.

The Panthers fans were going crazy, and there were so many of them.

I called a quick time-out. Looking at my team, I told them, "Settle down. We are still in good shape." I crouched down. "OK big guy, you know where you need to be?" I asked, looking at Nelson. Nelson was trying to sneak behind the defense to score, but we needed that big target in the middle. Nelson nodded, and we went back out onto the court.

We will get it right, I thought to myself, believing in my team and all the hard work they had done to get to this moment.

Well, for the next three minutes, Nelson Almodovar turned into Bill Walton. With his head up, he caught the ball, pivoted, passed, and we made layups. The Panthers were in the game, but with little time left, still trailing, they had no choice but to take three-point attempts.

Both teams kept battling, and in the end, we won the game twice. We were up by three points with just a few seconds left, and Cathedral inbounded a long pass to midcourt…

Before I describe this final sequence, I would like to say that over the course of thirty-six basketball seasons, I have witnessed many people step up to help the players of my team and students of HHS. Nelson Almodovar, in particular, has to be one of our community's all-time favorite players. He was a big kid who was unaware of his own strength. I am not sure he truly realized just how good a basketball player he was. Nelson was polite and kind, and it was clear he inherited these values from two very selfless people who helped him navigate through high school: Aunt Milagros Rodriguez and Mike "Eagle" Sullivan. His aunt provided Nelson with a roof over his head and a watchful eye. Mike, a local businessman and city council member, was always supportive of our kids and had a special place in his heart for our big center. Mike was at the top of the list of people who mentored our young adults and came through for our hoop program.

One summer, Mike sponsored Nelson so that he could attend an Outward Bound program where those selected learn to live off the land in the wilderness. The program's primary objective is to help young adults gain maturity and self-reliance. They are given a few rations and then left to navigate as best they can through the wilderness course. Nelson related to me that he consumed all of his provisions in the airport before he got to his wilderness destination. Like many teenagers, he tended to be perpetually hungry and a tad impulsive.

I share the above story because it provides more insight into the last few seconds of our championship game. As we were trying to close out the championship win, we needed to make one more stop. Nelson caught the desperate Panther pass in a crowd of players. Thinking he had won us the game, our center just took off and ran when he intercepted the inbound pass. He forgot that the clock does not start until someone touches the ball. The ball had been in the air for a few seconds, so even many of the fans thought, like Nelson, that the game was finished.

Instead, the ref blew the whistle and called Nelson with travel!

Nelson's misstep resulted in another opportunity for the Panthers to inbound the ball for another desperation shot. Luckily for Nelson and the Purple Knights, they missed. Another magical Western Mass Championship for HHS.

As I look back through years of score books and rosters, there is a common thread that stands out for each championship team. The teams that won (or almost won) were very talented, of course. However, talent was not enough. The world is full of teams with superior talent who simply cannot get the job done.

So what is the secret sauce, if not talent alone?

Quite simply, it is the acts of collaboration and sacrifice that see teams through to a championship title. The group of players who sacrifice their own game to benefit the team concept and culture greatly enhance their ability to win. Athas, Griffin, and Perez all could have scored more on the floor each and every night, but instead they did other things for the team, allowing us to be better.

Wilvaldo Cabrera and Nelson Almodovar scored, leading us to wins with raw talent and skill. Tony Zieja and JoJo Pollard were the perfect role players. Tony contributed defense and rebounding, while JoJo offered speed and scoring. Miguel Vasquez provided energy and pressure defense off the bench. Each player knew their role and contributed to the team's success. The economic situation, athletic ability, and social mobility of our roster varied greatly, but it did not matter to them. This team was all in, and when they stepped onto the court, they competed like champions all season long. When the playoffs started, they were ready to go. This group chose to empower each other, bringing out the best each teammate had to offer both on and off the court. It is because of the team's commitment to each other that they were able to win the title. They worked hard, played fair, and focused on bringing out the best in one other. In doing so, this group of Purple Knights pulled off memorable upsets against Chicopee and Cathedral to secure a championship and memories to last a lifetime.

A final note on Nelson: He could have easily traveled down the wrong path in life. Instead, he made good choices for himself, listening to his aunt and taking advantage of opportunities provided by community members. Many people recognized what a truly wonderful soul Nelson was, but Nelson also had the support and love of his teammates.

During Nelson's senior year, he was approaching the 1,000-point milestone. We were scheduled to play a weak team that night at our home gym. During the school day, Nelson came by room 108 wanting to talk.

"Coach, could you call the local TV stations to see if they could cover the game tonight?"

Trying to temper his excitement, I told Nelson, "You're still thirty points away. That's a lot. You don't want to put that kind of pressure on yourself."

"I know, Coach," Nelson continued. "It will be good."

Reluctantly, I called all of the local stations, but nobody came. They all agreed that he was too many points away but assured me that they would cover it the next game.

There were two things I did not know that day. First was the fact that the other Knights knew it was going to be an easy game. They had all agreed they were not going to shoot. They had conspired to feed Nelson the ball and get him to one thousand points. The second was more of a surprise. I had assumed Nelson wanted me to call the TV stations purely as a pitch to get his accomplishment some publicity, but that was not the case. Rather, because someone special in Nelson's life could not be at the game in person, he wanted them to be able to see it on the evening highlights.

Nelson scored his thousandth point with only two minutes left in the game. Everyone was happy for him. The media was not there that night, and Nelson was a bit disappointed that his milestone was not on TV that evening. The next day we sent a video of Nelson's achievement to all the local TV stations, who all graciously highlighted it on that evening's broadcast.

Esther Girl

(sung to Danny Boy)

Oh Esther Girl, you call, you call, you keep on calling
You need a ride to church, the hair dresser and the Mall at Ingleside
Jack Whelihan's gone and Mary Kane's old Chevrolet is dying
'tis you, 'tis you must go and we must give you a ride.

But call us back when basketball season is history
Or when you have finished the tale of the prince, your son, Danny
'Tis we'll be here because we forgot to unplug our telephone
Oh Esther girl, oh Esther girl, we sadly stayed at home

And if your linoleum is buckling and kitchen light is dying
And Paul Hogan and Tom Elisee are as dead as wish we
You'll come and find the place where we are hiding
And give us grief and shame until we agree

And when we hear that sweet soft voice sing, "hello it's me"
We know your scheme will become our nightmare as the case may be
And you won't fail to wake us from a rest so deep
We were in peace until you disturbed us in our sleep

Oh Esther girl, oh Esther girl, we forgot to unplug our telephone

Oh Esther girl, happy 70th birthday, we love you so

Owen Donohue's Esther Girl

CHAPTER 34

SHOT CLOCK, PHONE CALLS, AND THE SAME LETTER

Esther Baker Meehan was an influential presence in the Holyoke community, managing to get a lot accomplished in our city for someone who never had a driver's license. She worked the phones and encouraged her inner circle of influencers to work on her ideas and projects. Esther had her own fleet of Uber drivers before Uber was an IPO. Esther loved her family, city, Irish heritage, and the game of basketball. A sure sign that hoop season was approaching was the copious number of phone calls from Esther. One day the unofficial count approached the shot clock number (no kidding!)

Ring. "Who is Dylan playing today?"

Ring. "Do you think he will win the Lahovich Award?"

Ring. "What time are the Celtics on?"

Ring. "When do you play Central?"

Ring. "What was LeBron doing on that play?"

My mother-in-law moved a million times during the first few years Sandy and I were married. Thank God for my brother-in-law Paul Dubuc, who was indispensable over the course of Esther's many moves, which always seemed to be to the top floor of the building. Esther finally found her permanent home on Beech Street, a block from HHS. It was the perfect apartment for her family because it was in a prime location to view her beloved Saint Patrick's Day Parade. The first floor apartment was right along the parade route, which allowed her children, grandchildren, and great-grandchildren to gather as a family to celebrate the wearing of the green.

This apartment also supported our basketball-centric family members. As the parade festivities passed by, we could duck in and out of her flat to catch some of the NCAA basketball playoff games during March Madness. It was a perfect setup, and that apartment was a gift to all of our family members on parade day. Esther loved every minute of hosting her family as the Grand Colleen.

However, Esther Baker Meehan's greatest contribution to the Holyoke community was her drive to get a CYO (Catholic Youth Organization) program up and running at the Sacred Heart Church located in the Churchill section of Holyoke. She had to convince a lot of people to get on board, but as my daughter Alexa was fond of saying about her Nana Es, "she could sell you the shirt off your own back."

The reality was that a lot of work was needed at the old school gym: basketball hoops, scoreboards, upgrades to the hardwood court, a concession stand, and of course improved seating for the fans. Impressively, Esther motivated her inner circle to find bleachers and a scoreboard from Boyden Gym at UMass, which was undergoing renovation. Esther pushed to start the dream project to get kids a gym that they could feel proud to call their own. In the end Esther's Gym provided a safe place where kids could play in an organized league and develop fundamental basketball and life skills.

Nana Es honored.

CHAPTER 35

THE POWER OF TWO

During my teaching career, a writing prompt I used on many occasions was to ask students to discuss something in their life they wished were different. Initially, I thought I would read essays about being rich or famous, maybe having skills like LeBron James or Steph Curry. Maybe students would mention wanting to look different, be smarter, or own a luxury car. Although these types of essays were common, the response I saw most often and that stood out the most was students wishing that their mom and dad would get back together after a divorce, separation, or simple absence. The students I taught understood the time and score as it relates to family dynamics.

The power of true partnership between parents in raising children is a much stronger bargaining chip for them navigating the world. The challenges for the modern family are daunting and are tangled by the cracks in our safety nets, which have eroded over the past forty years. The end game for a single-parent family in all but the best of circumstances has become more complex and disadvantageous. Today, trying to go it alone as a single parent and caregiver can present significant roadblocks to the family unit being upwardly mobile in society. The power of two can be and often is the path to garner financial security, health care, education, housing, and the pursuit of happiness.

CHAPTER 36

JACK SEARS

Today, public schools are craving honest, hardworking, moral, and effective leadership. Our society has moved beyond Industrial Revolution jobs and stepped into the digital/technological age of manufacturing. Along with new AI work platforms, effective nonpartisan, nonideological school policy is required for modern-day education. There are a plethora of challenges facing school boards, superintendents, and administrators, so this is by no means an easy job. However, it is essential for schools to find leaders who embody a combination of common sense and twenty-first century skills to prepare students to compete in a global economy. Sounds like an impossible task to find such an accomplished individual, but it is not.

I am reminded of one of the best principals to lead at HHS, Jack Sears. Jack worked his way up the ladder of success one step at a time and not by stepping on people in his way to get ahead. In fact, Jack believed in helping drag others up the ladder, as all good leaders do. The HHS principal accomplished success through his skillful leadership as a teacher and administrator. His skill set was fueled by his love for and commitment to family and community. Jack Sears earned an associates degree from Holyoke Junior College and his BA in Math at Saint Anselm College in New

Hampshire. In the classrooms of HHS, John Sears taught all levels of math to students of various abilities. He reached out to all and spun his math magic. His pupils became more comfortable in the world of mathematics and more comfortable seeing themselves as lifelong learners.

In 1992 John Sears was named principal of HHS. This appointment was the culmination of a wonderful career in education serving the youth of our city. For the next seven years, Mr. Sears—I never called him by his first name—led the Purple Knights with a calm, dignified manner. He loved his family above all else and cared deeply about the faculty and students who walked the hallowed halls of old HHS. His wife Ronnie and their children John, Chris, Kathleen, and Patricia were the light of his life. Chris was a captain of the boys varsity team in his senior year. He was a great kid. Smart and humble, he had an excellent three-point shot. Jack and Ronnie Sears raised their children to value education and be respectful to all who crossed their path. For Jack Sears, it was his beloved wife Ronnie Frost Sears that drove his life. However, there were other aspects of his personality that stood out.

Mr. Sears was known for his temper, which was balanced by his heart of gold. He loved HHS and had high expectations for his students. He was often seen as tough, but he always tried to be fair. When he started out as principal, Jack Sears held the teachers accountable for being the best they could be for their students. One of his primary objectives was to improve discipline. This supported a school environment that provided teachers with more time for meaningful instructions and students with more time to learn. He did not make excuses for his students, regardless of ethnicity, economic status, or social standing in the community. All were treated with respect and given opportunities to learn, improve, and grow.

At the start of Jack Sears's principalship, Ramon Cosme and the Purple Knights were rolling. They were on their way to a beautiful 21-3 season. The three defeats came at the hands of Saint

John's in the state semifinals, Putnam in a tough loss, and Ludlow in a surprising upset.

No, that can't be right! We were playing basketball, not soccer!

Ludlow defeated our team and took us down with a great effort by the Knowles twins. At the same time, a sadness enveloped the team due to the tragic loss and passing of Mr. Sears's beloved wife Ronnie. Our players tried that night, but the surrounding sadness in our school was pervasive. Our players were gaining a tremendous amount of respect for their school principal. He had demanded good behavior and respect for their teachers, and attended most games to show his support. Many of our Purple Knights felt a part of the school community, a community that cared about them under the leadership of Principal Sears.

As a faculty, we were devastated for our principal and his family. We did not know how he would deal with this sudden tragedy. Jack Sears had lost his anchor in Ronnie. He had a new job that came with colossal responsibilities and time-sucking hours. On top of that, he still had to raise his children without his wife and their mom.

How would he get his own kids through such an enormous loss?

How would he get through himself?

Would John Sears still want to keep pushing to keep the high school a great place to send your kids and a wonderful place to teach ?

These questions hung over the HHS community. It is humbling to see a great man struggle, but it did not take long for all of us to get our questions answered. Like all great leaders, Mr. Sears did not let setbacks and stumbles keep him down. He rose up and kept moving forward. Jack Sears's courage and leadership remained a shining light for HHS and the entire community. He continued to lead as only a man of faith and conviction could. His resolve afforded the students, faculty, and staff, as well as the Purple Knight boys basketball team, a magical school year and season.

With Mr. Sears's leadership, the HHS faculty and staff were on a clear mission to provide the best possible education for our students. We were a staff who recognized time and score.

When Jack Sears walked into room 126 for the end-of-the-year faculty meeting, the entire room stood as one, clapping and cheering long and loud.

The faculty and kids were amazing that school year. Differences were put aside as we all pulled together. I will always look back on that time with incredible sorrow and joy. How could this one man give so much to others when he himself had lost so much?

I recently asked Chris Sears to send me some thoughts about the leadership skills of his dad. Chris shared the following:

> When I think of leadership and my dad, I think of commitment to both community and family. As a leader in the Holyoke school system, my dad had a vested interest in the community as all of his children spent all their years in the school system. He grew up in Holyoke and built his family around the city. He was deeply invested and that drove his decision-making on a daily basis. As he was well known as a disciplinarian and for "running a tight ship," he also would demonstrate a great deal of empathy at times which allowed him to connect with many students at HHS. While he was a VP and as Principal, he continued to tutor students after school and on weekends. He would make breakfast on Saturday morning for the students, then tutor for an hour or two. He also continued to teach math at Holyoke Community College, further demonstrating his dedication to the community at large. When it came to leadership, he walked the walk, using his experiences and values to guide him to the right decisions.

Anyone who had the privilege to work with or learn from Mr. Sears knows this to be true.

CHAPTER 37

CHET DUDLEY

Without a doubt, one of the most unusual and effective educators I came across during my teaching and coaching career was Chet Dudley. I first met Mr. D when I started teaching at Lynch Jr. High School. Or rather, I should say I first met Chet Dudley's inadvertent elbow to my left cheekbone.

Mr. Dudley served as one of the vice principals at the time. He was in charge of two things: discipline and organizing the Thursday after-school basketball games for the faculty. These gatherings tended to draw both good and bad players with all levels in between. Despite the basketball talent at play, one thing was sure: the combatants were working off a lot of stress after a day with junior high students.

One of the important skills I brought to these after-school matchups was my solid defense. I learned to guard without committing a foul at the old Holyoke Boys Club. This skill was drilled into me by my seventh and eighth grade coach, Wey Dotson. Wey was one of the all-time greats to wear a Purple Knight uniform. Wey played on some great Holyoke teams under Coach O'Connor. Championships, 1,000-plus points, rebounds, blocked shots, and individual defense were all aspects of Dot's career as a Purple Knight. My Boys Club mentor would push me to work on my footwork, reminding me "Don't reach!" Learning to not foul in basketball is a lot harder than you would believe. This is true for kids and adults.

During the Lynch pickup games, the skill of not fouling while defending was completely absent and useless, with countless infractions being committed inside our half-court game. My first competition demonstrated my colleagues' lack of self-control.

"OK!" Mr. Dudley shouted. "We have six today: Rigali, Lynch, Barrett, and I will play with Devine and Stebbins."

Just like that, Chet had picked the biggest and strongest player, Jim Devine, and the best quickest student, Bobby Stebbins. Mr. D always made up the teams. As the game got under way, I noticed Art Lynch would just hang on the perimeter and shoot. He was very accomplished at this strategy. Jim Barrett battled inside, so I settled on the role of trying to drive to the hoop and set up Art on the outside or drop it down to Jim Barrett for a layup. It was a bad choice on my part. The Lynch after-school pickup games had long since adopted a no-layup philosophy on defense. Who knew?

Instead, the Chet Dudley defense long preceded the bad boy Detroit Pistons. Dudley and Devine would have made Laimbeer and Rodman look like Tweedledum and Tweedledee. My first drive to the hoop drop-off to Barrett resulted in a layup. The second drive drew a hit, but I got the ball to Artie for another shot. Swish! Third drive did not end so well.

"Excuse me," I inquired, "could I use a phone? I don't want my wife to worry." The ER nurse handed me another ice bag for my headache and let me dial home.

"Hi, Sandy. Don't worry. I will be home in a bit. I need a couple of stitches."

"What happened? Did you get hit by one of your students?"

"Oh no!" I explained. It was nothing of the sort. "The vice principal caught me with his elbow going to the basket."

Back at the pickup game, we mopped up the blood. I picked myself up off the floor and was greeted by Chet announcing to all,

Get on the Purple Line

"Don't worry! He's OK! Besides, he can't stop playing. We aren't finished with the game yet!"

I reconnected (not by an elbow) with Mr. Dudley later on in our educational careers at HHS. Chet Dudley was strict, fair, and cared about kids. He loved to see our students participate in sports at HHS. He would encourage and push our athletes to behave and study. If my players and I heard it once, we heard it a thousand times: "Make up that assignment!"

In addition to his academic advice, he would chide our kids about their defense and always pointed out during passing time in the hallways, "Nice defense you almost played last night, Joey!" or "Good thing Wilfredo had your back!" or "Let's go pick it up! Putnam next week!"

The charismatic Mr. D was not going to let any school, community, or individual be disrespectful to any of our teams or players. His allegiance to his school and our athletes was on display every day. One particular example of this came when we were forced to postpone a home game due to the condition of our bleachers. Our sixteen-hundred-seat pullout scaffolding bleachers had seen their last game. Their condition was terrible as they would bend and break with each opening and closing. As a result our big game against Central had to be postponed.

No big deal, right? These things happen all the time.

On top of everything, a few days earlier, I had received a call from our athletic director.

"Coach, I'm sorry to break the news to you, but you are out a key player for a while. He is being suspended."

Now this is an unfortunate but not sn unusual predicament for a coach. Kids do dumb things all the time. It is up to families, coaches, teams, and players to get through it. The difference here was the conspiracy theories that circulated against our school as a result. Nobody labeled it "Bleachergate," but several surrounding communities felt that our school was postponing the game because we wanted to get our player back from suspension. Of course, nothing could have been further from the truth.

Mr. Dudley did not take kindly to the criticism and disinformation being handed out concerning the postponement, so in typical Mr. D fashion, he set everyone straight and stood up against the false allegations. The players and coaches loved it, and we loved Mr. D for having our backs. By the end of the week, apologies were rolling in from the different media outlets.

Mr. D raised a big family on a teacher's salary. For many years, he would work a factory shift after school to meet the financial demands to support his crew. He loved kids and sports, and he invested his time and focus on his community. He supported and loved watching the local high school kids play. Mr. D knew the time and score. I am glad I got to know and work for Chet Dudley. More importantly, I am glad many of the kids I coached came under his guidance.

Mr. Dudley and his dedicated career came during a time when the community's focus was centered on their local schools. Today, school communities have an uphill battle to gain support for their high school teams and events. Television, professional sports, and the digital age are an ever-present force field that schools must combat daily. The screens are winning, and our society is struggling to find the time and score. Technology is leading us away from authentic connection and relationships, while families are so busy with their schedules, with some parents working two or three jobs. Sometimes it can be difficult to attend games and go the extra step for our students and athletes. Indeed, support for our local teams is waning in the modern era, but I always remember Mr. Dudley during that after-school matchup. The game was not over, so I needed to keep playing. Play through whatever obstacle was in my way. As adults, we always need to make the time to give back to our kids, our schools, and our community.

CHAPTER 38

ZOOM CLASS

Taking a moment to pause and reflect on the context in which most of these remembrances were written is important. Much of this manuscript was written on Martha's Vineyard during the 2020 COVID-19 lockdown. Sandy and I spent the year on the island to provide childcare for our granddaughter, Marianela Juliet (MJ for short). This would allow our daughter Kiely to teach and our grandson Syius to do his remote learning in relative peace. Our family, like so many others, had to navigate new challenges during the pandemic. It was not an easy transition, but we were very lucky to maintain our health and be there for one another.

Kiely, like other teachers across the country, held remote classes via Zoom. Organizing and engaging the students was a constant challenge.

"Carlos, what are you doing here?" Kiely inquired to one of her students upon entering the Zoom class.

"I know, Miss! Sorry, I'm late!"

"No, Carlos. This is Cohort A; you are Cohort B—Monday, Tuesday, Thursday. Today is a Cohort A day," Kiely explained to her confused student. "But you can stay and do the work!"

Kiely went on to explain the complicated schedule in which Cohort A and B exchanged days every two weeks.

"In a few weeks, when we add grades, your Zoom classes will move to a block C scheduling," she concluded.

"But, Miss, I don't think my schedule is correct. I didn't sign up for your class!"

With a sigh, Kiely said, "Check in Friday. It's the only day all the teachers are available to Zoom and answer questions."

The conversation between Kiely and Carlos represented countless similar conversations between students and teachers transitioning to online learning. It was not an easy transition for anyone, and I am so happy Sandy and I were there to support our family.

CHAPTER 39
TITLE #3

Western Mass D1 Championship
March 3, 1999
University of Massachusetts
Mullins Center
Holyoke 54, Central 48

Holyoke: J. Hobert 5-1-1-15, E. Mattos 1-2-4, J. Yates 4-4-12, W. Cabrera 8-5-21, D. Matos 0-1-1, N. Almodovar 2-0-4. Totals: 20-1-13-54.

Central: J. Carroll 8-0-16, V. Davis 1-0-2, R. Panetta 1-0-2, B. McCombs 2-1-5-13, J. Sanders 1-0-2, A. Murray 2-0-4, A. Berrios 1-0-2, C. Morgan 1-1-2-7. Totals: 16-3-7-48.

The third title of my coaching career (seventh in our school's history) was very surprising and satisfying. I really did not know what to expect going into the season. We had lost key players the year before for discipline issues. The young men had not been all in. They struggled to be good citizens in school, so they were asked to leave with the promise that they would be reinstated in the program next season if they could tow the line in and out of school.

While this is challenging for some students, others know what it takes to be successful and take advantage of the opportunity. It worked out well for both the returning disciplined players and the Purple Knights varsity team. This group entered the championship game at the Mullins Center with a 19–4 record.

Whether out in the community, in the classroom, or on the playing field, kids need to know where the line is for acceptable behavior. They need to understand that they are accountable for their actions. Actions both positive and negative come with consequences. I have always believed that deep down inside, young adults want to have structure. In my experience, most kids respond well to it. This Knights team was no exception and it was great to witness these returning players committed to doing great things on and off the court.

As the playoffs approached, our opposition, Central, had come on strong at the end of the season. The Springfield juggernaut arrived at the title game with a 15-7 record. Any battle against Central is a challenge. We expected a hard-fought defensive contest. This group of Golden Eagles was coached by Tyrone Sullivan. Tyrone was a tough-minded, disciplined coach who had taken over the reins from Coach Howie Burns. Following in Coach Burns's shadow was no easy task as he won a lot with teams from both Tech High and Central. Whoever replaced Coach Burns at Central would face very high expectations to keep the winning streak alive each year.

No doubt the pressure was on Tyrone and all those who would follow him to keep producing championships.

The great basketball history of the Golden Eagles came about as a result of the closing of Tech and Classical High schools in the late '80s. The two schools were consolidated into CHS, a much larger entity. CHS produced a powerful basketball force in western Mass from its inception and possessed many attributes of high school programs that can compete for championships year after year:

- Enrollment that is much larger than the teams they compete against
- An affluent community that can supply all the extra resources to their children to develop their talent
- Exceptional coaches who understand the community's strengths and creative development of championship teams
- Positive school and community culture that has strong ties to the development of a particular sport (e.g., Ludlow High School soccer)

In this title match, the Purple Knights were down six at halftime (29–23). Central's James Carroll was having his way with us on the court, scoring ten points as he picked his spots on Jack Leaman Court.

The second half of the game was going to be an uphill battle for the Knights if we were going to have a chance of winning. Our problem was that our starting point guard, Dicky Matos, was playing through nagging, season-long injuries to both his ankles and hip. Matos, a smart, team-oriented point guard, was bottled up at the point by Central's speed. There were no shots inside for our bigs, James Yates and Julius Hobert, and our star wing player, Wilvaldo Cabrera.

I toyed with the idea of not starting Dicky in the second half.

What could we do to help him out and help us turn the game around?

We settled on using a triangle offense, having Dicky play in the mid post area of the triangle. This way he would not have to fight against the speed of Central but instead could use his size to hold off the defender. This would allow Dicky to pass out of the set to our cutters and post players. Not many high school kids would be able to make this adjustment midgame. It requires the player to be mentally tough and place winning over the possible discomfort of being exposed to failure by something unfamiliar.

Dicky Matos, with his ankles taped and an aching hip, rose to the challenge. Dicky passed out of the triangle set like Scottie

Pippen, helping Wilvaldo Cabrara score fifteen points in the second half on hellacious cuts to the basket. Dicky fed the ball to his teammates with pinpoint precision passing. Julius and James cleaned up the boards, Eric Mattos and Nelson Almodovar contributed key plays, and we squeezed out a 56-to-48 victory. Dicky scored one point, but did so much for the team. His second-half play was the reason we survived the game and came out victorious. From point guard to post passer, he knew the time and score: team first, me second.

Today, Dicky runs a very successful roofing and construction business. During his playing stint with the Knights, I thought he would end up a lawyer. My point guard was always working on give-and-take arrangements with the coaching staff. His negotiations focused on anything from conditioning sprints to the duration of practice, the time of practice, play selection, and uniforms. You name it, and Dicky had an opinion about it. He was never afraid to voice his opinion to staff or teammates. Dicky took on the role of public defender for the team. I actually had to invoke a Dicky Matos "no questions asked" day so we could cover all we had planned for our two-hour practice without interruption.

One February, walking into the gym from the back parking lot, Dicky noticed some damage to the back of my Dodge Caravan. There had been a lot of snow and ice the day before.

"Coach, who rear-ended you?" Dicky asked as he walked back to my car to take another peek at the damage. Then Dicky "Public Defender" Matos announced in his best Mark E. Salomone imitation, "Coach, not a penny less than $20K for damages and no charge for my services...and no sprints today at practice!"

CHAPTER 40

TOUCHDOWNS, STOP & SHOP, AND TWO CHARGES

Ken Gamble reminded me of Gayle Sayers on the football field. He was elusive, smart, and relentless in his dedication to be successful. Kenny was always looking to find ways to help his family and be a good example to his community.

On a bright Saturday afternoon, I watched Kenny Gamble run all over Roberts Field and score touchdown after touchdown. It was a remarkable display of athleticism. On my way home from the game, I made a quick run to the Stop & Shop on Lincoln Street in the Highlands section of Holyoke. When I got to the checkout line, I was surprised to see Kenny bagging the groceries.

Wait! Didn't I just see him on the football field?

The future Walter Payton Award winner had made a mad dash from the victorious locker room to make his shift at the grocery chain. On a day when most high school kids would be basking in the glory of hero worship from a great game, Kenny went straight to his job.

While Kenny was not as polished a player on the basketball court as he was on the football field, he brought a great competitive attitude to the court and he was an exceptional teammate.

Kenny played defense like an F-35 Lightning fighter pilot defending his nation's territory.

One sequence on the court epitomizes what KG was all about. The Knights were in a tough battle with one of our Springfield rivals. As the game approached the last few possessions, the Purple Knights held fast to a slight advantage. We were in a good position to win. Everything had to go right for our opponent to pull this game out now, and it was clear that they were feeling the pressure. From a combination of their erratic play, the referees, and our team's growing excitement, our opponents could feel the game slipping from their grasp. It all fueled their foul mood.

All we needed was a stop on defense or a conversion on offense and the game would be ours. The crowd was roaring as the Springfield player came streaking up the sideline right in front of our bench. It looked like he had a clear path to the hoop for a layup to tie the contest.

Suddenly, with a speedy sixth sense that all great athletes seem to possess, Kenny Gamble appears. Recognizing that his teammate has been beaten badly on the sideline, Kenny comes off his man and plants himself firmly on the sideline square to the offensive player driving to the hoop. The crash is imminent as the crowd and coaches are going crazy, emotions running high.

What's the call?

Offensive foul! On the opposing player!

What a great game ending play for Kenny, one would think. Alas, there is more! The call sent our bench into a frenzy of joy (naturally). However, the Springfield fans were less than happy. A Springfield fan came down from the stands, moving toward me at the scorer's table as refs and coaches discussed the call. He was big and could have very easily broken me like a twig if given the opportunity. Lucky for me, he never got the chance. They say speed can kill, but in this instance, it saved me and my hide.

Once again with his speedy skills, up pops Kenny from the heap of players involved in the previous play. He cuts in front of the emotional fan and takes another (unofficial) charge. Eventually, cooler heads prevail, the game ends, and the Knights win.

Kenny Gamble was not necessarily one of the best players on my team, but he always knew the time and score (and when Coach needed defending).

Note: Kenny Gamble was a three-time All American at Colgate University and member of the Colgate University Hall of Fame. During his college career, he won the Walter Payton Award for best player in D1AA. He owned 13 D1AA records when he graduated. After college, Kenny went on to play for the Kansas City Chiefs in the NFL from '88 to '90. After professional sports, he worked for Reebok as both VP and GM of the Sports License Division. But before all these accomplishments, he was a truly great Purple Knight and member of the HHS Hall of Fame.

CHAPTER 41

LARRY GILBERT: LAHOVICH WINNER AND ALL-TIME LEADING SCORER

Larry Gilbert was a key figure to the western Mass high school landscape during his four years as a Purple Knight. Each of Larry's four varsity seasons, his team reached the D1 Western Mass Championship game, winning two titles.

In the late '80s, I started to hear stories about this sixth-grader who could dunk the ball and was scoring and blocking shots at will. I always loved to do preseason clinics for the Boys Club, YMCA, and Parks and Recreation programs in the city. On the other hand, I made it a point to stay away from watching any grade-school youth games. I never talked with parents or the young adults in an attempt to persuade them to attend HHS and play basketball for the Purple Knights. This meant that I never saw Larry play basketball until he showed up for that first day of high school tryouts his freshman year.

However, there was no doubt from that first practice that the basketball court was where Larry shined. He faced obstacles going through school that could have gotten in the way of his basketball dreams, but he did not let that happen. Larry did an amazing job off the court to build a strong life for himself.

While he was in high school, Larry's time on our team and playing AAU ball garnered him plenty of attention. I was contacted by many D1 and strong junior college programs interested in recruiting Larry. Coaches always asked the same questions:

"What kind of a kid is he?"

"What are his grades and test scores like?"

"How does he get along with his teammates?"

Larry improved in all of these areas as he progressed through high school. By the time Larry was a senior, he was able to deliver a wonderful acceptance speech at the James Naismith Hall of Fame for winning the coveted Lahovich Award. He thanked all the people who had helped him on his journey and stood tall as he proudly accepted the award.

Many years later, in fall 2022, Larry Gilbert delivered another rousing acceptance speech from a different podium at his induction into the HHS Athletic Hall of Fame. The event was held at Wyckoff Country Club in Holyoke to a sold-out audience, with over four hundred people in attendance. Larry was then working in the financial sector in the NYC/NJ Metropolitan area. He had made an amazing journey from his Bridge Street home in the Flats.

Larry Gilbert's success both on and off the playing field is what any dedicated coach hopes for each of their players. In Larry's speech, he poked fun at Ramon Cosme. Ramon was a senior during Larry's freshman year, and they would go at it all the time in practice. Ramon wanted the best out of Larry as a player and person, pushing him to do better. Larry probably did not realize it, but when he reached his senior year, he would push our younger players to be their best just like Ramon had.

In his HOF speech, Larry also mentioned Adam Lunardini, a friend and high school teammate of his that we lost too soon. Adam worked in the same financial district as Larry, and they would talk about life, basketball, and what it meant to be part of a team. Through their time together on the court, in practice and in games, they formed a special bond and brotherhood. As Larry spoke that evening, he painted a picture of what those two hours of basketball meant to him, what his teammates meant to him, and what being part of a basketball family meant to him. These connections and relationships carried into adulthood. Adam and Larry's conversations were truly a gift to both as they were always and forever teammates.

⸺✢⸺

December 18, 1992
Holyoke High School
"Jinx" O'Connor Gym
Holyoke 66, Amherst 55

Holyoke: W. Cabrera 4-0-8, R. Cosme 2-1-0-7, J. Reyes 0-0-0, R. Sisson 3-1-7, S. Chatman 5-0-10, A. Lunardini 1-0-2, L. Gilbert 5-1-4-17, T. Neves 0-0-0, Mark Gubala 3-0-6, Matt Gubala 4-1-9. Totals: 27-2-6-66.

Amherst: Norkin 0-1-1, McDowell 7-4-18, Klewowski 1-2-5, Kortright 1-0-2, Stanton, 4-2-0-14, Loebl 3-4-10, Jackson 1-3-5. Totals: 16-3-14-55.

As previously mentioned, Larry Gilbert won the coveted Lahovich Award in his senior year. However, Larry achieved many other accolades as well. He was selected to multiple All State and Western Mass All Star teams and became the boys all-time leading scorer in the long history of HHS basketball, scoring 1,369 points. This record eclipsed Larry Westbrook's long-held record of 1,236. Larry played in three Western Mass Championship games and a D1 State final

Larry Gilbert's game was built on power and drive. He could get to the rack, elevate, and finish strong. His perimeter game was midrange, and his three-point shooting improved each year he played. Dunks, spins, slashing drives, and offensive rebounding— Larry could score in a variety of ways. His very first high school game was against Amherst High School, which would be the first of many teams to suffer an onslaught by one of the all time great Purple Knights.

His first career field goal was along the right baseline in front of our bench at HHS. Ramon Cosme hit him with a crisp pass in the corner off the tip. As Larry started to drive along the baseline, an Amherst defender came over and cut him off. Most high school kids would run over this guy for a charge. Not Larry! He spun back to his left and split two more defenders coming to help.

Then in a final attempt to stop Larry, the Amherst center retreating back from the jump ball circle approached, intent on blocking this rookie phenom. Elevating over the Amherst center, Larry rose up, shooting a sweet-as-can-be high-arching floater for two points. His journey had begun. Larry finished his debut with 17 points, 5 rebounds, 3 assists, and 1 block and steal. Not a bad start for a ninth-grader.

CHAPTER 42

GETTING OUT TO SEE THE WORLD

There is no shortage of basketball talent in the USA and around the world. As I was talking with Larry over the phone, he related the following: "High school basketball saved me."

His words meant a lot because as teachers and coaches, we want most to help our students and players navigate life successfully and happily. In order for Larry to continue to grow and develop as a player and a person, he needed to get out of western Mass and compete against the best talent from the AAU super teams. Two people were instrumental in giving Larry this opportunity. The first person was Wade Freeman, whose son Kevin played for an NCAA championship team at UConn. Wade and his entire family supported Larry in his AAU endeavors. The other person was AAU coach Wayne Simon. Wayne helped Larry get into some big national tournaments where he played against some pretty fair competition, such as Kobe Bryant, Tim Thomas, Richard Hamilton, Ron Artest, Lamar Odom, and Elton Brand. Larry had the opportunity to compete against the best players. This propelled him to come back with a passion and drive to get better. The all-time leading boys scorer at HHS understood basketball, so he knew he would have to keep improving if he wanted to compete at an elite level.

Larry's game grew over the years, and so did his emotional self-confidence. Like all teenagers, though, he had to balance his dreams with working out his college plans and looking out for family.

In his early years on the team, Larry struggled to find his footing off the basketball court. I don't think Larry said two words to me his entire freshman year. However, he could get his mouth open to eat pizza. No size or style was safe. Larry was a hungry growing teenager and loved the pizza parties after a game at our house. Sandy, Kiely, and Alexa always had a soft place in their hearts for him. There was always extra pizza or chocolate chip cookies steered his way or put aside to take home.

Although Larry was a man of few words at the start of his high school career, he got along very well with his teammates. We were all fortunate that a stellar collection of high school talent blended together during those years. Today, if you spoke with Larry, you would never know what a quiet kid he once was. Conversation and smiles flow easily from him now. He has undergone quite the transformation into the confident man he is. Larry has come such a long way from the kid who held everything inside except on the basketball court

"Why do you write like you're running out of time?"

The famous lyric from the Broadway sensation *Hamilton* always reminds me of how Larry played basketball. He never stopped on the court. He played hard and powerful all the time. On most nights he was unstoppable. You can see it happening today around our nation and the world. The Black Lives Matter Movement is empowering so many inner-city kids during their high school careers. These kids are full of passion, drive, and energy that pushes them in many different directions, both good and bad. This backlash at the social injustices they and their families endure each day can feel overwhelming. I think many inner-city youths ask themselves the same questions: *Can I change my life through basketball and sports? Do I have what it takes to earn a scholarship?*

The city player seemed to be railing at society through their efforts on the basketball court. Young kids expressed their angst through their playful creativity, passion, and sometimes disappointment on the blacktop and hardwood. Kids like Larry Gilbert knew the time and score not just for a game of basketball but for life. They knew at times it was going to be an uphill battle to get to a level playing field. Larry fought hard for every inch of ground gained.

After graduating from HHS, Larry Gilbert played for high-power junior colleges out West and for D1 Bethune Cookman in Florida. He did not let anything stand between him and a bright future.

D1 State Championship Game
March 18, 1995
Worcester Centrum
Holyoke 65, South Boston 78

Holyoke: J. Reyes 0-0-0, W. Cabrera 2-3-2-15, L. Gilbert 8-2-3-25, R. Sisson 4-4-12, P. Cavette 0-0-0, E. Davis 4-2-10, C. Washington 0-3-3. Totals: 18-5-14-65.
South Boston: M. Mack 4-6-1-25, I. Almedia 1-5-7, J. Depina 8-7-23, B. Lebron 1-0-2, R. Roberts 1-2-1-8, D. VanHennigan 1-0-2, C. Lewis 4-3-11. Totals: 23-5-17-78.

The powerful forward always played his best when facing top-notch competition. In our state championship game against South Boston, Larry was our leading player. Southie was lighting quick, led by future UMass stars Monty Mack and Jonathan DePina. We were fast, but they were faster at all positions. Except at Larry's small forward spot.

The game started, and Southie knocked us back with their speed. We turned it over against their pressure defense and had to use a couple of time-outs to settle our kids down. Slowly through the first half, the Knights adjusted to the fighter-jet speed of South Boston.

South Boston was built in 1901 in Telegraph Hill. It was one of the first public schools in Dorchester Heights. The school played an integral part in the Boston busing crisis of the '70s. There were days of violence, protests, and arrests. Sadly, violence in the summer leading up to this state championship season had reared its ugly head again. The South Boston team had lost a friend and teammate to street violence and had dedicated their season in his memory.

Their coach was Bill Loughnane, who would go on to win three D1 State Championships at South ('92, '95, and '96). Coach played for Jim Calhoun at Northeastern, so he had a wonderful pedigree and insight into the coaching elite. Coach Calhoun described Loughnane as follows: "He was like a coach on the floor. He played with a quiet toughness that you always find in a South Boston/Dorchester kid." Calhoun went on, "He was one of the fiercest competitors. He would never taunt someone, but if you were going to beat him, you had better bring your best." (*Patriot Ledger*, article by Paul Kenney, March 1, 2008).

Larry was ready to bring his best to the game that night, and his outstanding play brought the Holyoke crowd back to a place of belief: perhaps it was possible for HHS to win the game and deliver the first-ever state championship in basketball back to our school and community.

With just under three minutes to go in the first half, Larry slashed to the basket and made a Kobe Bryant finish at the rim taking on two South Boston defenders. The basket put us up by one point. It was a tough fight back in the first half for us, but our crowd went wild. In that instant we had a sense that we could hang in and win the game.

Then just like that, it was over. As soon as Larry scored, Southie executed the inbound pass into the prototypical Dean Smith sideline fast break. Ball to Depina, pushing it up the court. Mack sprinted to the three point area (I hesitate to say line because he shot from such length with such great accuracy that he was virtually impossible to defend). If you came up too fast on a close out, he would blow by you. One pass and one dribble by DePina, catch and shoot by Mack right in front of our bench. They were unstoppable. Even from what seemed like forty-five feet away from the basket. And that was the game. Our lead lasted a moment.

The rest of the night was like most of the first half—trying to catch up and compete. Larry had an amazing game in defeat and would set himself up for a great summer of travel hoop. His senior year would see him crowned the best player in our area, becoming only the fourth player from HHS to win the Lahovich Award.

CHAPTER 43

GILBERT VERSUS FREEMAN, TIME-OUT, AND NO FOCUS

Western Mass D1 Championship Title #2
March 11, 1995
Springfield Civic Center
Longmeadow 64, Holyoke 76

Holyoke: J. Reyes 1-2-4, W. Cabrera 9-1-1-22, L. Gilbert 4-5-13, R. Sisson 6-4-16, P. Cavette 2-0-4, E. Davis 5-2-12, C. Washington 3-0-6. Totals: 28-1-13-76.

Longmeadow: J. Heaps 4-1-4-15, T. Allen 2-1-2-9, R. Bryant 3-1-7, B. Cullinan 6-2-14, G. Berte 2-1-5, K. Freeman 3-2-6-14. Totals: 18-4-16-64.

Playing for the Western Mass Championship for the third year in succession was quite a thrill and a great tribute to the core of the Holyoke kids coming through our basketball program at this time. This outstanding group would go on to play in four consecutive finals, winning two and losing the other two in overtime battles. The Fab 3 of Larry Westbrook, Dave O'Connell, and Gary Grumoli had captured the Paper City fans' attention with three consecutive runs to the Western Mass finals at the start of the '80s. This group of Purple Knights won two of three titles but ran into some guy named Patrick Ewing in the state tournament each year, struggling to capture the elusive state title.

One of our championship games was against the Longmeadow High School Lancers. There were three things that made this Lancer–Purple Knight matchup interesting. First, Larry Gilbert, Wilfredo Cabrera, and Robert Sisson were accelerating their games at warp speed. Second, Gilbert would be facing a good friend and family mentors in the Freemans. Third was the number of excellent high school players and overall talent that took the court for this championship game. Longmeadow's roster consisted of Kevin Freeman (NCAA championship UConn and pro player), Jay Heaps (Duke University basketball and soccer player, and coach of the MLS Revolution), and Tim Allen (one of the smartest and toughest players to handle). Add in Bryant, an All Western Mass football player. Both Berte and Cullinan were exceptional multisport athletes, making the Lancers a highly talented team and fierce competition.

In comparison, the Knights' core was very solid. Robert Sisson went on to excel at Cushing Academy and was conference rookie of the year playing at Salem State. Joey Reyes attended Clark University. Cedric Washington was an All Star for Boston College Football, earning MVP at the Hula Bowl game. Wilfredo Cabrera played for Salem State and possessed an amazing jump shot. Eddie Davis, possibly the fastest human at dribbling a basketball from one end of the court to the other, was a great contributor, with additional role players in Cavette, Lawson, Langhorne, Barrett, Santos, Ortiz, and Sanchez.

Both teams were ready to play and win the game, so with tons of talent on display, the game commenced. The result was a down-to-the-wire contest. Yet believe it or not, it was the mascots that stole the show.

Yes! The Lancer and the Knight, both fan favorites, were great at entertaining the crowd with their mock jousting routine. During a time-out with about three minutes to play, trying to make a few critical adjustments to close the game, I realized that there was no focus in the huddle. My team was only interested in the buzz coming from the stands concerning the mascots. I had wanted to make a key point during the time-out: get the ball to Larry along the baseline. Kevin Freeman had been injured and taken off on a stretcher. Fortunately, he was OK, but Kevin's injury limited the Longmeadow interior defense. I stressed to our guys the importance of getting to the rim. No settling!

Every coach and player knows the clock always seems to go into molasses mode when you have a lead at the end of a game. Over time, I learned to stop thinking about winning or losing during the game. My focus needed to stay on the present and coaching the next play. I tried to take as much emotion out of the situation as possible. Being emotional clouds the decision-making process and sequentially hurts your team's chances to win. Stressing about an outcome not yet determined is a good way to lose track of knowing the time and score.

We had controlled the first half of the game fairly well, establishing a 35-to-27 lead. Wilfredo was shooting lights out, hitting one jump shot after the other off of our thumbs set. The play consisted of an old Kansas shuffle cut action with a back screen into an elbow post player who rolls to the hoop. This play, coupled with a screen, the screener action, was enough to put us over the top. Wilfredo would come off on a curl and nail his shot. There was not much the Lancers could do without putting pressure on the ball. This was our big advantage.

Just as Southie was a little faster at each position, so were the Knights when we were up against this talented group of Lancers. We could run our plays at our own pace. During the first half of the game, Will scored 15 points. I knew Longmeadow would try to adjust on Wilfredo during the second half, but Cabrera added another 7 points, finishing the game with 22 points. However, the closer of the game was Larry Gilbert, pouring in twelve points with drives to the hoop. As Longmeadow tried to get out faster on the shooters, it left their defense exposed, getting beat off the dribble. As usual, Larry made them pay.

CHAPTER 44

THAT SOUND AND MULLINS MAGIC

If we ever doubted the role sound plays during a sports competition, the COVID-19 vacuum clarified how important a live audience is in influencing a game. Whether it be cheers, screams, or boos, the noise from fans is a huge factor.

I always knew when that special sound of belief showed up to indicate victory in a championship matchup. At times, it was a dramatic event like Robert Sisson's out-of-nowhere three-pointer to beat Central for the Western Mass title in '93. The utter explosion and the sheer cacophony of joy that erupted from the Holyoke fans was undeniable. The disbelief and sadness on the opponent's side was heart-wrenching to be sure.

It is very different to what we experience on most of our days on this blue planet. That delivery of sound can emanate from a heroic shot or a well-designed play. And in two of our championship games, a "diamond slash" ushered in that sound.

The slash is a play we ran late in the game, hopefully so our opponent would not react well to it. We used it when inbounding under our own hoop and looking to score. The four Knights on the court set up around our foul line, spaced about five to seven feet from each other in the shape of a diamond. When our inbounder was handed the ball by the official, our four players slashed in four different directions, dissecting our diamond setup. Both a man and zone defense would have a hard time defending this play.

Eddie Davis finished off Longmeadow, and Tony Zieja did the same against Cathedral, running the diamond slash. Neither was a game-winning buzzer beater, but each time a basket was scored, indicating to our bench, our opponents, and our fans that the game was over.

It is done. You are finished. The title is ours.

When you coach in so many different types of contests, you come to realize that sound from the crowd signifies something special has happened and is collectively shared.

D1 State Semifinals
March 15, 1995
Mullins Center, UMass Amherst
Holyoke 76, Saint John's 65 OT

Holyoke: D. Sanchez 0-0-0, J. Reyes 0-3-3, W. Cabrera 4-2-5 19, L. Gilbert 5-2-8-24, R. Sisson 6-9-21, T. Lawson 0-0-0, P. Cavette1-0-2, T. Langhorne 0-0-0, E. Davis 1-2-4, J. Barrett 0-0-0, C. Washington 1-0-3, J. Santos 0-0-0. Totals: 71-5-27-76.
Saint John's: J. Taylor 2-0-4, M. Vicens 1-0-3, M. Teixeira 4-1-1-12, J. Demember 2-2-6, J. Frew 1-3-6, G. Donia 11-2-24, J. Brennan 5-0-10. Totals: 24-3-8-65.

In '95 we were on the ropes against Saint John's in the state semifinals at the Mullins Center on the UMass Amherst campus. The Shrewsbury-based all-boys private school was coached by the legendary Bob Foley. Coach Foley has not lost many games in his career and has secured over nine hundred victories to date.

Late in the game we began to press, rattling the Saint John's team. This led to a tie game in regulation, forcing overtime. Suddenly, there was that sound again!

The crowd was urging us on, believing in our ability to win the game. Thanks to Cedric Washington, who buried a Damion Lillard three-point shot that shook the stands right down to the Jack Leaman court. The Knights took the lead and went on to win the game, advancing in the tournament.

Then there was Wilvaldo Cabrera's baseline line drive late in the game, again at the Mullins Center, igniting that momentous sound as we topped Central for the Western Mass title. Or JoJo Pollard's press breaker layup at AIC, when we defeated Cathedral in the championship game. The sound erupted, roaring through everyone's ears and into their hearts.

Of course, this sound does not just occur during the playoffs. High school sports are very competitive, and the sound can be found during fierce regular-season games too.

That sound made itself known when the Knights snapped Central's eighty-five-game winning streak.

That sound appeared during Ramon Cosme's no-look pass to Matt Gubala for a streaking layup, which gave the team a double-digit lead in the fourth quarter.

Though elusive, that sound lingers in the air above the fans in the bleachers; like the beautiful fireflies lighting up a June night, it only lasts an instant before it is gone.

On a side note, here are a few sounds that I love and remember fondly:

- The Blue Angels air show (the sound of freedom).
- The high-pitch explosion of an Armory crowd at a Holyoke High versus Holyoke Catholic game.
- The crashing waves of the White Sands Beach, CT, shoreline.
- The USS *Nautilus* practice submerging in Long Island Sound (kaboom!).
- The frenzy from fans in Boston Garden when Havlicek stole the ball. When Russ inbounded off the guide wire, I turned to my dad in the upper deck of the old Boston

Garden. It was simultaneously the quietest and loudest place on the planet. On the call with Johnny Most was Al Grenert. As I've mentioned, Al Grenert was a scholastic basketball and baseball star at Holyoke High School. His sports career was interrupted by service in the marines during World War II. Grenert excelled in the same two sports at New York University, where he played for three seasons. Grenert played professional baseball and professional basketball. He was also a very successful head basketball coach for Nashua High school and Saint Anselm's College in New Hampshire (Pro Basketball Encyclopedia).

- The sound that rolls up from Arthur Ashe Stadium after an exciting rally at the US Open.
- The names of students being called out during high school and college graduation ceremonies.
- Crickets.
- Bhima's and Pete's barking.
- Waves rolling in on Lucy Vincent Beach.
- Basketballs dribbled during warm-ups.
- Sneakers squeaking on the court.
- The Fenway roar when Yaz or Big Papi hit one out of the park or over the Green Monster.
- Disney Joy.
- The crinching of a good kick serve.
- Max (our Yorkie) sleeping.
- The laughter of my grandchildren Syius and MJ when they wrestle.
- And of course, Washington's three-point shot in OT against Saint John's.

Note: In this state semifinal vs The Pioneers the Purple Knights converted 27 of 33 from the foul line. Cedric's game-winning three-pointer was the only field goal we made in OT. However, we made 16 of 18 from the foul strip in the extra session.

CHAPTER 45

ELECTION EVE

On November 2, 2020, ninety-three million Americans had already cast their vote. President Trump and the Republicans were banking on voter suppression, intimidation, and litigation to win a second term. All around the country, states had activated the National Guard to deal with any disturbances from one side of the ticket or the other concerning the outcome of the election.

The world was watching and hoping the great experiment could pull itself up from the mess we were in. Hope is such a powerful gift, and for so many people in the world, that is what America represents: hope for a better life.

On top of the election, COVID-19 was still surging, with the second wave sweeping across the country. Massachusetts had imposed a tightening up on gatherings and restaurant hours. In fact, a 10:00 p.m. curfew had been instituted across the Commonwealth. Meanwhile, the world struggled to find a new normal. Professional sports struggled to figure out how to play in a time of social distancing. College football was trying to get games in, as well as high school football.

During this tumultuous time, one wondered if anything positive came from the Trump presidency and the COVID-19 global pandemic. For certain, both exposed what many people in the front lines of society were up against on a daily basis. The struggles facing teachers, doctors, nurses, pharmacists, grocery store workers, municipal employees, and other essential employees started to emerge to the rest of society. On top of that, the various challenges facing American families to find work, feed their own, and keep themselves healthy were constantly under siege.

Like John Wooden preaches through his pyramid of success, the base has to be strong and in place to produce competitive excellence. John Wooden's base pyramid characteristics (industriousness, friendship, loyalty, cooperation, and enthusiasm) consisted of qualities needed for the chance to achieve excellence. Wooden's pyramid works in life as well as on the basketball court. The fabric of our nation is no different. In America our base of lifting up and strengthening our essential workers and families has been a neglected commodity for many years. A tearing down of the structural practices that block the poor, women, minorities, and low-to-middle-class Americans from having a fair shot is long overdue and necessary. Just like Hamilton belts out, "I am not throwing away my shot....I'm just like my country. I'm young, scrappy, and hungry. I am not throwing away my shot!" This election was the American public's shot to turn things around and head in the right direction of progress for all.

On election eve, my daughter Alexa sent me a poem by Langston Hughes titled "Let America Be American Again," in which he speaks to all the dreams of all the people who were here, who came here, or who were brought here against their own free will. Miranda, Wooden, and Hughes all knew the time and score about America and what made people want to be here. They understood those dreams because they were their dreams too.

CHAPTER 46

PAPO AND THE BIG MAN

D1 State Semifinals
March 9, 1999
Mullins Center, UMass Amherst
Holy Name 78, Holyoke 50

Holy Name: McClain 1-1-5, Lewandowski1-0-2, McGuirk 1-0-2, Latteir 1-0-2, Rauktis 2-1-7, McNamare 2-3-2-15, Moore 2-3-7, Nelson 3-1-9, LaFlamme 1-0-2, Collins 3-2-4-16, N. Fingleton 5-2-12. Totals: 20-9-13-78.

Holyoke: J. Hobert 5-1-13, E. Mattos 4-2-10, W. Cabrera 7-1-1-18, D. Matos 1-1-4, M. Vasquez 1-0-3, N. Almodovar 1-0-2. Totals: 17-4-4 50.

Miguel Vasquez, known as Papo to the Happy Valley, was a dynamic player for the Purple Knights. Not much taller than four-foot-eleven, he was a whirlwind of energy and speed. The Purple Knights version of Muggsy Bogues played the role of underdog because of his size. However, Miguel never played small. In fact, Miguel played like he was a six-foot-seven power forward. He scrapped for loose balls, got more rebounds than our bigs some games, and terrified the opposing guards bringing the ball up court.

"Coach, I never saw him coming" were words I often heard from opposing players after they went up against our Miguel. One time an opposing player who had just experienced the Vasquez defensive tornado expressed to me the hope that Miguel was a senior.

"Coach, what grade is Miguel? Please tell me he is a senior!" The tormented player had obviously seen enough of Papo and wanted *no mas*!

Miguel was a solid contributing member of our Western Mass Championship team in '01. Yet, it was a perfectly timed photograph that appeared in the *Springfield Union* newspaper that gained Papo national status in *USA Today* and other national publications.

In the state semifinals being played at the Mullins Center at UMass Amherst, we were up against an exceptional squad from Holy Name in Worcester, MA. Coached by Pittsfield native JP Ricarrdi, baseball scout for the Oakland A's and future GM of the Toronto Blue Jays, they were loaded with talent and size. Their tallest player, Neil Fingleton, stood at seven-foot-seven. Later on this high school baller played one of the giants in HBO's *Game of Thrones* series.

Fingleton, who hailed from the UK, was going to attend Worcester Academy but ended up at Holy Name instead. He was enormous and suffocated anything within fifteen feet of the hoop. He was a problem, but not as much of a problem as the flu bug that was devastating school communities across the state. I attempted to convince the MIAA to postpone the contest but was unsuccessful. I really didn't know if we could field a varsity group to play in such an important game due to sickness. I can tell you it was not a fun bus ride to the game. Players threw up on the way to the game, during the game, and on the way home. Sometimes things are stacked against you and all you can do is clean up the mess.

However, one positive that came from that game was Papo's photo. Miguel had switched onto Fingleton for a pick-and-roll sequence. As the switch occurred, the photo was captured. Fingleton at 7-foot-7 was being guarded by Vasquez at 4-foot-11. They say a picture is worth a thousand words, and they are right.

On a sad note, Neil Fingleton recently passed away. I hope he had some happiness in his acting and college basketball stints, the latter of which began for him as a North Carolina Tar Heel and finished at the College of the Holy Cross in Worcester. As I've mentioned, *Big Smooth,* a Paul Stainthorpe–directed documentary on Neil Fingleton, was released in 2023.

CHAPTER 47

9/11 AND SOTOLONGO

Everyone remembers where they were and what they were doing on September 11, 2002. I was teaching on the third floor of HHS. It was a class in which students studied both the Holocaust and Apartheid. Racing into the room, my coteacher Gilberto Sotolongo told us that the United States was under attack. He explained a plane had just crashed into one of the Twin Towers, soon followed by another plane into the second tower.

Gilberto Sotolongo was from the school of hard knocks. Gil made it out of the Bronx and a troubled neighborhood life, which carried over into a challenging high school experience. But challenges were something Gil never eschewed. By the time he finished his teaching career in public education, he was one of the most respected members of our community. Sometimes the most challenging students can make the best teachers, which is exactly what he was.

Gil was an outstanding teacher, husband, father, grandfather, and community activist. His wife Esther was also a teacher, and together they represented hope and success to our growing Latino community in Holyoke. They raised three great kids (Joshue, Cindy, and Salene). I even got to coach one of their grandchildren at HHS, Justin Colon. Justin was a very good player, had a strong drive to the basket, and always worked hard on defense. I also remember him giving me a hard time about his favorite team, the LA Lakers.

It was a benefit to my teaching career to encounter and work with many diverse educators. Each individual offered something special and unique that made them truly successful in the classroom. For Gil, it was his street cred. He had seen it all. He had found his way to the Pioneer Valley through his USAF assignment to Westover Air Force Base and formed roots. At this time, the base was a booming part of US Strategic Air Command.

Not far up the road, in the "Town That Fell from the Stars," Gil enrolled in the University without Walls program conducted on the UMass campus. I am not sure how many made it through this program, but I am thankful Gil did. He raised his family in Holyoke, and they were all contributing members of the community.

My experience coteaching with Gilberto was not the first time we had crossed paths. Gil was a regular in our Lynch after-school basketball games. I always tried to get on his team. Why? you ask. First, Gil liked to pass the ball and I liked to shoot. Second, he was the only guy who would accept the challenge of guarding Chet Dudley. As I mentioned before, I met Chet's elbow on a number of occasions. I became tired of going to the emergency room for stitches, so anyone who wanted the job was OK with me.

Like on the basketball court, Gil took no prisoners in class. It was his way or the highway. He was not buying into the "Oh, woe is me" philosophy that has crippled so many educators and students in public education. He held all students accountable for their work and behavior in our class—black, white, Hispanic, Asian, or Native American. If a disruptive or unmotivated student was disrespectful in class, he would quietly ask them to step outside for a conference. This worked most times, and as tough as Gil was, he absolutely never raised his voice or threatened students.

Gil presented a calm, determined dressing down of the student with direct instructions on what he expected from them. His short podcast to the offending student would always culminate with a follow-up visit or phone call to the student's household.

A long career in teaching produces many memorable days in which the outside world invaded the routines of a normal day at school. Teachers had the tough job of helping kids through the day and creating a calming environment that was safe for students. Beyond 9/11, there were many days that I encountered as an educator and coach that demanded such leadership and guidance from all staff, including the *Challenger* disaster, a school strike, the murder of Officer John Dinapoli, the funeral of Officer Dave O'Connell (a Purple Knight basketball legend), budget cuts, 245 teachers being laid off, Proposition 2 2/12, weapons of mass destruction, RIFs, receivership, the O. J. Simpson trial, and the crushing memories of our students whom we lost far too soon but who inspired us and had a profound impact on our community.

When you are an educator and a coach, there are always days when school is not about the subject taught and practice is not about the game played. Rather, it is about helping your community stand up when everything and everyone wants to knock you down. My students were always the best part of my career. When they hurt, I hurt, but I tried not to show it. I always tried my best to be present and show them a way forward.

When Gil raced into class that day, no doubt the kids looked nervous about what was going on in our country. Gil grabbed a TV and rolled it into the classroom. As he was doing this, he calmly explained what was happening and told the student not to panic.

At this time, our school system had many Latino and Hispanic students enrolled. Many had families and friends in NYC, and they were understandably scared for them. Gil knew that they would be worried about the tragic events of the day and how it would affect their loved ones. He swung into action, and like so many other Holyoke teachers had done for so many years in the Holyoke Public Schools, he put his students and their needs first. The Bronx native accomplished this by continually talking, reducing the high anxiety level that only grew as more reports on the attack came in.

Note: At the time this is being written, the CDC had just given approval to start rolling out the COVID-19 vaccines. The global pandemic showed us how much we have cut from our infrastructures. At the top of the list was our commitment to public health. As I listened to NPR reporting on this topic, they mentioned the city of Detroit. They noted that before the 9/11 attack against the USA, the Motor City employed over seven hundred public health workers. As of today, December 11, 2020, they employ five. Our nation's funding switched heavily to our military after 9/11. The net result was a drastic decline to health education and the general infrastructures of our nation, which are desperately needed to produce a healthy quality of life.

CHAPTER 48

A REGIONAL SCHEDULE FOR THE PURPLE KNIGHTS, THE WHALERS, AND COCA-COLA TO HOOP HALL

The Knights played at least one game against five of the six New England States during my tenure as boys varsity head coach (somehow we missed the Granite State). We also took on five teams from New York and one from Florida, the Sunshine State. In the Bay State, we competed against four schools from the Berkshires, five from central Mass, four from the South Shore and Cape, and thirty-seven different schools from Hampden and Hampshire counties. I believed it was important for our players to see other teams and different players from all walks of life. It made us a better program in the long run, and it definitely made me a better coach.

From New England, we competed against Vermont's Brattleboro High School, Connecticut's Warren Harding High School in Bridgeport and New Britain High School, Maine's Deering High School in Portland, and Rhode Island's Classical High School in Providence.

From New York, we took the hardwood against All Hollows, Monsignor McClancy, East Elmhurst, Haldane Central, and Wings Academy.

From Florida, we went up against Pine Crest Academy.

From Massachusetts we competed against the Berkshires' Pittsfield, Taconic, Hoosac Valley, and Drury; central Mass's Saint John's, Holy Name, Leominster, Gardner, and Groton Dunstable; the South Shore and Cape's New Bedford, Brockton, Dennis-Yarmouth, and Cardinal Spellman; Boston's South Boston, Boston English, East Boston, and Jeremiah Burke; and Hampden and Hampshire counties' Central, Cathedral, Commerce, Putnam, Tech, Classical, Chicopee Comp, Agawam, West Springfield, Minnechaug, Westfield, Longmeadow, East Longmeadow, Amherst, Chicopee, Northampton, South Hadley, Greenfield, Ludlow, Belchertown, Holyoke Catholic, Sci Tech, New Leadership, Sabis, Dean Tech, Pope Francis, and Pioneer Valley.

In total, I faced fifty-six different opponents during my coaching career, all of whom tested the Knights' skill and determination.

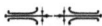

Our basketball staff and fans were always excited to get a peek at our upcoming schedule. We played against great teams from the Berkshires to Cape Cod and many others throughout our great state of Massachusetts. One special in-state rivalry was our thirteen-game series against New Bedford High School. The Whalers were always one of the strongest programs in the state. The Big Three of Brockton, Durfee, and New Bedford were so much larger than most schools in our state that they were placed in a league all their own. In fact, at one time they represented the three largest high schools east of the Mississippi River. The MIAA amended scheduling rules to help them find games.

The Whalers were coached by fellow Assumption Greyhound Eddie Rodrigues. Eddie and I both graduated from Assumption College in Worcester. We followed each other's coaching careers even though we were in different parts of the state. Like Steven Wright once said, "It's a small world, but I wouldn't want to paint it."

Few of our trips to the southeast coast produced wins, but we did get a victory once or twice on their home court. Overall, the Knight's record against New Bedford was 5-8. One of our most memorable victories achieved there could be directly attributed to a size and length advantage we had over the Whalers, which dismantled their vaunted diamond press (1-2-1-1). Eddie's teams pressed the entire game and wore opponents out at the end. They were not always big, but they were strong, fast, and in great shape. Coach Rodrigues was smart with the pressure defense. He would move the press around to full court and then back to three quarters and finally a half-court trap. The Whalers mentor never let you or your kids feel like they had things figured out.

In spite of the Whalers' pressure defense, this particular group of Knights played with poise and control, using their height to pass out of traps and not dribble into double teams, which often resulted in the dreaded live ball turnover. Julius Hobert and James Yates scored inside and on layups when we broke the full-court press. It was a tense game, and Coach Eddie was miffed with the refs. A number of close calls went our way at the end, and it didn't sit well with the coach. Most coaches and fans feel that the home team will get some close calls when a game is coming down the stretch, but that was not the case that day.

On the way out to the bus, our assistant coach Jim Hobert stopped to talk with one of the officials. Coach Rodrigues entered the conversation,

"Boy, it sounds like you know that guy!" he said to Jim.

"Yes, I do. That's Eddie Hurley." His family was from Holyoke, and the Hoberts and Hurleys had been friends forever. "Little Eddie," as his family called him, had a roots in Holyoke and a heritage of officiating as his grandfather was a major league umpire in the American League.

"Nao acredito nisso," Rodrigues said in Portuguese, then shook Jim's hand and walked away mumbling something about a home court advantage.

It is a small world after all.

Today, Coach Rodrigues is a member of the MBCA Hall of Fame. He brought two state championships to his hometown, along with tons of guidance and love to the youth of New Bedford. After stepping away from duties as New Bedford coach, he served as athletic director at Wareham High School and assisted longtime friend Brian Baptiste in the UMass Dartmouth men's basketball program.

CHAPTER 49

RINGS, RINGS, RINGS, AND MORE RINGS

It felt like my hand was being crushed. There was no room to latch on to the man's hand to greet him. The five rings were enormous, bright, and shiny. I am not sure, but I think he had a few rings on the other hand as well. Charles Bentley and his five rings were quite a sight. I really needed a pair of Oakleys just to dim the shine emanating from the man. Each ring represented a Connecticut State Championship. Each ring was earned through Coach Bentley's interesting coaching style: five in, five out, and substitutions every four minutes. His goal was to wear you down and get you in the end.

On this day our seven core, rotating players were strong enough to best the Bridgeport Five. They were a good team, but a far cry from the elite teams led by Charles Smith. Yes, the same Charles Smith who played for the New York Knicks. Coach Bentley and Smith dominated the Nutmeg State for years.

A buffet was provided for both teams after the game, so I had an opportunity to talk with Coach Bentley a bit about his city. I asked him what the difference was between his past teams and his present group of kids.

"No difference!" he exclaimed. "They are all good kids. Love to coach 'em all." Then he paused a minute and said, "Well, they did tear down the projects."

Coca-Cola Classic
December 27, 1995
Springfield Civic Center
All Hollows 44, Holyoke 35

All Hollows: Lacayo 1-1-5, McCay 1-0-2, Thompson 4-1-9, Harley 3-0-6, Gist 3-1-7, R. Gibson 5-2-12. Totals: 17-2-4-44.
Holyoke: L. Gilbert 4-0-8, C. Washington 3-0-9, P. Cavette 2-0-4, M. Hobert 1-0-2, E. Davis 4-0-8, J. Barrett 2-0-4. Totals: 13-3-0-35.

Before the now enormously successful Hoop Hall Classic held in Springfield, MA, over Martin Luther King Jr. Weekend, there was a much smaller event named the Coca-Cola Classic. The tournament paired two local high school programs against two quality out-of-state teams. The Purple Knights were in at the beginning of this event. It was a great experience for players to compete against quality out-of-state opponents.

In our first game in the Classic, we took on All Hollows, which included future Georgetown star Reese Gibson. The team, coached by John Carey, was extremely well disciplined. I think our fans were expecting a wild game with players racing up and down the court as in the style of NYC basketball. Run and gun! I had been given a heads-up on Coach Carey's style by Jim Powell, head coach for the men's basketball program at AIC and recently retired advance scout for the Indiana Pacers.

"Nope, not with Coach Carey," Jim explained to me at his Shamrock Hoop Camp in Springfield. "Coach doesn't recruit, and he feels the only way he can compete with the big boys in the Catholic league is to control tempo."

The shot clock was set to forty-five seconds for the event, and Coach Carey's players made us play defense for all of it. A couple of late three-pointers from Cedric Washington got us close, but in the end, it was not enough to get us the win. In fact, we only scored thirty-five points the entire game, the lowest number of any varsity team I coached. It was a great coaching lesson for me. Again, it demonstrated for me the beauty of Dr. Naismith's game. There are so many ways to play, so many ways to get things done.

I had the opportunity to ask Coach Carey why he chose this style of play. He certainly had very good players who could play at a faster pace. While he agreed, he explained that his team competed in a very tough league.

"I don't go after kids. Too many kids in the city jump around from school to school each year. It's the discipline...that's what their families see and want from me and my basketball program." In the state of New York, players did not have to sit a year if they transferred as was required in some states, including Massachusetts, so shuffling players around was not uncommon.

Coach Carey went on, "They are hoping it transfers to help them stay away from trouble on the streets."

The other standout from this game was the foul shots. If you are a hoop fan, you have heard the cliche "Games are won and lost at the foul line." I usually did not have to worry about this. In more than eight hundred games as a varsity coach, this was the only game where my team shot absolutely zero foul shots.

That's right, you read correctly: Zero. Zilch. Nada. Nothing. Zip.

Mike Deary, an exceptional official from Longmeadow, had this to say about the contest: "Coach, they didn't come within three feet of fouling any of your kids." A block call when they tried to step in was about it for the All Hollows team. This was what I loved about coaching high school basketball. No two games were ever the same. Each night was different, and each night you learned something about coaching and yourself.

Certainly one of the many blessings I received through my coaching career was the wonderful people I met from the coaching ranks. Playing a regional schedule exposed me to many different styles and interesting people who brought different perspectives about the game and life.

On the occasions when a Purple Knight foe had to travel a good distance to play at our gym, I would always like to send the team back on the bus ride home with some pizza. During one of these games, Tom Brassil, hall of fame basketball and baseball coach, was working as the site manager. The horn sounded to start the second half of the game. Tom brought to my attention that a number of Spaulding 1000s were missing from our ball rack. The warm-up balls were placed in the shooting rack for the teams to practice with before the game and at halftime.

"Coach, your rack is empty, but I will check some things out," Tom said to me.

After some investigation, Coach Brassil found a number of our balls had gone into the visiting team players' travel bags. After the game, I mentioned this to our visitors' assistant coach and he assured me he would get on it. The coach retrieved the missing balls, and all was well.

As our guests boarded their bus to return home, four party-size, sizzling-hot pizzas arrived compliments of John Silvestri, owner of Italian Friendly Restaurant in Holyoke.

"Enjoy, guys!" John piped up. The head coach thanked John and invited his assistant and team manager to come to the front of the bus to get some slices before the hungry teenagers devoured the four boxes.

"Smells great, Coach! Seniors first!" a player voiced from the back of the bus.

Then the visitors' coaching staff did something that indicated that they were tuned into the time and score of coaching high school basketball. As the hungry teenagers inched closer to the hot pizza, their head coach handed the boxes of pizza back to me. "Coach, take these to a shelter. Our team isn't very hungry."

You would have had to see the looks of disbelief on his players' faces, but little did they know that they had just discovered the meaning of knowing the time and score. A lesson their head coach had long implemented into his playbook of life lessons for his team.

Coca-Cola Classic
December 28, 1995
Springfield Civic Center
Holyoke 74, Harding 56

Holyoke: Langhorne 0-1-1, L. Gilbert 7-0-14, C. Washington 1-1-1-6, P. Cavette 3-1-7, M. Hobert 4-2-10, E. Davis 10-4-24, J. Barrett 6-0-12. Totals: 31-1-9-74.

Harding: Gregory 4-1-9, Counts 1-0-2, Geter 1-0-2, Marshall 6-0-12, Williams 7-1-2-19, Doss 3-0-6, Hatton 1-0-2, Upchurch 3-1-2-10. Totals: 26-2-9-56.

CHAPTER 50

MLK WEEKEND

At the local level, Greg Procino is a fine basketball official. On the national level, he is the one person high school programs want to get a call from. Encompassing elite level programs and the local high schools, Greg put the Hoop Hall Classic together. I was very fortunate to coach the Knights in a number of Hoop Hall Classic contests. We had some interesting match-ups to test our program. There were great battles against the neighboring South Hadley Tigers. Coach Guiel was always a challenge to play against, with a team of great kids: Dubuc, Lacey, Lopes, Lunney, and O'Rourke. The games against South Hadley were a lot of fun.

Another memorable matchup was our win against Maine state champs Deering High School, from Portland. Then there was the night Eddie Almodovar carved up New Bedford. Two good wins for the Purple and White.

Regardless of when you got the call, when Greg was on the other line, you answered. One year Greg reached out to us about a game against Pine Crest, Florida, and future NBA star Brandon Knight. Another team had backed out, and the Hoop Hall was in a bind. A great feature about the hall of fame event was that Greg was able to pair teams for a fair contest. His goal was to make all the games as competitive as possible, resulting in a good, positive experience for the teams, coaches, and players involved. The opportunity to play a game on the wonderful Springfield College campus and James Naismith Court was always an enriching opportunity, win or lose.

I was happy to help Greg out and provide my team with an incredible chance to play an out-of-state team, and we played as hard as we could against Pine Crest. Mike Rohan did his best to guard Brandon Knight, but the Florida player put on quite a show. Mike had a moment or two against Brandon, crossing him over for a nice reverse layup and a clean strip of the future NBA first-round draft pick. In addition to Knight, Pine Crest had plenty of other outstanding players on their team. They beat us easily.

As a coach in Massachusetts, you are always aware of that ten-game victory mark as state teams are allowed to schedule twenty nonexemption games. To qualify for states, a team needed to win 50 percent of their schedule or finish first or second in their league. Today, teams can also qualify under a state power ranking formula. It was not without reservation that I accepted the invitation. It was an opportunity to help the hall of fame event and give something back to the game of basketball, which had been a positive influence in the lives of many Holyoke kids.

In making up our independent schedule, we usually had three or four games to fill. My rule of thumb was to try to schedule one independent matchup where we would be the favorite, one or two that would be competitive, and one where we would be considered the underdog. As Coach Yoast (Will Patton) said to Herman Boone (Denzel Washington) in the film *Remember the Titans*, "Leave no doubt." There is no doubt we were the underdogs in our game against Pine Crest, but even those games can help you learn both the time and score on the court and in life.

CHAPTER 51
ENGLISH CLASS

February 18, 1996
Holyoke High School
"Jinx" O'Connor Gym
Holyoke 114, Boston English 87

Holyoke: J. Athas 0-2-2, T. Langhorne 1-0-2, D. Guzman 2-2-4, L. Gilbert 11-13 33, C. Washington 7-2-1-21, M. Hobert 2-2-6, E. Davis 15-7-37, A. Rosado 1-0-2, J. Barrett 1-0-2, T. Steele 0-3-3. Totals: 39-2-30-114.

English: R. Wilshire 1-0-3, K. Andrews 5-10-0-3-43, T. Campbell 2-7-11, J. Rice 1-1-3, M. Russell 2-0-4, W. Evans 2-1-3-10, H. Alverez 2-0-4, M. McGriff 1-1-0-5, N. Molynneux 2-0-4.

Eddie Davis was the fastest human being I ever coached. To this day, Boston English is still trying to figure out what that blur was moving up and down the court, scoring bucket after bucket. The Boston city powerhouse team had traveled to Paper City and met its match for fast break basketball on this Saturday matinee in the cold month of February. English was accustomed to being the one giving out the fast break headaches to opponents.

With the incredible speed and talent of our power three, they were not able to get away with it this time. Eddie Davis, Larry

Gilbert, and Cedric Washington put on quite a show with the three Purple Knights scoring 91 points combined: Eddie Davis scored 37 points, Larry Gilbert 33, and Cedric Washington 21. It was racehorse basketball at its best. During time-outs, we could hear the English coaches telling their players to get back on defense, but they could not keep up with our players' speed.

This group had a great season but came up a bit short with an overtime loss in the Western Mass Championship to Commerce. The Knights had taken on a great regional schedule competing against All Hollows from NYC, Warren Harding from Connecticut, and English from Boston.

CHAPTER 52

"START LIKE THIS" AND FOUR HUNDRED WINS!

D1 Western Mass Preliminary Road
February 28, 2012
Holyoke High School
"Jinx" O'Connor Gym
Holyoke 79, Pittsfield 60

Holyoke: G. Godreau 1-1-2-7, A. Keeler 2-7-4-29, L. Vasquez 0-0-0, J. White 4-2-11, T. Cason 4-3-3-20, J. Sanchez 0-0-0, J. Lane 2-1-5, E. Rivera 1-0-3, J. Pabon 0-0-0, N. Rodriquez 0-0-0, M. Whitelock 2-0-4, M. Girard 0-0-0, R. Rodriquez 0-0-0. Totals: 15-12-13-79.
Pittsfield: B. Hamel 7-0-14, Cross 3-2-2-14, Adopo 6-1-4-19, Bradley 3-0-6, Hanford 1-0-2, Conant 1-1-3, Hopkins 0-2-2. Totals: 21-3-9-60.

A basketball game can be won at any point in the contest. Sport as theater tends to focus on last-second margins of victory. But if you want to win a game early and not stress out the entire game, I suggest you have a player like Austin Keeler start. The magic in Austin's game against the Pittsfield Generals was amazing that night. When the ball was in his hands, there was very little the opponent could do. He was a wonderful passer. Austin had great vision and timing to deliver the ball at just the right time to the right teammate. He was also ahead of most high school players at this time with his willingness to launch a three-point shot from just about any distance. When I first started coaching Austin, I thought he was trying to infuriate me by shooting the ball from way behind the three-point arc. The reality was he really believed he could make any shot from any distance. But over the course of the season, I learned to live with a few of his ill-advised heaves from what felt like Roberts Field.

During this preliminary round matchup in the western Mass state tournament at O'Connor Gym, both teams entered the game with a good chance of winning. The Generals were always tough competition and played fiercely. The excitement in the gym that night was electric, and the fans on both sides were ready to rock.

The jump ball tip went to Austin. He took two dribbles over half court and launched the ball. Swish. The Purple Knights fans went wild, while the Generals fans looked at each other in utter astonishment, thinking, *What just happened? What was that kid doing?*

If I am being honest, I was thinking the same thing myself.

High school playoff games can often get off to inconsistent starts, with the players' adrenaline taking over. Sometimes it works in your favor; sometimes it does not. He made the basket, but I was pretty sure he just did not understand where he was on the court. As the game continued, the team was off to a great start with multiple stops on defense. We kept pushing the ball up the court to Austin. The goal was to get some easy transition baskets right. Or so I thought.

Wrong again. As Austin Keeler crossed over half court, he was letting the shots fly.

Five attempts. Five three-pointers. Thank you very much, Dr. Stietz.

O'Connor Gym was bedlam. The Generals, their fans, and coaches were in triple F mode: free fall frenzy! At the end of the first quarter, Pittsfield changed strategies and doubled Austin whenever he got the ball. The Pittsfield coaches and players did their job of adjusting to make it a close contest, but Austin adjusted too. He passed out of the double teams, and our other Knights scored just enough to get us into the next round of the playoffs.

Austin finished with 29 points, including 7 three-pointers. The win over the Berkshire team was also an important game for me as it marked my 400th win as a coach for the Purple Knights. I did not mention it to the papers because I did not want to take anything away from our kids' nice playoff win and Austin's amazing game.

The last contest I coached for HHS was a playoff loss against Commerce High School in a Western Mass state quarterfinal. We had a couple of double-digit leads but could not put the Red Raiders away. We were without our top scorer Darius Diaz due to a sprained ankle, and his absence made a difference down the stretch when we needed some clutch shots to stop Commerce.

It is like I always say: *Sometimes the basketball gods have a mind of their own.*

At the time of our loss, I did not know that was going to be the last game I coached for the Holyoke Knights boys varsity basketball team. I would never lead a basketball team again after that night. In essence, my coaching career officially ended on April 15, 2015. My team had lost by a score of 8 to 3 when the State Board of Education voted to place the Holyoke Public Schools into Receivership.

Wood carving of Ramon Cosme by teacher Jim Barrett

CHAPTER 53

RAMON COSME

Family. Champion. Lahovich Winner. Pro player. HHS hall of famer. These are just a few things that come to mind when I think about Ramon Cosme. Ramon started off as a student and player, and became an important part of our family. He is a trusted, respected, and loved member of the Rigali clan.

The first time I witnessed Ramon playing basketball was at a clinic I did for the Holyoke Boys and Girls Club. Two things stood out right away. One, he was small. Two, he was incredibly skilled in most facets of the game. Slight and only about five-foot-three on a good day, he dominated the high school landscape for four seasons. Ramon had admiration from the entire Pioneer Valley because of his skill set on the court and his humanity off of it. He was accurately perceived as the ultimate underdog, and his smile, energy, and love for the game were infectious. He was inspiring to both his teammates and younger fans. As Holyoke's Hispanic population grew, Ramon became a symbol of the great promise of success and acceptance.

As is the case with all shining stars, not everyone wanted Ramon to succeed. There were letters and snide remarks that needed to be addressed and repudiated. Ramon dealt with the naysayers and bigotry the best way he knew how. He played harder, he improved his game every day, and he was respectful to everyone on his high school basketball journey. The old-timers who came from all over to watch him play were delighted by his willingness to reach out to them for a quick chat or advice. Ramon would sit with the veteran fans before a game and make them know how appreciative he was they had come to watch some high school basketball.

On top of his amazing attitude and gratitude, Ramon was a fierce competitor. He loved to win and hated to lose. Even when he had had a great game, he always took a team loss hard. Many high school kids are less upset with a loss if they have had a good game. They focus more on their stats than the overall outcome for the team, but not Ramon. He wanted the team to win, and so it is wonder his great play often made his teammates better. In addition to the help Ramon provided to our basketball program as an exemplary basketball player and teammate, he also enriched me personally by helping me understand the many structural and social injustices facing our minority community today.

Throughout his high school career, Ramon took many physical hits. One game, he sustained an elbow to his mouth. His lip was cut, and blood was everywhere. In the locker room, our trainer said he should go to the ER. Like most ERs on a Friday night, Holyoke's had the potential for a long wait. On the way out the door after the game, my wife Sandy caught Ramon.

"Let's see that lip," she demanded.

"I'll be fine, Mrs. Rigali." Ramon said. "Ice will be good."

Well, that was not good enough for Sandy. Over the course of her life, Sandra Meehan Rigali had engaged in many careers—mother, licensed practical nurse, preschool aide, elementary school teacher, and coach's wife. Taking matters into her own hands, she navigated Ramon to our van and up the street to the ER. My unofficial official assistant coach for life was concerned that with the ER so busy, they would gloss over the cut and send Ramon home without stitches. She knew the cut would need to be closed to heal properly. And the Irish mom with her Puerto Rican adopted son in tow was not going to leave that ER without the stitches. She was not going to chance the possibility of Ramon being dismissed simply because he was Hispanic *and* a teenager. Ramon got the stitches, and his lipped healed.

Another lesson came at the end of the basketball season. As I've mentioned, after our last game, I would always have the players and coaches over to the house for pizza, cake, and a batch of Kiely's famous chocolate chip cookies. At one such gathering, Ramon arrived a bit late to our house. He had to park on a side street some distance from our home; the city was resurfacing our circle, so there was not a lot of room near our home to park.

Ramon burst in the front door, "Coach! Sorry I'm late!" Ramon started. "It took a bit to walk around the neighborhood."

"Ramon, why didn't you just cut through the backyard?" I asked. "It would have saved you fifteen minutes of walking."

He looked at me like I was a chupacabra.

"Coach, we can't do that!" Ramon exclaimed. He continued to explain that a couple of Puerto Ricans cutting through someone's backyard at night in a predominately Anglo neighborhood would likely not end well. "Someone will call the cops if they see us!"

His comments made me think about how many of our minority kids have to think about taking that extra precaution so as not to draw any attention to themselves.

Ramon went on, "I didn't want anything to spoil your party, so we walked around." As if he was the one who needed to apologize!

Ramon's first year on varsity was challenging. We did not have a strong team, with the Knights only winning four games that season, the lowest win total in a season during my coaching career. Without having to worry about a championship run, we gave Ramon the keys to the car. It was a choice to build for the future. We would be as competitive as we could be that season, but we were playing a long game to see what could happen down the road.

1993 state sectional championship team. Ramon Cosme, Lahovich award winner, is pictured in the middle of the front row.

During that season, I saw special attributes in Ramon. He had arrived from Puerto Rico during his grade-school years. His family struggled with meeting the challenges of relocation to a different country. A great deal of the responsibility to assimilate into a new culture fell on Ramon's shoulders. His ability to be there for his family was one of the first admirable things off the basketball court I saw in him. He cared for others, like his family, and made them the priority in his life. He did this even when he was going through the same difficult transition from a warm tropical climate and Caribbean island culture to our bustling New England culture and cold winters. Ramon Cosme did not run from problems; he tried to solve them. That was the guy I wanted to run my team for four years.

Even in a short season like high school basketball in Massachusetts, where schools are limited to a twenty-game regular season, a lot can go down. You need a player leading your team who can keep things afloat and make adjustments when they are needed. You need a player who can deal with game situations that do not always go as planned. You need a player to motivate the rest of the team when competition gets heated. Ramon was this type of leader—he absolutely refused to give in and refused to let his team go into self-destruct mode.

Paul Dubuc, the exceptional high school coach for the South Hadley girls basketball program, would rave to me about Ramon (Paul had coached him in a city program at the Lawrence School gym): "Billy, no one, I mean no one, will ever take the ball from this kid!" No worries about live ball turnovers. No worries about being pressed. No worries about him playing great defense on the opposing point guards.

"So what can't he do?" I asked.

"Well…" Paulie thought for a minute. "He can't dunk!"

Ramon was lucky to run across Coach Paulie in his development. Ramon gained a true understanding of the most effective way for a point man to play. That is and always will be to get the ball to an open teammate. Point guards must be selfless and look for their teammates first, while sacrificing their scoring to benefit the team. Ramon was the only player I ever coached who could dominate a game without scoring a point. His trademark strengths were passing, ball handling, and pressure defense.

Surprisingly, the most community crowd refereeing toward Ramon occurred not in his first varsity season when the team won only four games but later in his career when he experienced more success. I suppose those who wanted to see the little Hispanic kid fail took solace in the team's poor record that year. The vitriol toward Ramon spilled out during his sophomore and junior years, when our team was very good, with the jealousy and spite ramping up significantly. Some people in our community were not accustomed to the new kids on the block (i.e., the Hispanic athletes) taking on the star roles.

In the past, Holyoke had been represented by great Euro ethnic stars such as Archie Roberts, Bob Zwirko, Dave O'Connell, and Gary Grumoli or our fantastic African American athletes like Waymond Dotson, Randy Watkins, Moyes, the Westbrooks, and JJ Jennings. I am sure the road for the latter was not smooth, but they were accepted in many more circles possibly because they were not going to be the majority minority. Additionally, many of these black athletes had families with deep, established roots in the city. Holyoke had many amazing athletes who were embraced despite their skin color. However, at this time in our city's sports history, the Hispanic athlete as star was troubling to some.

If I threw away one nasty letter, I threw away fifty. People think trolling is a new phenomenon, but I can assure you it is not. Our means of putting out negativity to others is the only thing that has changed. Today, people can easily post hateful comments online. Back when Ramon played, it was sent through the USPS. I never shared the snail mail with Ramon. I would check in with my principal and AD to let them know what was going on.

My conversations with Ramon focused more on his responsibility to himself and his team. "Ramon, as your success grows, there will be people out there who don't want you to succeed. How are you going to handle these situations?"

Ramon would be a bit down about it at times, but it seemed to only fuel his desire to achieve more. He never reacted outwardly to this small-minded group. The diminutive point guard focused on his studies, family, friends, and the game he loved. The team was building success throughout Ramon's sophomore and junior seasons, and nobody could deny the infectious spirit and energy that was being brought to the gym each night number 11 took to the court.

Ramon Cosme is one of many great Hispanic players to grace a Purple Knight uniform. Another was Isidro Roman, who played a significant role as a Purple Knights hoop star. The flashy perimeter player was recognized on local and regional levels for his talent and skill. However, Isi was not the focus of a western Mass basketball community as Ramon was. He definitely received less scrutiny from the community crowd referees. Isi was an excellent high school player for the Purple Knights. He was at the start of the wave of excellent Hispanic athletes who would grace the HHS playing fields. Ramon was El Jefe en la ciudad! When I graduated from Holyoke High school in 1970 with a class of more than five hundred graduates, we had only one Hispanic student in our class. That's it!

Ramon faced the haters with dignity because he was a brave, kind, and caring kid. Never was this more apparent than one night in downtown Holyoke.

"Ramon! Get over here!" Sandy yelled across the street to my starting point guard. She had spotted Ramon walking down to the corner of Sergeant and Maple on her way to pick up Kiely from CCD class at Sacred Heart. "I thought you were going home," she said.

Ramon had been at our house using our computer to work on a research paper earlier that night.

"No, Mrs. Rigali. I was just visiting my aunt. She lives on the top floor." Ramon replied, pointing up to the building on the other side of the street. Sandy told Ramon to hop into the back seat as Alexa was sitting shotgun and offered him a ride home.

Suddenly, a loud "Pop! Pop! Pop! Pop! Pop!" rang through the night air. Ramon and my wife threw their attention to the corner diagonal from where Sandy had pulled over to lambaste Ramon for being out by himself in a notoriously tough section of Holyoke. Down the road, illuminated under the streetlight, a body lay crumpled on the ground as two other figures ran swiftly away into the darkness.

"Mrs. Rigali! Go! Get out of here!" Ramon commanded, his first instinct to protect my wife and youngest daughter.

"No, Ramon. I have to help," my wife replied. Sandy's first instinct as a mother, nurse, and teacher superseded the danger emanating from the corner. She turned back to Alexa. "Stay in the car!" she ordered. "Keep the doors locked. I will have my eyes on you at all times. I need to help."

Together, Sandy and Ramon ran over to the corner to see the young man lying on the ground and bleeding badly. Sandy flagged down an off-duty ambulance coming up Sergeant Street. A crowd formed quickly. Police arrived and asked a few questions about whether they had seen anything. Ramon got Mrs. Rigali returned safely to our van, and Sandy drove around the corner to the Sacred Heart parking lot to pick up Kiely. She was mystified as to why she had to wait an extra forty-five minutes with Sister Mary to get picked up. Ramon came back to our house to just clear his thoughts, then we got him home.

I often think about how so many lives changed in those few seconds of gunfire. One young life lost, two young men sent to jail, and the pain for all of their families.

And what about Ramon and my family?

What if they had arrived a few minutes earlier?

Would the outcome have been different?

One thing was for certain: the event had a lasting impact on our family. Alexa wrote an essay in high school about the bravery of her mother going over to help the young boy shot on the street corner, as well as a personal narrative about that evening for admission to Assumption College (now University). The events of that tragic night further reinforced who Ramon Cosme was and is today as part of our family.

During Ramon's senior year, his team was ready to rock on the basketball court. It was to be the start of a wonderful run of four consecutive trips to the Western Mass championship game and a D1 state final. The team was balanced with proficient players in all aspects of the game necessary to compete for a championship, but the key was Ramon "El Jefe" Cosme.

CHAPTER 54

LUCKY 13

Western Mass D1 Final Title #1
March 6, 1993
Springfield Civic Center
Holyoke 55, Central 54

Holyoke: W. Cabrera 4-1-6-17, C. Washington 0-0-0, R. Cosme 2-2-6, J. Reyes 0-0-0, R. Sisson 8-1-3-22, S. Chatman 1-1-3, L. Gilbert 0-0-0, R. Diaz 0-0-0, T. Lawson 0-0-0, Mark Gubala 0-3-3, A. Lunardini 0-0-0, Matt Gubala 2-0-4. Totals: 17-2-15-55.
Central: R. Smith 4-0-8, D. Denson 3-1-7, S. Smith 6-1-0-15, A. Dickenson 2-2-1-11, D. Gotzendonner 2-0-4, J. Gee 2-1-0-7, R. Williams 0-0-0, R. Marquez 1-0-2, K. Collins 0-0-0, J. Moore 0-0-0, W. Johnson 0-0-0, D. Clark 0-0-0. Totals: 20-4-2-54.

It took me thirteen seasons to coach the Purple Knights to a championship game. When I took over the position as head coach from O'Connor, he had ended his twenty-seven year tenure on a wonderful run of championships. His final teams graced our community with great memories going up against Cambridge Rindge and Latin, led by Patrick Ewing, in state competition. Holyoke had always been known as a good sports community. Nestled in the valley beside the Connecticut River winding through the rolling hills, it was recognized as a tough working-class city that produced exceptional football and baseball talent each year, along with great boxing champs reared at the Holyoke Boys Club.

Basketball also captures the imagination of our fans, and they have had plenty to cheer about over the years. During the '50s and '60s, HHS graced the crowd with great players like Wey Dotson, Archie Roberts, Don Whelihan, Fran Skwira, Dave Bennett, Skip Clayton, Jack Skypeck, Randy Watkins, the Hurleys, Al and Ron Westbrook, Tom Rohan, John (Elgin) Downey, Kevin O'Connor (one of Coach's sons), Mike Dean, and Greg Dennett. In the '70s and '80s, fans were entertained by the amazing Larry, Gary, and Okie Show (Westbrook, Grumoli, and O'Connell), along with tough big men like Dunn and Allen. Throw Dennis O'Connor (the youngest of the O'Connor clan) into the mix, and the HHS boys basketball program was showcasing some great basketball that helped Coach O'Connor finish off a brilliant basketball coaching legacy with the Purple Knights. And let us not forget the incredible Lahovich winner John "Abe" Collomore's hardwood excellence.

Purple Knight hoop fans have had their fair share of great kids and teams to follow over the years. This great foundation and tradition of basketball excellence continued with Ramon and his team as they ushered in a new wave of Purple Knight basketball dominance, which resulted in sending the Knights to four title games in row.

The history of HHS basketball is long, rich, and successful. Many sources cite HHS as the first high school in America to have its own organized team, as I've discussed. Springfield schools played organized basketball competitions first; however, I have been told they drew from multiple city schools. Additionally, the Knights basketball résumé includes a New England Championship and victory over the Yale freshman team.

The roster the Knights brought to Western Mass for the '92–'93 season was talented, balanced, and cohesive. Our guards were led by Ramon. His back up was Joey Reyes, the ultimate team player waiting his turn. He would go on to have a very nice career at Clark University. Today, Joey is one of the area's top high school and college basketball officials. Then there was Cedric Washington, whose strengths included both defense and scoring. At one time, this phenomenal athlete even held the state football rushing record. Cedric went on to a great football career for the Boston College Eagles. Then there was Sean "The Glove" Chatman, our super defender, named in honor of pro great Gary Payton; Raul Diaz, who was tough and team driven; and Adam Lunardini, who was a smart, all-around player. We tragically lost Adam recently, and our hearts and prayers go out to his family. Finally, in the backcourt, the perfect complement to Ramon, was Wilfredo Cabrera. He was one of three future 1,000-point scorers on the roster. Wilfredo was one of the few high school players at this time who could shoot a pure jump shot. His form was perfect: elevate, elbow in, and release at the top of the jump.

Our forwards were led by Robert Sisson, who went on to play for Cushing Academy and Salem State College, and Larry Gilbert, future Lahovich winner and D1 collegiate player. Tim Lawson and Tony Neves were the perfect team orientated players and could battle inside for us and pushed our starters every day in practice. Finally, the Gubala brothers cleaned up everything inside. Matt and Mark were tough, skilled, and raring to go. They never backed down from a challenge, whether it was from an opponent or each other! One of the biggest challenges we had with Mark and Matt was keeping our practice time to two hours. As is often the case with brothers, they would argue, fight, and fool around with each other. But boy, when the chips were down, you could count on them to get a big rebound, make a key shot, or send the perfect pass.

No doubt the '92–'93 Purple Knights team was a complete roster ready to win a Valley League Championship, along with a State Sectional Title.

The regular season was special, with sweeps over Cathedral, Commerce, and Central. We suffered defeats at the hands of Ludlow (around the time of Principal Sears's wife passing) and Putnam. Putnam was a tough matchup for us. They would beat us up physically and would try to get our bigs into foul trouble. At their court, we squeezed by them at the buzzer. To this day, Putnam Coach Dan Butler swears the winning field goal came after the horn. In my heart, I think he is correct. On the way out to our bus, I stopped by Coach Butler's office. I wanted to let him know his team probably deserved a better outcome that night. When I walked in, all I saw was the coach's game notes shredded in half and his suit coat turned inside out, lying on the office floor.

Where is Coach Butler?

It reminded me of the scene from the motion picture *The Rock* when the FBI director (played by John Spencer) asks Dr. Stanley Goodspeed (Nicolas Cage), "Where is he?" referring to British agent prisoner John Patrick Mason (Sean Connery).

"Vaporized," Goodspeed responds.

A wise man once told me that the basketball gods can do crazy things to our minds and souls. If you have ever coached high school basketball, at some point along your journey, Goodspeed's response has accurately described that feeling after a soul-crushing loss—vaporized. Danny and his team deserved better that night. His kids outplayed us the whole game, but we caught a break at the end. Danny Butler was a wonderful man and coach who cared deeply about his Putnam players.

The Purple Knights' championship run produced good play-off wins over the Mike Labrie–coached Chicopee Pacers in the quarterfinals and Cathedral in the semifinals. Our victory in the championship game over Central gave us a three-game sweep that season over the Golden Eagles. That final victory almost did not happen as the game reached its final 4.3 seconds. But the Knights prevailed, and their special season ended in the state semifinals at the Springfield Civic Center with a hard-fought battle against Saint John's of Shrewsbury.

Central was led by All World athlete Sean Smith. He had been terrorizing the Purple Knights on the gridiron and basketball court for what seemed like an endless run. Smith doled out one gut-wrenching defeat after the other in both sports. Daryl Denson (future Central coach), Anthony Dickenson, Rudy Smith, Doran Gotzendonner, and James Gee completed a well-rounded Central squad that was accustomed to victory on the big stage.

I always try to build my life in a positive direction by finding balance between my family life, work, and dreams. The feeling of pride that we had going into this championship game brought all of those feelings together in one setting.

When the day of the championship game arrived, the team was ready and had the full support of our community. Bill and Chris Kane did a great job filming the team throughout the season and even recorded some wonderful footage of the kids celebrating in the locker room after the miracle win. The emotion of the final winning shot brought out sheer, unscripted joy as we had undergone a gauntlet of emotions. As the team swung from near victory to assured defeat back to a miraculous victory, all within the last ten seconds of the game, the Kanes caught all the drama on camera. They captured the emotion on and off the court as they continued rolling into the locker room, showing both the relief and exhaustion of our players, who were mentally and emotionally worn out from what they had just experienced. You could almost read their thoughts in bubbles overhead: *What just happened? Did we just do that? Are we really champions?*

On the other hand, on the film you can see the crushed reaction from the Central players due to Jim Hobert's perfectly designed play, aptly named "home run," practiced over and over again at the end of each practice. The team executed the play to perfection. First was Matt Gubala's perfect inbound pass with Assistant Coach Jim Hart reminding us all to make sure everyone was in the righ spot. Next, Robert Sission caught the long ball down court, turning to shoot his arching, game-winning shot. As the ball floated toward the basket, the silence in the arena was like something out of the Twilight Zone. In our deepest moment of despair, when all seemed lost as we huddled together during our last time-out, we chose to hope. We were not going to turn on each other and lay blame. We were going to think, and we refused to shrink from the enormity of our situation. We had prepared for this play all season, and we believed in in each other. The last words spoken as we broke the huddle and faced the last 4.3 seconds of the game were from Matt Gubala: "We can do this!"

And we did.

The ball left Robert's hands, the buzzer sounded, and the ball swished through the net. The Holyoke coaches, players, and fans erupted in pure, unchecked joy and celebration. *That sound* exploded throughout the Springfield Civic Center arena. I can tell you it was one hell of an epic way to win my first championship as a basketball coach.

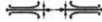

The game itself was pretty much a defensive battle. Central tried to pressure us on the ball and make it tough to get into our sets. Our tight zone defense was designed to force Central to shoot from the perimeter. A big arena can be challenging for outside shooters with the lack of depth perception behind the baskets. The Knights would set up in a 2-3, and then after the first pass (Syracuse 1) the strong side guard would go to pressure the ball while our other guard would find number 23, Shawn Smith. The box or diamond was designed to limit the touches for Central's top player.

At halftime, the game was tied at 21 points. We started to control the pace a bit in the second half, with Sisson and Cabrera scoring 23 of our 34 second-half points. Our zone did two things. First, it kept Central off the foul line. Central only attempted five foul shots in the game. Second, it kept the Knights out of foul trouble. We were only whistled for eight fouls the entire game. As we inched ahead and kept a small lead down the stretch, we arrived at the crossroad of victory. Ramon was on the foul line shooting a one and one with just under eleven seconds remaining. The Purple Knights were up by one. Ramon, the player who had been the most vilified and honored for the Knights, was on the clock. It was his time. Swish, and we were up by two. Swish, and we were up by three.

Our crowd was joyous. We could feel the title within our grasp. To their credit, Central thought differently and did not give up. Like a lighting bolt, Sean Smith gathered the inbound pass and dribbled down the right sideline as three Knights chase him into the corner. Trapped with nowhere to go and falling out of bounds, he banked in an incredible three-point shot. Now the game is tied.

The Central players were in an uproar and still on the attack. We inbounded quickly to Ramon, who lifted his head slightly to peek at the bench to see if we wanted a time-out. This split-second decision created enough time for Sean Smith to steal the ball from Ramon and drive to the hoop for a layup. Suddenly, Central was up by two.

Time-out Knights with 4.3 seconds left.

How did things go so wrong so fast?

I cannot honestly say whether it was the basketball gods, kids, or just the nature of Dr. Naismith's great game. What I do know is that it only takes mere seconds for one's life to change. The important thing is to get back in the game. Have a plan, but be willing to improvise. Believe in yourself and those you have entrusted around you to come through.

You already know how the game ended, but there is one more thing to share. During the final play, a Central defender went for the interception of Matt's pass to Robert but missed. The action unfolded right in front of our bench. The coaches and all players on the bench were screaming for Robert to drive in for the tying layup—there was no defender in front of him! It would have been an easy layup to tie the score. Instead, Robert just turned and shot the ball. The rest is HHS basketball history.

Many times, I have reflected on the events of that game and those final moments. I do not know if I would have continued to coach had we lost from that position. It all would have seemed so unfair to our players, to Ramon, but that is life. It's not fair. It is everything to live moment to moment, giving the best of ourselves and, hopefully, in the process making the world a better place for as many people as possible. Even if the basketball gods see our fate differently.

Nonetheless, on this cold, snowy night (it was fun getting bombarded with snowballs on the bus by the Central fans as we pulled away), the basketball gods did seem to recognize both the time and score.

Note: Robert Sisson's D1 championship three-point shot was the only three-point shot he attempted all season. Additionally, in 2021 Ramon Cosme was inducted into the HHS Athletic Hall Fame. Needless to say, El Jefe received the longest and loudest greeting of the night when introduced to the audience. Wilfredo Cabrera joined him in the hall in 2023. I hope at some point Robert is inducted and that the team is recognized. Each member of my miracle team deserves it.

CHAPTER 55
HOME RUN—THE WINNING PLAY

The home run set is like a full court 1-3-1 formation. We would have the player with the best arm and accuracy throw the pass (Matt Gubala). Our point guard (Cosme) would start at the opponents foul line and curl back for the ball in the event that we could not throw long or to half court. Our forwards (Cabrera and Gilbert) would set on each wing around the hash mark, fake back to the baseline, and then sprint to half court for a pass going up the sideline. Our center (Robert Sisson) would start on the low block of our basket and sprint to the top of the circle looking for the long pass. He would have the option to catch and shoot, drive to the hoop, or tip pass to either of our forwards racing down the sideline. It is basically the same set and shot that Duke employed to beat Kentucky in the NCAA playoffs the year before. Can you say Christian Laettner!

CHAPTER 56

YOU CAN'T DO IT ALONE AND MORE *PICCOLI MIRACOLI*

Piccoli miracoli is Italian meaning "little miracles," and it is precisely what your assistant coaches do. It is also what the managers, scorekeepers, custodians, video, and stat people do all season long. Together this wide-ranging group of people made my coaching life so much better. Collectively they added color, fun, and camaraderie to help build a cohesive basketball program at HHS. The basketball roster is small, and I had to cut young adults every season I coached. This was a difficult task, and it never got easier. In fact, it only became more difficult year after year. That is why I was so happy to honor a request from a student to help the team in any capacity.

Over my career, I was blessed with wonderful, dedicated assistant coaches. They represented the best ideals of developing our student athletes. We had remarkably little turnover in our staff over the years. This consistency through the freshman, junior varsity, and varsity teams was a stabilizing factor for the success of our program and the individual players. These coaches confronted many of the socioeconomic problems that sought to derail many of the kids who came through our program, and they did not allow that to happen.

My basketball s staff included Bob Lastowski, Tim Collamore, Wayne St. Peter, Rashid Milledge, AJ Lajoie, and Steve Dubilo. This group handled our freshman program (when the school budget allowed). They provided our kids with the structure of learning how to be part of a team along with a great focus on the fundamentals of the game. At the JV level, Jim Hart, Mike Athas, Tim Dunn, Ramon Cosme, Mark Dulude, Don Moye, and my longtime assistant Jim Hobert taught this group to compete and earn their playing time.

Then there were the many volunteers who took players to the Troy Summer League games, offered their insight into the game, and let them know that people in the community cared about their success. These people modeled the importance of giving back to others by using their own valuable, personal, and family time to support our kids. Steve O'Brien, Marvin Dotson, Miguel Diaz, Harry Melendez, Richie Miranda, Jose Ortiz, Adam Meehan, Kiely Rigali, and Mrs. Coach—my wife Sandra Ann—were among the many people who supported the team through the years.

James Hobert was with me for more than thirty seasons of coaching. We let each other into our families' lives, and the basketball season just seemed like an extension of the good things that crossed our paths. Coach Hobert worked hard at his craft. He played for HHS, Saint Thomas Moore in Connecticut, and Boston College. He loved the game and our kids and coached with both passion and discipline. Jim did a million things for the kids he did not have to do. Coach Hobert went above and beyond the lines of the basketball court to help our players succeed on the court and in life.

Over the years, we kept this promise to each of our players: We will work hard every day to be the best possible coaches we can be for our you. We will never promise a spot on the team, playing time, or a starting position. Whether you are in our program for one year or four years, we will always be there for you.

We communicated to our team they could call us about anything. If we could not help them, we would find someone who could. Even after our players graduated, former Knights who needed a job, a recommendation for school, or just someone to talk with would be supported. Once a Purple Knight, always a Purple Knight. Many of our kids came from families where the father was not around much. Then all of a sudden, Dad would climb back into their life when his son was on the court. It is no wonder that so many kids associate their self-worth with their basketball experience.

One of my favorite memories of coaching with Jim Hobert took place in the locker room at the Mullins Center at UMass Amherst. We were preparing to play Saint John's from Shrewsbury and legendary coach Robert Foley in the D1 state semifinals. I customarily went over the game plan with the team five or six minutes before we would take the court. All the coaches could sense the Knights were ready to go. The nervous energy, the fake stretching, anything to pass time. Talk, wait, stop. Overtime!

Greenfield High School was playing before us in their state semifinal game led by All-State star Angelo Thomas. The Greenies were in a dogfight to get to the D2 state finals.

"Settle down, guys!" I coaxed Wilfredo, Robert, Joey and the other Purple Knights. My players were jittery and jumpy as we waited to take the court. A few more quick words, and we would be ready to go. Nope. Another overtime!

I thought our kids were going to go crazy. I could see their focus leaking out of their pours with each passing minute our game was delayed. Then out of the corner of my eye, I saw Coach Hobert pushing the right buttons to relax our stressed-out teenagers.

"All right Robert, tell me the truth—you really love number thirty-three!" Coach Hobert teased, referring to Celtic great Larry Bird.

"Cut it out, Coach!

"Wilfredo told me you guys think he is really better than Jordan, but Joey said you can't root for him because if you did, you would lose considerable street cred." Suddenly, the rest of the team began to shout out their personal favorites: Patrick Ewing, Clyde Drex, Dominique Wilkins, and Tim Hardaway. All the Knights were chiming in on their favorite NBA players, and the stress of the upcoming battle was dissipating. John Stockton, Dennis Rodman. Charles Barkley, Reggie Miller. This unmoderated debate sparked by Coach Hobert did the trick! Collectively, we all wanted to succeed, but by this time we had done too much thinking about what was at stake. Coach Hobert had riled the team up with a great distraction in order to settle them down.

When the Purple Knights finally took the court, like Greenfield before us, we had to play overtime to advance to the championship game. Needless to say, it was a physically and mentally exhausted group of players and coaches who boarded the old yellow school bus traveling back to Holyoke with a victory in hand.

CHAPTER 57

THE COW PLOP

There were a few times when I really doubted if sports would be offered to HHS students. I learned early on that coaching was not the only thing I was going to have to worry about. On a number of occasions, fiscal issues stretching out from local, state, and federal government presented budgeting challenges, resulting in major cuts to the public schools. I started my varsity coaching career the same year that the Holyoke Public Schools riffed close to 250 teachers. These economic downturns left athletic budgets on the chopping block. At times, we vacillated between no funding and very limited funding. This resulted in reduced playing schedules, no equipment, no uniforms, no freshman sports, and no transportation. User fees were even implemented for students in a "pay-to-play" policy. Fortunately, people from our community stepped up many times to support the student athletes of our city. These people selflessly raised funds and donated money in order to fill the financial gaps left from budget cuts. These were extremely difficult and bleak at times. It was challenging to see a way forward for the high school athletic programs. And the truth was I never knew what we could count on from year to year.

Luckily countless parents, families, friends, and community business leaders kept fighting to keep our Purple Knights on the playing fields in some capacity. The first angel I encountered during one particular crisis was John "Murph" Murphy. John's son Cory was an excellent baseball player. Murph did not want to see his son and the other kids he watched come through Holyoke's youth leagues miss their high school season. Cory's dad was the driving force behind a number of successful fundraisers that provided monies to keep our athletes on the playing fields and off the streets.

The most fun and daunting fundraiser was the great cow plop raffle. For those not familiar with a cow plop, it consists of the following steps: secure a venue (preferably an open field), rent a cow, divide the field into numbered squares, and sell raffle tickets with designated square numbers. Fingers crossed La Vaca poops on your spot. Holyoke Hall of Fame baseball coach Joe McCarthy and alum Eddie Jackowski worked on the idea to get HHS alumnus Mark Wohlers back to Holyoke to help out with the extravaganza. Eddie had been Mark's battery mate in high school, so it was a great connection. Mark Wohlers was just getting started with his career as an all-star closer for the Atlanta Braves. It was a fun night, and the cow plop group went above and beyond the call of duty. Additionally, that year high school athletes cleaned streets and picked up trash to pledges for hours worked. Needless to say, it took a lot of fundraising that year to get the kids their high school sports memories.

Our basketball team contributed by running a 50/50 raffle on game nights. These funds were used by the team to help out with scholarships on Class Day and gifts for the seniors given out at their last regular-season home game. Volunteering for many seasons to greet the fans as they entered the lobby to purchase a game ticket was William Dulude. No one could get by Billy at the door without a short but sweet conversation. He would get your attention, turn on the charm, talk about a big winning prize, and then ask how many tickets you wanted to purchase that night. Billy was a natural!

One time, I overheard a fan who had just purchased a number of tickets announce, "He could sell water to a whale!"

William Dulude's work at our 50/50 raffle was a hit with the fans and a huge help to our program. Of course, Billy was not above convincing a well-off raffle winner to donate their winning share back to the Purple Knights. It was people like William Dulude whose small but meaningful acts of kindness helped out the kids in our community. Not only did they help to raise funds; they also helped raise our spirits. Search and you will find our better angels. They are all around. All you have to do is look.

CHAPTER 58

HOW DID WE GET HERE?

When DESE took control of the Holyoke Public Schools, they took away a part of the community's democratic process of self-governing. Some would argue that the state takeover of the Holyoke Public Schools created division in our community that failed to create a rallying force to move our schools in a better direction. I feel the real culprit holding back gateway communities revolves around the challenges of peeling back failed social policies and legislation enacted over the previous forty to fifty years; improving these antiquated systems would take real work. Much easier to blame teachers (he says sarcastically). Add in a confluence of change both old and new: old industry moving out, new digital age moving in, and structural policies to navigate—you get the picture. Improving school performance was not going to be an easy task.

Decades before the Holyoke receivership, in the late '60s, HHS won the Bellamy Award. The award was a national recognition given by the Bellamy family. They did this in honor of Francis Bellamy, who penned the original draft of the Pledge of Allegiance. Schools who represented the American spirit and embodied the characteristics of patriotism, citizenship, service, and scholarship could contend for the honor.

During my teaching career, I witnessed Holyoke Public School students being taught by an exceptional group of professional teachers. My colleagues had advanced degrees, teaching licenses and certifications, and copious amounts of professional development. Many hailed from the community. They lived in our city, sent their children to Holyoke Public Schools, and had a vested interest in seeing our students succeed. They were not the problem, as many would infer through the state takeover.

Ineffective welfare laws, school of choice, high stakes testing, public schools for profit, Proposition 2 1/2, bad zoning laws, the constant shifting around of our K–8 setup, white flight (along with Hispanic and Latino middle class flight), and absentee landlords have all contributed over time to hinder Holyoke's recovery into a healthier community. Holyoke housing's structural design, with numerous spacious big-city apartment blocks built in its industrial golden age of wealth, ironically led to many problems that still exist today. A number of housing units originally needed to house the families of the factory workers were eventually left vacant as our city's population dropped from 60,000 to 38,000/39,000 residents. Landlords counted on the poor and elderly to fill these vacant apartments. Many who occupied these units were on some segment of government assistance. It became evident that far more poor-to-impoverished people were living in Holyoke than in other communities of the Pioneer Valley. Communities that the city was competing against for resources, business, and tax dollars (the most valuable resource, though, is people).

Given all of these failed even if well-intended local, state, and federal policies enacted over the past forty-plus years, wasn't the government just as responsible for the problems our community was facing? Yet the blame landed squarely on the shoulders of the schools and the teachers. First, they limited the power of school board members. Next, the state's answer was to punish teachers by taking away their union, contract rights, and autonomy in the classroom. Teachers, who were already working with an overflowing caseload, were asked to do more without compensation. Like all people, educators deserve a life in balance where they can provide for their families. We should not be taking away quality time with our loved ones; we should be increasing it with healthy working hours and expectations. All of this occurred while our nation was rallying around better working conditions and health care for our essential workers.

Since the state started to take over our schools eight years ago, the city of Holyoke has lost an abundance of excellent certified teachers. Teachers who passed the state teacher exam, teachers who took part in professional development, and teachers who earned a master's degree. DESE set their requirements, and the Holyoke teachers provided instruction that offered a quality education for any student who wanted one. Instead of harnessing the experience and wisdom of a community of veteran educators, the state implemented the receivership, with many teachers retiring early. Those who could not retire chose to work in neighboring communities' school systems. Some just left the profession out of frustration.

You can slice it any way you want, but the impact on a school community placed in receivership is that they are left with a significantly less experienced group of educators to deal with very difficult learning situations. I hope the state, DESE, and our community can work together to return control of the Holyoke Public Schools to the capable hands of the city's educators. I believe it will greatly benefit all, especially and most importantly the students.

CHAPTER 59

GET ON THE PURPLE LINE!

In late November 1982, I began my career as the boys varsity basketball coach for HHS. My first order of business was to conduct tryouts. More than one hundred candidates poured into the gym. Due to budget cuts and late resignations, I was the only coach there to pick a varsity and a junior varsity team. We would have no freshman program for a while at the school. My teaching and coaching gigs started with a confluence of shortcomings and challenges that society threw at students and educators, all with the expectation that we just make things happen. It was a good thing that I did not know any better back then. I did my best and attempted to select the most deserving candidates to play in the basketball program that season.

With so many kids trying out for the team, very little room, and a ridiculous time slot to select the team, this was not an easy task. Running drills, playing scrimmages, and even communicating to the kids all presented challenges. Still, that was the hand I was dealt.

Over the years, the tryout process evolved into a much more organized and evaluative structure. However, the one aspect that never changed, even as participation in school athletics dropped, was the hardship of making cuts. So many of our kids would tie their self-worth to a spot on the team. Many of our kids had already endured a lot of disappointment in their young lives. I knew it took a lot of courage for them to put themselves on the line, to risk rejection in order to play a game they loved.

The truth was it was never really hard to pick the varsity team. Picking the best ten to twelve athletes on the court was pretty easy. The same can also be said for the freshman team. The real skill came in putting together your junior varsity squad.

Which younger kids do you move up?

Can an older player, say a junior, help you in his senior year?

Who improved enough from their freshman year to contribute this year?

And what about the new kids? The transfers or the student who chose not to try out the previous years? How do they fit into the mix?

Junior varsity was where you would place kids who needed to develop their skills and maturity. Coach Hobert did a masterful job season after season putting together this key developmental step for the Knights.

Basketball tryouts and practices provided a lot of information about our students' skills and athletic abilities beyond the hardwood. On multiple occasions, hall of fame track coach and official for the Atlanta Olympic summer games William Kane would wander through the gym to scout out new track-and-field talent. Bill would say a quick hello as he looked for potential candidates for his track team come spring.

One practice, I was watching my team pass the ball to any of the following: the water cooler, the banners hanging on the back wall, the team manager. I ordered them to drop the ball and get running. They had no focus.

"OK, guys! Line up and let's run!" I shouted.

After a while Coach Kane came over to me. "Can I speak with you a minute?"

"Sure! What's up?"

"You know running is supposed to be a joyous experience. Your kids don't seem to be enveloped in the joy."

Spoken like a true cross-country and track coach.

Reflecting back on my first day on the job with over a hundred kids trying out for the team, I should have known that coaching high school sports was not for the faint of heart. From day one, I faced challenges big and small. Our practice was scheduled for 4:00 to 6:00 p.m., but at about 5:30, the parents of grade-school kids and basketball officials started entering the gym. Apparently, a suburban league game had been scheduled, and the already overcrowded practice had met its melting point.

The basketball court at John "Jinx" O'Connor Gymnasium was encased by a very thin purple line. This was not the problem. It was all the other lines distributed that ran north, south, east, and west all across the main court that presented an issue. There were lines for the volleyball court, lines for two smaller basketball courts bisecting the main court, and others that seemed to have no purpose whatsoever except to confuse players. I thank God every day that pickleball was not around until after I was fired! And of course, the lines were all different colors, to make matters even more difficult. It was quite confusing to opponents over the years to decipher the baseline out of bounds. The maze of lines was always good for a few turnovers from the visiting teams, but later on in my career, we convinced the powers that be to encase the court with a single thick purple sideline.

At times over the years, when it seemed impossible to get through to my team with a lecture, demonstration, review of plays, or scrimmage, I found the best motivating tactic to get our players to work harder and focus was running a "17." This was a sprint from sideline to sideline repeated seventeen times that needed to be completed in a set amount of time by all players or it did not count.

Looking back to the first tryout, I can still see the custodians as they moved through the crowded gym. They had started to pull out the bleachers and set up for a grade-school game, ending my first practice as a varsity coach. At this point, I realized the time and score. I was outnumbered by one hundred teenagers trying out for the team, custodians trying to do their job, suburban parents with kids in tow waiting to watch their children play, and referees wanting to get the show on the road.

The practice ended before I was ready, much like my career as the boys varsity basketball coach at Holyoke High School. It was not fair and certainly not the plan. I had the gym till six, but outside forces made staying impossible. There was so much I wanted to do before I ended the practice that night, but unlike the final buzzer at the end of a game, life does not always provide us with neat endings.

At this point, I had a choice about how to proceed. Even though things did not unfold the way I wanted that first night as coach, I was still responsible for the kids in the gym. Just as I was responsible for every student and player I encountered over the course of my thirty-six year coaching career. I never took for granted the great privilege and trust people place in you when you work with their kids. Through it all, I sought to help young kids learn about themselves and life through my words but even more so, through my actions. The best way to empower our students and our players is to help them know the time and score, whether they are in the classroom or on the court.

Show up for yourself and do your best. Show up for your team and help them up. Do the work. Find your joy. Time and score.

Only one thing left to do before finishing for the night: "Get on the purple line!"

EPILOGUE

My good friend and best man Robert Baron always talks about ideas on our weekly phone conversations.

"Some are good; many are not so good," Bob-o always reminds me.

Bob, a chemical engineer by trade, WPI and MIT graduate, and beloved member of the aforementioned Elmwood 5 (Baron, Sullivan, Lucey, St. Germain, and Rigali) is probably one of the smartest people I know.

"The key is to figure out which is which."

Sometimes, I really do think Bob spent his career as an officer for the CIA, but that's another story for another time.

The state takeover of the Holyoke Public Schools changed many things for our community. It also led to some big changes for me and my family. On the one hand, it gave one of my daughters the courage to move away from her fifteen year teaching career for HPS and start over on Martha's Vineyard. Kiely had been an activist for Holyoke's failed Save Our Schools Movement. The constant challenges that she and other urban teachers faced under the receivership were a contributing factor for her decision to leave.

Luckily, the change has been good for her and her family. I pray and hope every day that she can continue to build her career and contribute to the Martha's Vineyard island community.

As for me, the revolving door of people that the state flooded into the Holyoke school system as experts was the beginning of the end for my coaching career. That dynamic made me come to the realization that for me to move forward with my life in a positive manner, I needed to leave many parts of my hometown behind.

I am sorry the receivership felt my contributions were no longer needed or of value to the Holyoke community. I would have liked the opportunity to finish my coaching career in Holyoke on my own terms and in some capacity continue with applied hope for a better future for the city.

Other communities across the land have also struggled with the concept of a state takeover of their schools. Adam Urbanski, president the Rochester Teachers Association in New York, which was taken over, is adamantly opposed to state laws that give receiver superintendent cart blanche: "Replacing local control makes the very harmful assumption that 'outsiders' know best how to fix our schools." Urbanski goes on to say that receivership is largely driven by the perception that teachers are standing in the way of reform. "My daughters are fond of saying that you resource people out of tough learning, living, and working situations." For many decades Holyoke teachers did an amazing job for their students while being under resourced!

On March 22, 2022, Boston Mayor Michelle Wu spoke out against the idea of state receivership for Boston public schools at a meeting for the Department of Elementary and Secondary Education (DESE), stating "I firmly oppose receivership" as it "will be counterproductive in light of progress we're making in collaboration with the state."

Many teachers have made their feelings known about their opposition to state takeovers. Boston public school teacher Samantha Laney has explained, "We will not allow Boston to suffer the same fate as our sisters in Lawrence, and if DESE actually wants to improve schools, they will call off any attempt to put Boston or any district under form of top-down control. Instead, you will listen and provide the resources that the communities say they need" (WCVB.com).

I need to look no further than my own family to see what teachers do for their students. Sandy taught twenty-three years for Holyoke Public Schools, Kiely taught fifteen years for the same system and eight years for MVRHS, and Alexa taught twenty years in the English Department at Randolph High School. Our family has always embraced the diversity of their students and worked above and beyond the call of duty to provide a quality educational experience. Receiverships timeline school districts have been under resourced for years and in many instances have been the victims of global change in how people work, live, and try to gain upward mobility.

I have been very fortunate in life. Sandy and I have been able to spend more time closer to our daughters' families. Saiid and Josh are wonderful and caring partners for our girls. Following the exploits of our grandchildren Syius William and Marianela Juliet is a full-time, enriching experience. I have even learned to get along with Max, Kiely and Saiid's bold-as-brass Yorkie. I coach tennis in the spring at MVRHS. I have coached both the boys and girls teams, and it has been a great experience. I have been fortunate to coach and volunteer on some important projects that give back to the Martha's Vineyard community. I have met some truly amazing kids and people along the way. As the *great* Nelson Mandela famously said, "Wherever you are in life, there is always more to the journey."

APPENDIX

HOLYOKE HIGH SCHOOL HALL OF FAME ACCEPTANCE SPEECH

In November 2022, I was inducted into the HHS Athletic Hall of Fame as a coach. I was not sure if I should attend, but in the end I did. It was an opportunity to thank the committee, my players, other coaches, and most of all my family in public. I ended my acceptance speech with these words:

> To my wonderful and beautiful Irish colleen, Sandy, and my two intelligent, passionate, and beautiful daughters, Kiely and Alexandra. The three of you made my teaching and coaching career possible. You sacrificed time and again to allow me to complete the many demands which my profession placed on me. I couldn't have done it all those years without your continued love and support. Also to my daughters' partners, Saiid and Josh. My joy of joys, my grandchildren Syius William and Marianela Juliet. My sisters Johanna and Meg and all of my extended family members who showed so much support over the years. And of course, my mom and dad, Pego and Chick, for getting me started on the right road in life.

To Sandy, Kiely, and Alexa, accept these words. I wish I had written them, but I quote from one of my favorite authors Robert Kurson when he dedicated his work about the Apollo 8 Mission "to my family": "My Family is my everything. They guide me in the dark. They are my stars."

HHS Hall of Fame induction gathering with some of my former Purple Knights.

Later that night I received a text from Tim Lawson, who was a member of our '95 D1 state finalist team. I had sent Tim a text thanking him for making the trip back from Boston and taking time out of his busy schedule. Tim works in the financial sector and travels to many different parts of the world to do business. I also mentioned to him just how important a role he played for us that year and during his career. Our team was talented and so was

Tim, though he never got big minutes in games. Still, he was consistent and always performed well, practiced hard, and made us a better team. He was an exceptional teammate. What he wrote back to me blew me away:

> Hi Coach! Thank you for your message. I loved the words of affirmation. It means a lot to me. Saturday was an amazing night. It was really great to reconnect with everyone. A few people mentioned it Saturday, but our early/mid 90s teams always seem more like a family than a team. You were the leader that created that atmosphere by teaching as much about life as basketball. Years later with the ability to have a larger view of the world, it's astounding what those teams accomplished, the changing demographics of the city, massive budget issues (threat of cutting sports), closing the last big factories (and the local newspaper), all the socio economic issues that plague families that go through those circumstances. To overcome all that and create an atmosphere of family & winning is a remarkable sports story. However, the best part of the story is the kind of adults all of us on the team became. Thank you for all you did in those times. I have never forgotten it, and none of the other players that I played with have forgotten.
> Talk soon,
> Tim

Alexa, our youngest daughter, at her teacher's desk.
Randolf High School is very lucky to have her!

Bill, Sandy, and Max our beloved Yorkie at Aquinnah on MV.

Marianela (MJ) Kiely, Saiid and Syius.

For the record section collage of schedule cards, some of the players who were responsible for any success I achieved!

THIRTY-SIX YEARS OF VARSITY COACHING HIGHLIGHTS

- 484 wins
- 1 D1 State final appearance
- 7 Western Mass finals
- 5 Western Mass Championship victories
- 28 state playoff appearances
- 31 state playoff victories
- 4 Valley League Championships
- 5 MBCA Coach of the Year awards
- 5 IABBO Team Sportsmanship awards
- 2 Lahovich Award winners
- 3 D1 players
- 8 one-thousand-point scorers
- 250-plus academic and athletic All-Star selections

FOR THE RECORD
(Purple Knights Stat Leaders over My Career)

1000 point scorers: Larry Gilbert 1369, Wilfredo Cabrera 1209, Maxwell Perez 1208, Robert Sisson 1119, Nelson Almodovar 1105, Tim Dunn 1095, Eddie Rodriguez 1058, JJ King 1051.

900 points: Julius Hobert 960, Wilvaldo Cabrera 942.

800 points: Eddie Almodovar 851, Justin White 835, Eliezer Vazquez 831, Josh Almodovar 827, Juan Galdon 808, Mike Tully 803.

Most points in a single season: Larry Gilbert 530.

Most points scored in a single game: Wilvaldo Cabrera 45.

Assists: Ramon Cosme 657, Max Perez 374, Devante Wardell 316, Austin Keeler 260, Juan Galdon 247, Eddie Rodriguez 223, Guillermo Godreau-Rivera 201, Chris Montemayor 187.

Rebounds: Nelson Almodovar 912, JJ King 842, Tim Dunn 670, Justin White 616, Larry Gilbert 575, Justin Sarabaez 516, Dave Zieja 502, Devante Wardell 493, Jerry Cruz 464, Elizer Vazquez 451, Matt Gubala 380, Eddie Anderson 361, Dave Pratt 302.

Blocks: Tim Dunn 278, Mike Laplante 197, Julius Hobert 195, Jerry Cruz 143, JJ King 141, Justin White 111, Justin Sarabaez 106, Dave Zieja 101, Mark Gubala 87.

Steals: Ramon Cosme 423, Maxwell Perez 302, Eddie Rodriguez 179, Devante Wardell 176, Guillermo Godreau-Rivera 152, Austin Keeler 143, Juan Galdon 137, Derek Biriell 123.

Three-point field goal career: Eddie Rodriguez 139, Austin Keeler 118, Max Perez 100, Luis Vazquez 90, Taylor Cason 83, Darius Diaz 78, Wilfredo Cabrera 73, Juan Maldonado 72, Emmanuel Rivera 66, Guillermo Godreau-Rivera 59, Jack Keane 56, Dereck Biriell 54, Eddie Anderson 52.

Three-point field goal season: Emmanuel Rivera 49, Luis Vazquez 49, Eddie Rodriquez 48, Julius Hobert 47, Austin Keeler 46, Jamal Warren 44, Taylor Cason 43, Cedric Washington 41, Juan Lopez 40, Nathaniel Pollard 39, Max Perez 36, Austin Keeler 35, Eddie Almodovar 34, Juan Maldonado 33, Darius Diaz 33, Guillermo Godreau-Rivera 32.

Three-point field goal single game: Eddie Rodriquez 7, Austin Keeler 7, Luis Vazquez 7, Emmanuel Rivera 6, Chris Sears 6, Wilvaldo Cabrera 6, Nathaniel Pollard 6.

FINAL NOTE FROM THE AUTHOR

I wrote most of these pieces while spending the COVID-19 lockdown year on Martha's Vineyard. Sandy and I were there to help our daughter Kiely's family (Saiid, Syius, and MJ) navigate through a year of remote learning, childcare, and work. I wrote about both my teaching and my coaching career at HHS with markers for each of the five sectional championships my teams won. The basketball focus was about some unusual games, which I hope represented the uniqueness and beauty of Dr. Naismith's wonderful game. Additionally, I included stories about the remarkable people who shared my journey with me, from coaches to players, community members, colleagues, friends, and of course, family. Whether in the classroom or on the hardwood courts, I have met some wonderful people along the way.

Change is never easy and can have both positive and negative effects in one's life. Through my coaching and teaching career, I experienced both. It was amazing to witness how the kids, parents, coaches, and teachers handled all that was thrown their way. The people and events I wrote about were special to me, different, and in many ways reflected the enormous challenges and upheaval in our community and society as it transitioned to a new normal during the global pandemic. In the classroom stories, I changed some of my students' names. The names of the players in my sports remembrances remain unchanged.

ACKNOWLEDGEMENTS

To my family, your love and support were always there from the start to the finish of my story. To Billy Greaney Holyoke's own master artist, illustrator and teacher for his amazing cover design and interior sketches, they captured the essence of my memoire! To the Naismith Basketball Hall of Fame for allowing me access to displays with special thanks to Head Curator Matt Zeysing and Director of Operation and Facilities Jim "Moon" Mullins. To award winning authors Mark "Pathfinder" Epstein and Jim Price for their time and advice. To my wonderful and skilled publishing team at Elite Authors, Jenny Chandler and Neena Laskowski, who were always there to answer my questions. To Atty. Mark Beauregard who provided his legal expertise on getting my work to publication. And finally, to the young adults I had the privilege to teach and coach, YOU were always the best part of my journey. TO ALL, thank you from the bottom of my heart.

Credits: to the Transcript Telegram (Ziggy Sears) and the Springfield Republican for photos used to help create the design for my book cover.

www.ingramcontent.com/pod-product-compliance
Lightning Source LLC
Chambersburg PA
CBHW071735150426
43191CB00010B/1577